Dalits in Neoliberal India

Exploring the Political in South Asia

Series Editor: Mukulika Banerjee
Associate Professor, Department of Anthropology, London School of Economics and Political Science

Exploring the Political in South Asia is devoted to the publication of research on the political cultures of the region. The books in this Series will present qualitative and quantitative analyses grounded in field research, and will explore the cultures of democracies in their everyday local settings, specifically the workings of modern political institutions, practices of political mobilisation, manoeuvres of high politics, structures of popular beliefs, content of political ideologies and styles of political leadership, amongst others. Through fine-grained descriptions of particular settings in South Asia, the studies presented in this Series will inform, and have implications for, general discussions of democracy and politics elsewhere in the world.

Also in this Series

The Vernacularisation of Democracy: Politics, Caste and Religion in India
Lucia Michelutti
978-0-415-46732-2

Rise of the Plebeians? The Changing Face of the Indian Legislative Assemblies
Editors: Christophe Jaffrelot and Sanjay Kumar
978-0-415-46092-7

Broadening and Deepening Democracy: Political Innovation in Karnataka
E. Raghavan and James Manor
978-0-415-54454-2

Retro-modern India: Forging the Low-caste Self
Manuela Ciotti
978-0-415-56311-6

Power and Influence in India: Bosses, Lords and Captains
Editors: Pamela Price and Arild Engelsen Ruud
978-0-415-58595-8

Why India Votes?
Mukulika Banerjee
978-1-138-01971-3

Dalits in Neoliberal India

Mobility or Marginalisation?

Editor

Clarinda Still

First published 2014 in India
by Routledge
912 Tolstoy House, 15–17 Tolstoy Marg, Connaught Place, New Delhi 110 001

Simultaneously published in the UK
by Routledge
2 Park Square, Milton Park, Abingdon, Oxon OX14 4RN

Routledge is an imprint of the Taylor & Francis Group, an informa business

© 2014 Clarinda Still

Typeset by
Glyph Graphics Private Limited
23, Khosla Complex
Vasundhara Enclave
Delhi 110 096

All rights reserved. No part of this book may be reproduced or utilised in any form or by any electronic, mechanical or other means, now known or hereafter invented, including photocopying and recording, or in any information storage and retrieval system without permission in writing from the publishers.

British Library Cataloguing-in-Publication Data
A catalogue record of this book is available from the British Library

ISBN 978-1-138-02024-5

To David, Hazel and Gaby, with thanks

Contents

Maps, Figures and Plates	ix
Tables	xi
Abbreviations	xiii
Foreword by Mukulika Banerjee	xv
Acknowledgements	xix

Dalits in Neoliberal India: An Overview *Clarinda Still*	1

1. Dalit Entrepreneurs, Globalisation and the
   Supplier Diversity Experiment in Madhya Pradesh   44
   Sudha Pai
2. Trajectories of Dalits' Incorporation into the
   Indian Neoliberal Business Economy   70
   Kaushal K. Vidyarthee
3. Locating Caste in a Globalising Indian City:
   A Study of Dalit Ex-millworkers' Occupational
   Choices in Post-industrial Mumbai   107
   Sumeet Mhaskar
4. Legislating for Liberation? Dalit Electoral
   Politics and Social Change in Tamil Nadu   133
   Hugo Gorringe
5. A Book Also Travels: Circulating Small
   Booklets in Dalit Poorva   162
   Badri Narayan
6. Low Caste Elites and Re-traditionalised Responses:
   Status and Security in an Economically Uncertain Time   184
   Jordan C. R. Mullard

viii द *Contents*

7. Dalit Women Becoming 'Housewives': Lessons from
   the Tiruppur Region, 1981–82 to 2008–09   208
   Judith Heyer
8. Finding One's Place among the Elite: How Dalits
   Experiencing Sharp Upward Social Mobility Adjust
   to their New Social Status   236
   Jules Naudet

About the Editor   259

Notes on Contributors   260

Index   263

Maps, Figures and Plates

Maps

2.1	Proportion of SC Population, 2001 Census	83
2.2	Proportion of SC Enterprises, 2005 Census	83
2.3	Enterprise Growth, 1990–98	84
2.4	Enterprise Growth, 1998–2005	84
2.5	Enterprise Growth, 1990–2005	85
2.6	PI for 1990	86
2.7	PI for 1998	86
2.8	PI for 2005	87
2.9	PI (Agriculture and Livestock) for 1990	89
2.10	PI (Agriculture and Livestock) for 1998	89
2.11	PI (Agriculture and Livestock) for 2005	90
2.12	PI (Non-agricultural Business) for 1990	90
2.13	PI (Non-agricultural Business) for 1998	91
2.14	PI (Non-agricultural Business) for 2005	91
2.15	PI (Manufacturing) for 1990	92
2.16	PI (Manufacturing) for 1998	93
2.17	PI (Manufacturing) for 2005	93
2.18	PI (Trade, Hotel & Restaurants) for 1990	94
2.19	PI (Wholesale Trade) for 1998	94
2.20	PI (Trade — Wholesale and Retail) for 2005	95
2.21	PI (Education) for 1990	96
2.22	PI (Education) for 1998	96
2.23	PI (Education) for 2005	97

Figures

2.1	Enterprise Growth in India, 1990–2005	79

x ᚷ *Maps, Figures and Plates*

3.1 Distribution of Ex-millworkers by Caste, Religion and Post-textile Mill Closure Occupation, Row Percentages — 119
3.2 Distribution of Ex-millworkers by Caste, Religion and Post-textile Mill Closure Occupation, Column Percentages — 121

Plates

4.1 Government Issue TV — 145
4.2 Land Rights Conference Rosette — 149
4.3 Ambedkar, Periyar, Sonia Gandhi, Karunanidhi, Thirumavalavan, and Stalin — 153
4.4 VCK Trade Union Board, Madurai — 154

Tables

1.1	Number of Dalit/Tribal Suppliers and Manufacturers Who Have Adopted the 30 per cent SD Policy in 50 Districts of Madhya Pradesh	52
1.2	Targets Set and Achieved in the RDS for the State of Madhya Pradesh between 2004 and July 2007	53
1.3	Dalit/Tribal Entrepreneurs Registered as Suppliers to the State Government under the Thirty Percent Scheme in Bhopal DTIC	55
1.4	Capital Invested and Annual Production by Dalit/Tribal Entrepreneurs under the Supplier Diversity Policy with DTIC Bhopal	57
1.5	Socio-economic Background of the Selected Dalit/Tribal Entrepreneurs in Bhopal	59
1.6	Investment and Income Gained from Business by Entrepreneurs Registered with the Bhopal DTIC	60
2.1	Distribution of Enterprises by Size, Employment and Enterprise Type	80
2.2	Distribution across Sectors of Private Enterprises in India	81
2.3	Regional Patterns of Economic Incorporation of Dalits	88
2.4	Regions of Differential Incorporation for Various Sectors	97
3.1	Distribution of Ex-millworkers by Caste, Religion and Post-textile Mill Closure Occupation, Frequency	118
6.1	Ownership and Average Revenue Patterns for the Largest Landowning Castes and Families in the Village	191

xii द *Tables*

7.1	Male/Female and Dalit/Non-Dalit Occupational Distributions, 1996 and 2008–09	219
7.2	All Females, 2008–09	225
7.3	All Dalit Females, 2008–09	226
7.4	All Non-Dalit Females, 2008–09	227

Abbreviations

AIADMK	All India Anna Dravida Munnetra Kazhagam
ASI	Annual Survey of Industries
BAMCEF	(All India) Backward and Minority Communities Employees' Federation
BC	Backward Classes
BD	Bhopal Document
BMOA	Bombay Mill Owners' Association
BJP	Bharatiya Janata Party
BSP	Bahujan Samaj Party (Majority People's Party)
CAT	Common Admission Test
CPI(M)	Communist Party of India (Marxist)
DIR	Defense of India Rule or The Defence of India Act 1915, also referred to as the Defence of India Regulations Act
DMDK	Dravida Munnetra Murpokku Kazhagam (National Progressive Dravidian Federation)
DMK	Dravida Munnetra Kazhagam (Dravidian Progressive Federation)
DPI	Dalit Panther Movement
DTIC	District Trade Investment Centre
GDP	Gross Domestic Product
GIS	Geographic Information System
ICDS	Integrated Child Development Services
IAS	Indian Administration Service
IFT	Indian Institute of Foreign Trade
IIM	Indian Institute of Management
IIMA	Indian Institute of Management Ahmedabad
IIT	Indian Institute of Technology
IMF	International Monetary Fund
INR	Indian Rupees
IPS	Indian Police Service

xiv Ⱬ Abbreviations

IRS	Indian Revenue Service
JNU	Jawaharlal Nehru University
LPG	Liquid Petroleum Gas
LTTE	Liberation Tigers of Tamil Eelam
MLA	Member of the Legislative Assembly
MNS	Maharashtra Navanirman Sena (Army for the Construction of New Maharashtra)
MP	Madhya Pradesh
MSME	Micro, Small and Medium Enterprise
NGO	Non-governmental Organisation
NREGS	National Rural Employment Guarantee Scheme
NRI	Non-resident Indian
NSS	National Sample Survey
OAE	Own Account Enterprise
OBC	Other Backward Classes
PCS	Provincial Civil Services.
PDS	Public Distribution System
PI	Indices of Participation
PMK	Paatali Makkal Katchi or 'Toiler's Party'
PT	Puthiya Tamizhagam or New Tamil Nadu Party
RDS	Rani Durgawati Scheme
RMMS	Rashtriya Mill Mazdoor Sangh (National Federation of Mill Workers)
RSS	Rashtriya Swayamsewak Sangh
SC	Scheduled Caste
SCP	Special Component Plan or the Scheduled Caste Sub Plan (SCSP)
SD	Supplier Diversity
SHG	Self-help Group (part of women's micro-credit programmes)
ST	Scheduled Tribe
TNUEF	Tamil Nadu Untouchability Eradication Front
TTS	The Tamil Nadu Theological Seminary
UP	Uttar Pradesh
UT	Union Territory
VCK	*Viduthalai Chiruthaigal Katchi* (Liberation Panther Party)

Foreword

The persistent discrimination and subordination of Dalits, people born into the erstwhile caste of 'untouchability', despite India's constitutional ideals of equality, liberty and fraternity is without doubt one of India's greatest challenges. 'Untouchability' and caste identity is based on an ideology inherited from Hinduism that ranks groups of people according to birth and this ideology affects all other religions on the Indian sub-continent,such that they too display similar rankings in their communities. This caste system was also manipulated and used by colonial powers to serve their own interests, thereby entrenching an already iniquitous system in new ways. In 1950 however, the Indian Constitution written for a newly independent India, deemed this odious phenomenon illegal, putting in place a new conception of universal citizenship that granted all Indians equal rights and gave each citizen of India a vote of equal value. Nearly seven decades later, the lived-reality of the people who belong to this erstwhile category however continues to remain subordinate and shamefully stigmatised.

The term 'Dalit' is used as a shorthand to describe this group, a vast population of 160 million spread across the breadth and diversity of India, in which people speak different languages, live with neighbours from a variety of religions and physically look very different to each other. Members of this community do not use the term Dalit as self-description, and indeed all Dalit communities rarely unite under a single political banner. Their enthusiastic embrace of electoral politics as a bargaining tool in the current phase of Indian democracy has also led to a greater fragmentation and ethnicisation of the group across different regions of the country. But like any historically marginalised group in the world, they share a basic common cause around which political movements have attempted to unite them. At the heart of the struggle is the desire for a meaningful citizenship in which their Constitutional right to political equality is also matched by everyday social equality.

xvi *ढ Foreword*

However, despite the difficulty with nomenclature, the term 'Dalit' when used in scholarly literature has a fairly unambiguous meaning and is therefore a useful term to bring together a number of different academic writings on the subject.

This volume brings together some of the best research and writing on this topic. It presents a selection of papers presented at a conference organised at the University of Oxford by Clarinda Still who is also the editor of the volume. A social anthropologist by training, her own work on this topic and continued engagement with scholars from a wide variety of related social sciences, has led her to bring together this excellent collection of chapters that makes a timely and valuable contribution to the literature. Set in the context of a market-oriented political economy of contemporary India, the chapters are written by scholars who have all spent considerable years in studying particular communities of Dalits, and are therefore able to bring a temporal perspective to judge the nature of change in these communities. The chapters present a diverse range of perspectives but there are perhaps five key themes that emerge in this collection. First, what impact does a changing and liberalising economic environment have on Dalits who overwhelmingly belong to the labouring classes? Do new labour regimes, job opportunities and scope for migration lead to economic empowerment? Do Dalits have access to full economic citizenship in an India of high growth rates? Second, how does India's rapid urbanisation affect inter-caste dynamics? Are the traditional rules of residence, kinship, commensality and division of labour challenged as a result and does this bring any advantages to the Dalit communities? Third, is there scope for genuine social mobility for Dalits? Given the social practice of caste has considerably lessened since independence, has this also led to a reduction in the traditional stigma of ritual pollution? Do Dalits have fair access to freedom, justice and physical security? Do they have opportunities for education and jobs to improve their life chances and increase their capabilities? Or, as Still asks, is social stigma the new ritual pollution? Fourth, what examples do we have in contemporary India in which political will and institutional structures have enabled social change and the creation of opportunities for Dalits? What can we learn from these examples and can they be replicated elsewhere? This leads

Foreword ᵹ xvii

to the final and over-arching theme of the opportunities created by electoral politics on the one hand and the difficulty of social mobility on the other. This issue is reflected in the title and the provocation is deliberate because it addresses the contradiction at the heart of Dalit politics in India today.

Bhimrao Ambedkar — the most famous and erudite of all Dalits — anticipated this contradiction at the time of the writing of the Indian Constitution. As the chair of the large committee that drafted the Constitution and as a political thinker in his own right, he pointed out that India's adoption of a liberal democratic agenda in writing would need a much bigger effort to put into practice. This was because he pointed out 'Political democracy was only a top-dressing on an Indian soil which is essentially undemocratic'.[1] There was a real danger that the introduction of democratic ideals of liberty and justice in such a context could lead to India paying mere lip service to these ideals while entrenched inequalities continued to persist. There was, thus, a need to achieve social and economic equality alongside the political equality that the Indian Constitution had legislated for. Ambedkar blamed Hinduism as the source of the undemocratic or the anti-egalitarian ethic of India and argued that it was not really religion but 'really law, or at best legalised class-ethics ... The first evil of such a code of ordinances, misrepresented to the people as religion, is that it tends to deprive moral life of freedom and spontaneity, and to reduce it (for the conscientious, at any rate) to a more or less anxious and servile conformity to externally imposed rules. Under it, there is no loyalty to ideals; there is only conformity to commands (Ambedkar 1936, in Roy 2014). It was for this reason, Ambedkar warned 'We must remove this contradiction at the earliest possible moment or else those who suffer from inequality will blow up the structure of political democracy which this Constituent Assembly has so laboriously built up' (Ambedkar 1948, in Guha 2012: 323).

This volume provides a valuable assessment of how far Indian democracy has got in addressing this contradiction. The question that remains is whether Dalits have had the opportunities to achieve

---

[1] Constituent Assembly Debates 1989: VII: 38 in Betéille (2008: 36).

xviii द *Foreword*

a greater economic and social equality, i.e., have they gained greater mobility or do they continue to be marginalised? As India is about to institute her sixteenth Parliament, this question remains as urgent as it was for the first one.

May 2014   **Mukulika Banerjee**
                                                                        London

References

Betéille. Andre. 2008. 'Constitutional Morality', *Economic and Political Weekly*, 43(4): 35–42.
Guha, Ramachandra. 2012. *Makers of Modern India*. Delhi: Penguin Viking.
Roy, Arundhati. 'The Doctor And The Saint: Ambedkar, Gandhi and the Battle against Caste', 1 March. http://caravanmagazine.in/reportage/doctor-and-saint (accessed 10 May 2014).

Acknowledgements

I would like to thank all the participants of the 'Dalits in Neoliberal India' conference that took place in Oxford in July 2010, especially those who travelled long distances to be there. I especially wish to thank those who prepared papers for the event, and the discussants who offered such insightful commentary on the papers. Thanks to Professor Gopal Guru who gave the keynote speech and Professor Craig Jeffrey who summed-up on the last day. I am grateful to Oxford University's John Fell Fund for providing the grant which funded the conference, and to Professor David Gellner, Kate Atherton and the Institute of Social and Cultural Anthropology (ISCA) who gave us the venue. Thank you to Sarah Rank in who provided invaluable administrative and practical support for the conference; Louise Gordon at Wolfson College for providing dinner and accommodation to our guests, and Mitra Paraiyar, Kaushal Vidyarthee and Sumeet Mhaskar who helped me enormously on the day. I personally want to thank my mother and my aunt who looked after my (then) four-month-old baby and brought him to me at intervals to feed. I am grateful to all the contributors and the editorial team at Routledge, New Delhi for all their work on the manuscript; together they have made it a pleasure to work on this volume.

Dalits in Neoliberal India

An Overview

The title of this volume asks a deliberately provocative question: has the position of Dalits improved or deteriorated in contemporary India? Are Dalits more socially mobile than ever, or rather have recent changes to the economy and society marginalised Dalits in new ways? On the one hand, it seems obvious that Dalits are not only better off than earlier generations, they are a rising power in India today. Through electoral politics, organisation in civil society, social movements, affirmative action, conversion away from Hinduism and global campaigning against caste discrimination, Dalits are spearheading radical change. Indeed, in terms of sheer numbers (160 million), Dalits are set to profoundly influence the future of India's democracy. And, yet on the other hand, there are indications that despite significant progress, in certain respects, Dalits are persistently and increasingly excluded in the market-oriented political economy of neoliberal India. To anticipate my argument in this introduction, then, the answer to any question about mobility or marginalisation must be that there are elements of both, not just in terms of variation within the Dalit population but also because mobility and marginalisation themselves are closely related.

This contradictory situation is fuelling special interest in the effects of liberalisation and globalisation not just in India but in rapidly developing economies across the world, compelling scholars, activists, policy-makers and engaged citizens to assess how historically-marginalised groups will fare in the foreseeable future. This concern was the motivation for the conference for which the chapters in this volume were prepared. In different ways and from different perspectives, all of the participants were interested in how rapid change in India is affecting Dalits. Rather than attempting an exhaustive treatment, this collection is instead made up of a selection of contributions from the lively discussions that took place. Drawing on insights from different disciplinary perspectives (anthropology, political economy, politics), the

2 ढ *Clarinda Still*

authors seek to describe and reflect on the processes that are shaping and constraining Dalit choices in neoliberal India.

In using the word 'neoliberal' in this introduction, my intention is not to repeat arguments for and against liberalisation from a Dalit point of view, something already done eloquently and comprehensively elsewhere.[1] Neither do I attempt to draw direct, causal links between Dalits' current position and economic liberalisation *per se*. Rather, I use the term neoliberal more broadly in order to understand not just Dalits vis-à-vis India's economic reforms but how Dalits' position is being affected by the shifts in society, culture and politics associated with the current market-oriented climate in India. As Shyam Babu says, 'for many Dalits the response to liberalisation transcends the narrow confines of economic reforms and includes social and political concerns as well' (2004: 4). This forms the subject of this introduction, which in turn should help to frame and contextualise the chapters in this book.

In order to address these broader questions, the book is organised into three parts. The first part deals with Dalits in the economy, the second part deals with Dalit politics and the third deals with social mobility. This chapter and the following one (Vidyarthee) set the scene by discussing Dalits at the all-India level, arguing that Dalits continue to face discrimination and marginalisation despite impressive advances in some areas. Vidyarthee's chapter, in particular, highlights areas of serious disadvantage and the policy implications of this finding. Subsequent chapters take the form of in-depth case studies in particular sites across the subcontinent, focusing on Uttar Pradesh, Tamil Nadu, Mumbai, Madhya Pradesh, Rajasthan and nine cities in north India. As qualitative studies, these chapters cannot (and do not) claim to make over-arching conclusions about all Dalits in India. Rather, using rich empirical material from long-term field-based studies, each chapter provides a detailed snapshot of the ways in which Dalits are managing forms of upward mobility or persistent marginalisation.

---

[1] For more on this, see Babu (2004); Debroy and Babu (2004); Jodhka and Newman (2007); Jogdand (2000); Nancharaiah (2000); Teltumbde (1997); Thorat (2002); Thorat, Aryama and Negi (2005).

An Overview द 3

Before considering these issues, we need to interrogate the subject of our enquiry itself: Dalits. What exactly is this term referring to in the first place?[2] Can we even talk about such a large and diverse sub-population with any kind of empirical accuracy? At the outset, we have the problem that today many people to whom we might apply the label 'Dalit do not use it themselves'. As a politicised term, some associate the word 'Dalit' with ideologies from which they distance themselves. Just because a person's ancestors suffered untouchability does not automatically mean that he/she identifies with those political groups that employ the term Dalit. Indeed, some Dalits refuse to refer to themselves as 'broken'; they do not wish to be defined in terms of oppression or called by a name that reminds them of an abject past (Paik 2011: 229). Moreover, as Dalits become increasingly politically fragmented, the term 'Dalit' may become more and more problematic. Dalits in different parts of India are engaged in internal conflict with other Dalit castes to the point where they are defining themselves not against non-Dalits but against one another. This has resulted in greater usage of *jati* names and a rejection of the unifying term 'Dalit'. Just as the Gandhian term, 'Harijan' (Children of God) has been largely rejected for its patronising overtones, so Dalit may be losing relevance for many of those so described.

To avoid these problems, some scholars have opted to use the word 'Untouchable' instead. Mendelsohn and Vicziany (1998: 5), for instance, justify this on the basis that most readers outside India would recognise this word and that it is evocative of 'one of the more pernicious forms of subordination encountered anywhere'. This may be true but many activists, scholars and ordinary Dalits find the use of the term 'Untouchable' (and its vernacular equivalents) deeply reprehensible. The Delhi-based publisher, Navayana, for example, prints much Dalit-related literature but will not allow Dalits to be referred to as Untouchable.[3] If most Dalits refuse to be referred to as Untouchable in their own languages, it seems inappropriate to apply a rejected

---

[2] 'Dalit' is a Marathi word popularised by the Dalit Panthers in the 1970s, literally translated as 'downtrodden' or 'broken'.

[3] Personal communication with S. Anand, Navayana Publishers.

4 ॒ *Clarinda Still*

name. 'Scheduled Caste' is another possibility and many Dalits prefer this bureaucratic term. But the use of this appellation is not universal either so to use 'Scheduled Caste' here would be to reify a government category. For want of alternatives and in spite of its problems, most of the contributors and I use the term 'Dalit' simply because at the time of writing it seems to be the least offensive and most widely-used name in the Indian media, literature and in academia. This may change in years to come but for now it will have to suffice.

The Construction of Caste and Untouchability

This difficulty with nomenclature strikes at the core of the issue of the Dalits' sociological existence, an issue which needs to be considered seriously, especially in light of the 'anti-Orientalist' critique of caste.[4] According to this school of thought, Dalit distinctiveness, is in fact, a product of historical processes. Charting this history, Charsley (1996) argues that 'Ex-Untouchables' were constructed, census by census, political movement by political movement, until they were fashioned into the shape they are in today. Each change of the Dalit status and identity over the last century or so has inaugurated the use of a new name. Untouchables, ex-Untouchables, Harijans, Panchamas, Chandalas, Avarnas, Antyajas, Adi-Hindus, Adi-Dharms, Adi-Dravidas, Pariahs, Dalits, Scheduled Castes (SCs) are all terms that can be used to refer, very broadly, the same 160 million people in India but each name implies a slightly different political stance. Charsley asserts that the production of the concept 'Untouchable' consolidated a previously diverse mixture of social groups. These processes produced the naturalised view we have of Indian society today. That there is a pan-Indian standard which dichotomises people as Untouchable or not, that it

---

[4] The 'anti-Orientalist' critique of caste criticised earlier scholarship which, scholars claimed, had both exaggerated the importance of caste and described it within an Orientalist framework (see Appadurai 1996; Cohen 1996; Dirks 1992, 2001; Inden 1990). Following Said (1978), these scholars suggested that the emphasis on caste was part of Western tendency to exoticise India and unearthed evidence to suggest that caste was actually the product of political and social processes in the colonial and post-colonial period.

An Overview द 5

emphasises one particular disadvantage over others (Untouchability) and condemns it as a negative practice: these are all historical rather than natural processes, he argues, which have served to suppress the diversity that exists (and has existed) in reality.

Charsley is surely right to emphasise the diversity of people who fall under the category of 'Dalit'. Indeed, it is often impossible to see what is distinctive about Dalits as compared to everyone else. Dalits do not live isolated from the society, they are not immediately identifiable physically; they speak the language of those around them. They may even have similar rituals and marriage practices, they often share a religion with people of other castes, and they may live according to similar norms and values. Conversely, Dalits are by no means a homogeneous group; they are divided by region, religion, gender, class and political affiliation. These axes of differentiation at times may give Dalits more in common with those outside their caste than those within. To what extent then is the classification of 'Dalit' artificial?

This question is not to be posed lightly. As Fitzgerald (1996) points out, Ambedkar himself would have been seriously troubled by the suggestion. Fitzgerald shows how the similarities between Ambedkar and Dumont's idea of caste (both judged Untouchability an essential feature of the overall caste system and believed political power to be 'encompassed' by religious values) prompted Ambedkar's campaign for the annihilation of caste and his conversion to Buddhism. Thus, for Fitzgerald, viewing the unity of Dalits (and the institution of caste) as a fallacy is not only inaccurate, it is also politically disabling.

There is some consensus that Untouchability (like caste) is neither the 'immutable essence' of Indian society nor is it a colonial fantasy (Bayly 1999: 11). Importantly, any view that over-determines the effects of colonial rule runs the risk of neglecting the role of present-day politics and policies on the ascendance of caste in contemporary India. Galanter (1971) and Dudley-Jenkins (2003: 4), for example, have argued that programmes devised to eradicate caste have served to strengthen it, leading to a paradoxical situation in which people must claim to be 'backward' in order to move forwards. This situation is found in politics too. As Suri (2002: 59) puts it, 'the paradox of modernity and democratic politics in India is that while they have contributed to weakening the caste system, they have tended to reinforce group

6 ৱ *Clarinda Still*

solidarities based on caste identity'.[5] Dalits, those who have suffered most from the caste system, are now using caste as an instrument of advancement (Kothari 1994: 1589).

Dalits, then, should not be seen as part of a pan-Indian ritual system that has existed since time immemorial but rather a group moulded by the concrete hand of modern law, the compulsions of Dalit politics, the active work of collective memory and the social processes of identity formation. Entitlements that flow from the classification 'Scheduled Caste' in themselves ensure that this group is kept alive and well. The re-inclusion of caste in the 2011 Census, brought back in after a gap of 80 years, as well as the re-publication of the ethnographic survey of SCs, bears testament to this.[6] These actions force fluid social realities into shapes, which people themselves use and imbue with meaning. When Dalits name themselves 'Scheduled Caste', they animate that category and in doing so, they produce social reality. As long as politicians appeal to voters on the basis of caste and as long as caste exists in law and policy, it is difficult to envisage its demise.

Features of the Dalit Experience

But Dalits are more than simply a category produced by identity politics and legal categorisation; there are indeed aspects of Dalit experience and history that make them unique, not least their subjection to some of the most severe forms of oppression found anywhere in the world (Mendelsohn and Vicziany 1998: 5). This oppression stems from multiple axes of denigration which combine to interpellate Dalits as systematically subordinated subjects (Mosse 1996; Oommen 1990: 255).

For Dumont (1970), of course, Dalits represent the permanently impure, the counterpoint to Brahmins in the ritually-organised caste hierarchy. While people of all castes are temporarily polluted, for Dumont, superiority is the high castes' ability to pass 'out' and 'down'

---

[5] See introductory chapter of Michelutti (2008) for a review of the debate on caste in Indian politics.

[6] Though this has more to do with OBCs than SCs or STs who have always been in the census as separate categories (based on personal communication with Alpa Shah, Reader in Anthropology at the LSE, 3 July 2012).

An Overview द 7

ritual impurity to the Untouchables, who, by absorbing pollution perform the function of a sort of ritual sewer. As is well known, in classical Hinduism, their status is justified by the notions of *dharma* and *karma*. Untouchability is part of the moral order of caste and the punishment for sins committed in a previous life.[7] This does not mean that Dalits are kept out of the ritual sphere but when they are included it is in the lowest position (Fuller 2004: 137–39). Even Dumont's critics rarely say that Dalits are anything other than the lowest of the low. Quigley (1993) and Raheja (1988a, 1988b) whose models of caste are based on kingship (not ritual purity), still assert that as dependents, Dalits are at the bottom of the hierarchy.

Taking both the Dumontian and Hocartian view into account, it is possible to argue, as Mosse (1994, 1999) does, that subordination is the defining feature of Untouchability. Subordination is not just a part of the Dalit experience; it is 'ideologically constitutive of Untouchable identity' (Mosse 1994: 74, 1999: 68). This subordination is a result of several interlocking sets of values or 'fields', in Bourdieu's terms. In each field, Dalits figure at the bottom. Subordination then must be understood as what Oommen calls a system of 'cumulative deprivation' (1990: 255). Poverty, economic dependency, lack of knowledge, lack of education, landlessness, powerlessness, a perceived lack of morality, self-control and 'culture'; physical 'dirtiness' and ritual impurity, these are all used to explain and justify Dalit inferiority. When grouped together, these elements help to explain the force of Untouchable subordination.

Although it is the religious basis of Untouchability that make Dalits 'truly a category apart' (Deliège 2010: 18), as Béteille (1972), Klass (1980), Mosse (1996: 74) make clear, poverty and material deprivation should not be underestimated. Poverty is so intertwined with subordination that some argue that a rich and powerful Dalit can no longer be considered Untouchable in the strict sense of the term (Deliège 2010: 18). This point is important and shall be discussed further later.

---

[7] Even so, ordinary Hindus rarely invoke the notion of *karma* to explain the low status of the Untouchables.

8 ठ *Clarinda Still*

For the most part though, to be Dalit is to be poor. We know that Dalits are disproportionately represented among India's poor (Bhaumik and Chakrabarty 2006; Borooah 2005; Gang, Sen and Yun 2005; Kannan 2011, Kijima 2006; Sundaram and Tendulkar 2003; Thorat and Newman 2007).[8] The Government classifies 48 per cent of rural Dalit households as 'Below Poverty Line' and 22 per cent as in severe poverty (Mehta and Shah 2003: 12). But according to Kannan (2011), as much as 85 per cent of the *adivasi* and Dalit population live in poverty in 15 states of India. Dalits still have some of the lowest incomes of any social group in India and are overwhelmingly present in the lowest paid occupations. This is related to other kind of disadvantages, such as high infant mortality, insufficient nutrition and low life expectancy (Borooah 2010). Dalits suffer disproportionate levels of deprivation (Harriss-White and Subramanian 1999) and are acutely lacking in what Amartya Sen calls 'freedoms' and 'capabilities' (Drèze and Sen 1995; Sen 2000). This is especially the case in the sphere of education. Although Dalit literacy rates and educational levels have improved hugely over the last half century, they still fall short of the national average (54 per cent versus a national average of 65 per cent according to the 2001 Census). Dalits constitute a large part of the agricultural workforce and perform most of the menial work. In villages, Dalits are mostly landless, their well-being often depends on upper-caste landlords and because they have limited access to credit, many rely on exploitative moneylenders (Mendelsohn and Vicziany 1998: 29–36; Reddy 2012; Shylendra 2006). Evidence suggests that practices of Untouchability are still alarmingly prevalent in rural areas (Shah et al. 2006). In cities, Dalits engage in casual and wage labour, domestic services, and generally do the filthy, degrading jobs such as sweeping and waste removal. In rural Tamil Nadu, Heyer (2000, 2010) describes a 'standard of living paradox': while real wages increased several-fold, Dalits' standard of living has not increased at the same rate. Despite improvements, Dalits remain severely disadvantaged in material terms. Together with *adivasis*, it is clear that Dalits are still worse off than all other social groups in almost every part of the country.

---

[8] See Corbridge et al. (2005: 75–76), Deshpande (2001), Gang, Sen and Yun (2005), and Mehta and Shah (2003) for analyses of caste and poverty.

An Overview **द** 9

Dalit Economic Mobility/Marginalisation

All of this is by now well established. But the question is whether economic liberalisation improves Dalits' situation. Insofar as Dalit subordination is rooted in material deprivation, some argue that it should. Economists such as Dollar and Kraay (2002); Wood and Calandrino (2000) Sundaram and Tendulkar (2003) and the World Bank's World Development Reports all advocate growth alongside reforms to reduce poverty.[9] Using this work, one might assume that liberalisation may solve many of Dalits' problems. But as Dalits are not simply poor people and cannot be analysed as such. What are the effects on Dalits specifically then? Here we run into trouble as it is difficult to tell how much liberalisation *in itself* can account for changes in Dalits' situation and there is much less known about Dalits in the economy generally (Babu 2004: 8).

Looking at the economic position of Dalits more generally from 1980s onwards, there have certainly been some shifts in their economic situation. These include improved pay, working hours and working conditions; a move out of agricultural/bonded labour into other kinds of work; migration out of villages and other shifts which in part can be attributed to a changing economy. Economic growth has also allowed state governments to invest more substantially in programmes for the poor. A raft of welfare measures for Dalits have been introduced in different parts of the country in the last two decades while earlier ones have been advanced or modified. Perhaps the most important of these has been the provision of subsidised food and basic household provisions through the Public Distribution System, the Midday Meal Scheme in state schools and the National Rural Employment Guarantee Scheme in 2005. These, in addition to specially-designed schemes for child and maternal health, the establishment of the National Commission for Safai Karamchari (a statutory body that deals with legislation on manual scavenging), housing projects for the poor, sanitation, electrification,

---

[9] See McCartney (2010) for a more detailed discussion of liberalisation in India.

10　द　*Clarinda Still*

roads, community buildings, micro-credit schemes for women and even state-supported projects for the construction of statues of Dalit icons. Despite patchy provision, problems of implementation, corruption and discrimination within the system, in some measure, the welfare programmes have contributed to a rise in Dalit living conditions and life chances in some parts of the country.

Although not linked to liberalisation *per se*, education and affirmative action were also clearly having a considerable impact on Dalits during this period, even though Dalits still lagged behind (Chalam 2007). Having been previously denied entry to schools altogether, Dalit parents were now able to send their children to school and were sending them in their numbers. Although the dropout rate remained high, girls were not getting very far, the poorest families remained excluded, the quality of primary state education was in question and discrimination and segmentation in schools was still rife, Dalit literacy levels leapt up in the 1980s and 1990s in spite of all this (Desai, Adams and Dubey 2010; Kingdon 2001; Kingdon and Muzammil 2001; Nambissan 1996, 2010; Seenarine 2004). With a greater section of the Dalit population now able to read and write, many Dalits had a chance to escape the occupational destiny of their parents. Education armed them with the confidence to extract themselves from exploitative employers and seek better employment (whether or not they found it). As the works of Jeffrey, Jeffery and Jeffery (2004a, 2004b, 2005, 2008a) and Ciotti (2006) show, although the majority of the Dalit youth do not find jobs to match their education, it is still regarded as having a transformative potential, engendering a sense of entitlement altogether absent previously. Dalit access to reserved places in government colleges and universities improved, and during this time a minority of educated Dalits obtained salaried state employment and began to form an influential Dalit middle class.

At the same time, severe criticisms were being levelled at the reservations system. Among them, that reservations were only benefiting an already-privileged, self-perpetuating Dalit elite (the so-called 'creamy layer') while doing little to change the lot of the vast majority; that the policy was encouraging dependency on the state rather than enabling the cultivation of Dalits' own independent capacities and that it only permitted their entry into the lower echelons of state

An Overview ᄃ 11

employment, not the higher positions. Reservations were implicated in the conflicts between Dalit sub-castes and were blamed for creating politically-disabling class division among Dalits themselves.[10] The very fact of jobs and education given on the basis of caste was criticised for inhibiting meritocracy and hindering efficiency.[11] These objections had violent manifestations across India in the years following the Mandal Commission's report. But during the 'mandalisation' of politics in the 1990s, commentators noted that liberalisation was rapidly shrinking the state sector anyway, thereby substantially reducing the number of government jobs available to beneficiaries in the first place.

This focussed the debate more closely on the effects of liberalisation and globalisation on India's Dalits. Many were realising that energy was being wasted on the struggle for a fair share of government resources when the state itself was being rolled back. There was serious concern that as the private sector grew, Dalits would be cut adrift from the lucrative and growing sectors of the economy and marooned in low-level government employment, agriculture and wage labour. Without the forms of capital (financial, educational, social, political) to succeed in a free market economy, and most importantly, without affirmative action policies to ensure them equality of opportunity, Dalits would be marginalised all over again, so some argued (Jogdand 2000; Thorat 2002; Thorat and Newman 2007; Teltumbde 1997; Walker 2008).

Moreover, others have suggested that Dalits' revitalised marginalisation would be more extreme with the increasing social inequality and steeper stratification that liberalisation was bringing with it. The works, of Datt and Ravallion (2010), Dev and Ravi (2007), Patnaik (2007), and Himanshu (2007) provide persuasive evidence to show that 'inequality increased significantly in the post-reform period' (Dev and Ravi 2007: 509) and that the growth of the market economy was

---

[10] See Balagopal (2000, 2005) and Jodhka and Kumar (2007) for more on this topic.

[11] For more on the reservations issue, see Chalam (1990), Deshpande and Yadav (2006), Ghosh (2007), Ilaiah (2006), Mohanty (2006), Thorat, Aryama and Negi (2005), Weisskopf (2006) and Shah and Schneiderman's 2013 special issue of *Focaal* on affirmative action.

12 द *Clarinda Still*

resulting in greater cleavages between the rich and the poor. Early on, Teltumbde (1997) anticipated that strategies of 'flexibilisation and informalisation of labour; corporatisation and depeasantisation of farming etc. will release vast numbers of people in the job market' which will increase competition and exacerbate caste prejudice. The concern was that this would aggravate and intensify Dalits' already marginal position and that without protective measures or affirmative action, Dalits would have little chance to enter or succeed in business, industry or the professions in the private sector. Examining poverty levels between 1993 and 2004, Das (2010) argues that the risk of poverty for Dalits, STs and Muslims actually grew in the period of market reform. Economic growth, in this analysis, was *not* resulting in improved conditions for Dalits. Indeed, the government's emphasis on 'inclusive growth' in the Eleventh and Twelfth Five-Year Plans can be read as indicative of precisely these concerns.

Simultaneously, Dalits were now newly exposed to an upper-caste backlash, which some suggested were linked to statutory reforms. The elites of the old caste system had remarkably effectively reinvented themselves and converted their traditional assets into modern advantage (see, for example, Fuller and Narasimhan 2007;Upadhya 1988, 1997). Some suggested that liberalisation with its urban and upper-caste bias directly bolstered their position (Babu 2004: 5). Among these caste-shaped middle and upper classes, affirmative action policies have produced strong feelings of resentment, and some openly express the view that too much favouritism has been shown to the so-called 'Backward Classes' (Still 2013). This attitude has seemingly acted as a justification for new forms of nepotism among the middle-class upper-castes who have responded by turning inwards to protect themselves and advance their own interests. In addition to looking after their own, they also boycotted those Dalits who attempted to enter 'their' spheres of work (Froystad 2010). This made Dalits especially vulnerable in a brave, new, liberalising economy where the state was paying less and less attention to the provision of reserved employment, the mitigation of poverty, the advancement of social justice and development, and the protection of rights.

These new forms of discrimination as well as the interlocking set of Dalit disadvantages, described earlier, may account for Dalits' current exclusion from important parts of India's economy, which new

An Overview द 13

studies have revealed. Using Planning Commission and National Sample Survey (NSS) data, Thorat and Dubey (2012) show that while there has been a general decline in poverty from 1994–2010, the rate of decline has been lower for SCs than for the rest of the population in both rural and urban areas. Even in self-employed and non-farm households (which experienced the highest decline in poverty), SCs lagged far behind everyone else (ibid.: 50). SC farmers, SC agricultural labourers and other SC wage labourers seem to be doing particularly badly (ibid.: 51). Deshpande's recent book also draws on a wealth of econometric analyses to show the persistence of caste disparity and discrimination in the urban, formal sector and the economy more generally, a finding that strongly militates against any optimism about the 'trickle-down effect' of growth (2011: 213). Similarly, a recent edited collection entitled, 'Blocked by Caste' has showed just how severe and extensive economic discrimination against Dalits really is. Thorat and Newman (2010) discuss a gamut of contemporary mechanisms through which Dalits are persistently excluded and disadvantaged while other contributors present findings that show that Dalits with similar or higher qualifications than their higher-caste counterparts are significantly worse off in the labour market (Thorat and Attewell 2010; Deshpande and Newman 2010). Examining hiring practices, for instance, Jodhka and Newman (2007) show how managers' image of an ideal candidate implicitly disadvantages the low castes and Dalits (as well as very high-caste applicants), whilst favouring those in the middle. What makes matters worse is that the advantages of non-Dalits are so naturalised and imperceptible that they often judge Dalits to be unfairly rewarded when it is they who have the natural but invisible advantage of birth (Deshpande 2011: 212). Far from being neutral or objective, ideas of merit appear to be strongly caste-inflected.

This substantiates the work of Barbara Harriss-White (1996, Harris-White and Subramanian 1999, 2003, Harris-White and Nillesen 2004), which has consistently shown the 'embedded-ness' of caste, gender and religion in rural, semi-rural and urban labour markets. We know that Dalits face severe discrimination not only in the purchase of agricultural land, employment as agricultural labour, non-farm wage labour (Thorat, Mahamallik and Sadana 2010) but in business too (Das 2010; Jodhka 2010; Thorat, Kundu and Sadana 2010). Controversially, Prakash (2010)

14 द *Clarinda Still*

shows that the proportion of Dalit-owned firms in Tamil Nadu actually *declined* by 15 per cent in the 1990s. Dalits are often refused sites in the marketplace or rented rooms; they may be untrained in the etiquette of offering bribes, they may be avoided by consumers as well as potential business allies, they may lack knowledge about trade practises and access to facilities, they may lack capital and the ability to effectively secure credit. They are often excluded from the business networks of the service sector, trade, transport and hospitality. This leads Harriss-White and Prakash (forthcoming) to suggest that caste is operating as a 'civil social institution of capitalist accumulation' which continually disfavours Dalits. They argue that the discrimination practised against Dalits, adivasis and Muslims by the state, markets and civil society amounts to a denial of 'economic citizenship' (ibid.).

Presenting the results of different but related research with Barbara Harriss-White, Kaushal Vidyarthee's chapter (this volume) also shows the erratic and uneven nature of economic opportunity for Dalits. Using data from the Economic Censuses 1991, 1998 and 2005, Vidyarthee's paper maps the effects of discrimination on Dalits in different regions of India and in different sectors of the economy. This pioneering work suggests that there are serious barriers preventing Dalits entering the business economy and shows regions of relative advantage and disadvantage for Dalits. In doing so, Vidyarthee highlights avenues for exigent comparative research.

Mhaskar's fieldwork material (this volume) from Mumbai illustrates these themes. Mhaskar examines Dalit ex-mill workers' responses to the closure of Mumbai's textile mills since the late 1990s. Compared to other caste groups, he finds that while caste plays little part in determining Dalit opportunities in wage labour, caste plays a significant role in the small businesses. Here, Mhaskar shows how local politics combined with the social institution of caste shape Dalit ex-mill workers livelihood opportunities in the context of wider urban transformation. Together, these studies point to the resilience of caste in the economy and a denial of Dalits' 'economic citizenship' in the era of liberalisation (Harriss-White and Prakash 2012). It is not only that liberalisation is not helping Dalits, there are in fact signs that it is worsening their situation.

An Overview द 15

Sudha Pai's paper (this volume) documents Dalits' reaction to this and provides an encouraging example of a proactive government response. Pai's chapter is concerned with the 2002 Bhopal Conference, which brought together Dalit intellectuals, activists and the government officials to formulate ways to facilitate Dalit economic empowerment. Pai's chapter discusses one of the outcomes: the creation and adoption of an experimental policy called 'Supplier Diversity' by the Congress government under the leadership of Digvijay Singh in 2002. This ambitious policy set out ways to actively create Dalit entrepreneurs who would be supported by the government to enter business and industry. Pai evaluates the success of this policy and discusses its wider significance. More broadly, her paper suggests a move from the political empowerment of Dalits towards the economic empowerment of Dalits. In a climate of competition and hostility, Dalits are clearly determined to ensure that they are not excluded from the fruits of India's economic growth.

Dalit Social Mobility/Marginalisation

But the economic story cannot be separated from the social story. For part of the reason why Dalits continue to be under-represented not just in business but in almost every prestigious profession is because they lack the social skills and attributes requisite in the high-earning professions and are quietly debarred from networks of industry. As studies of 'enterprise culture', education and the middle classes show (Gilbertson 2012; Gooptu 2009; Jeffrey, Jeffery and Jeffery 2004a, 2004b, 2008a; Upadhya and Vasavi 2006), this is not just a matter of qualifications. It is also a matter of 'educated-ness', demeanour, manner, way of talking, fluency in English, 'exposure', confidence, dress, body language and even attitudes. Now taught in private schools and on expensive 'personality development' courses, these attributes are becoming characteristic of the privileged (high-caste), middle, and upper classes, meaning that the forms of distinction that lead to economic success are out of Dalits' reach all over again. This brings us back to Bourdieu (1984) who showed how the forms of cultural distinction wielded by the educated, French middle classes acted as one of the principal mechanisms for class reproduction. It is no co-incidence that the things that are enabling

16 *द* *Clarinda Still*

the traditional elites to succeed in the new economy are precisely the things that continue to elude the Dalits.[12]

This makes the rare cases of social mobility among Dalits even more noteworthy, a topic that forms the subject of Jules Naudet's chapter (this volume). Not only is it especially difficult for Dalits to obtain qualifications and well-paid jobs in the first place, when they do, Naudet shows they face peculiar pressures that emanate from the transition itself. Naudet argues that socially mobile Dalits are 'torn' between the attachment and obligations towards their original community and the desire for social legitimacy in the new group. Unlike affluent upper-caste students, upwardly-mobile Dalits cannot rely on financial support from their families. On the contrary, they often bear the burden of supporting their families even when they are studying (Thorat and Newman 2010: 24). Those who do succeed in moving class position often report carrying a psychological shame that prevents full adaptation to their new position while also feeling ambivalence towards the community they left behind. Naudet suggests that this tension presents a major challenge for socially-mobile Dalits.

This experience of upward mobility may help account for the persistence of caste endogamy even among middle-class Dalits who have the option of marrying into those families unconcerned about caste background. Present-day endogamy may not just be a matter of upper-caste families refusing Dalits as their children's marriage partners. It may be that Dalits are also actively seeking out those with the same 'culture', attitudes and experiences as them. If, as Naudet says, the experience of being both middle-class *and* Dalit is so particular, that shared experience may assume more importance in the choice of spouse. Dalits may choose to self-consciously separate themselves.

But it would be incorrect to say that the relatively low instance of marriage between non-Dalits and Dalits is solely Dalits' own choice. On the contrary, marriage with Dalits is still widely condemned and

---

[12] That said, as a personal communication with Hugo Gorringe, Senior Lecturer in Sociology, University of Edinburgh, 31 January 2012, suggests, the rise of Dalit millionaires suggests that Bourdieu's theory must be applied cautiously in the Indian context and that closer attention needs to be paid to this issue.

An Overview द 17

'upper-caste' families often go to great lengths to prevent it. Certain factors make inter-caste unions more or less acceptable, of course: a Dalit girl may be more easily incorporated into a higher-caste family than a Dalit boy, especially if there is a tradition of hypergamy (marrying up) between certain castes; a well-educated, affluent Dalit has more chance of being accepted into a middle-class family than his/her less-educated counterpart; the personal circumstances of the couple (whether or not the union is public or has already caused a scandal) and the adaptability of the individual concerned (political opinions, dietary habits, etc.) may persuade the parents one way or another. But on the whole, while rules about marriage have relaxed among almost all of the castes above the 'pollution line', inter-caste marriage with Dalits is, for many, still seen as beyond the pale. Increasingly widespread ideals of 'love marriage' and companionate marriage seem to halt at the boundary between Dalits and non-Dalits. This lends weight to Bayly (1999: 312, 340) and Parry's argument (1999, 2001, 2007) that while the caste divisions between the upper caste has merged and diminished, the division between Dalits and non-Dalits has become more rigid.

One of the most prosaic indicators of this is the continuing residential separation of Dalits and non-Dalits, what Dalit activists describe as 'India's apartheid' (Béteille 1965; Deliège 1999; Gorringe 2005; Searle-Chatterjee 1981). In my own fieldwork site in Andhra Pradesh, villages are colloquially referred to as *pallituru*, reflecting the fact that a village is constituted of two related but separate parts: the *uru*, the place where the non-Dalits live and the *palli*, the Dalit hamlet. This residential segregation marks out Dalits from other villagers and keeps them in a geographically-bounded locality so that however wealthy a Dalit becomes, he/she cannot move into the non-Dalit part of the village. This is observable in villages across India and there are parallels with urban India too, in that Dalits make up a large proportion of the urban slum population. Dalits may go in and out of the city for work but they do not live in the centre, they live on the outskirts, often in squalid, impermanent and illegal dwellings. In villages and cities, Dalits are ambiguously related to wider society: they are both in and out of the mainstream; contemptible but depended upon; marginal and crucial (Deliège 1999).

18 द *Clarinda Still*

Although termed 'the pollution line', distance is rarely justified on the basis of Dalits' polluted-ness but rather in terms of socio-economic, cultural and political difference. It is not just the fact of being the most poorly-remunerated; it is also that Dalits are in the most stigmatising occupations. Just as the high castes are uniquely positioned to take advantage of the opportunities presented by liberalisation, so Dalit professions have converted in the new economy. This is not always disadvantageous: erstwhile leather workers in Karnataka and southern Maharashtra, for example, have now become successful urban financiers of international leather production (Parameshwara 1990; Kumar 1998 cited in Charsley 2010: 159). More often, however, Dalits' low position in the traditional order finds its equivalent in the neoliberal economy (Hariss-White and Prakash forthcoming). Dalits may no longer have to manually remove human faeces but they tend to be the ones who work in sewage works; Dalit leather workers may no longer make a living from tanning hides and but they may gravitate towards shoe repair or wage labour in shoe manufacture; Dalit midwives are now undertaking training in hospitals but families still pay them to deal with the most defiling aspects of birth. Dalits still do those jobs which necessitate contact with death, dirt and waste, whether in their traditional roles in villages or as workers in urban municipal councils. Social stigma becomes the new ritual pollution; it is this that gives social separation renewed force.

The two are not unrelated. I argue elsewhere (Still 2013) that beliefs about ritual impurity have morphed into a powerful discourse about the Dalit's 'dirty habits', laziness and disease. This discourse, I suggest, is linked to atavistic concerns about pollution/contamination and functions in a similar way. Poverty may mean that some Dalits do indeed live in cramped slums or hamlets, without proper sanitation or water. But the hygiene discourse sees this as an intrinsic part of Dalit character and a product of their perceived 'innate laziness', thereby misrecognising the structural conditions of Dalit poverty and stigma, attributing it instead to an ascribed social or caste character of a stereotyped Dalit 'Other'.

Neoliberal discourses dovetail with these ideas in surprising ways. One of the more pernicious aspects of neoliberalism for Dalits pertains to the construction of poverty itself. Gooptu (2009) examines the implications of neoliberal development discourses, showing how the poor are framed as responsible for their own impoverishment. She shows how the urban poor (many of whom are Dalits, as we know) are both represented as, and coached to be, 'entrepreneurs': self-maximising individuals who make something of themselves through their own initiative. In this framework, poverty is reduced to a problem of individual attitude rather than the result of the systemic inequalities produced by liberalisation. Gooptu (2009) further argues that in framing the poor in this way, the state and development agencies de-politicise poverty and abdicate responsibility for ameliorating widening and deepening stratification.

The characterisation of poverty as personality flaw gives non-poor, non-Dalits all the more reason to separate themselves. In some areas, upper-caste communities attempt to seal themselves off and clamp down on alliance, especially marital and sexual. As the title of Chowdhry's article, 'First Our Jobs and Then Our Girls' (2009) suggests, upper-caste communities perceive Dalit men to be encroaching not only on 'their' political, occupational and residential domains but gaining access to their sisters and daughters too. In places like Haryana, this has become an acutely sensitive issue: rather than viewing inter-caste relationships as personal matters of the heart, upper-caste families perceive them as a form of direct Dalit attack and use violent means to retaliate (ibid.: 438).

Dalits are not always innocent victims in this scenario. Rogers (2008) argues that Dalit college students compensate for their own structural disempowerment and caste humiliation through the 'sexual conquest' and 'eve-teasing' of upper-caste girls. Anandhi and Jeyarangan (1999, 2002) also show how young Dalit men in rural Tamil Nadu have adopted a model of aggressive masculinity detrimental both to gender relations within the Dalit community and caste relations outside it. Indeed, it may be that Dalits are acting in retribution for the historical exploitation of Dalit women by 'threatening the manhood of their oppressors' (Kannabiran 2002: 260). However, these perceived and real advances towards upper-caste girls often elicit an unjustifiably aggressive upper-caste reaction. Occasionally this has included retributive public rapes and murder of Dalit women (Dietrich 2003; Kannabiran

20 द *Clarinda Still*

and Kannabiran 2002). Sexual politics seems to be an important part of contemporary caste conflict and violence.

This brings us to one of the most depressing features of Dalits' situation: atrocity. In 1966, Srinivas predicted that, 'As more and more Harijans become educated and seek the enforcement of constitutional rights, local clashes are likely to increase' (1966: 93). 'Local clashes' have on occasion escalated to brutal mass murder, violent assault and destruction of Dalit homes as modern India witnesses an increase in Dalit 'atrocities'.[13] In his powerful book 'Khairlanji', Teltumbde (2008) argues that these crimes have often been perpetrated not by those at the top of the caste system but by those nearer Dalits in the traditional caste hierarchy (OBCs) who feel most threatened by Dalits' rise. News of these crimes is not always reported and even when it is, Dalits have sometimes been too fearful or unable to galvanise in response. In other cases, under certain conditions, atrocities have provoked outrage among Dalits, and in several states, it is these events that have precipitated militant political protests. Although there are stringent laws designed to protect Dalits from this ultimate form of discrimination, Rao (2009) argues that in marking out Dalits for special protection, paradoxically, the law also makes Dalits more vulnerable to it. This is especially so in light of caste-based political parties' current condemnation of Dalits 'over-use' of the Atrocities Act. The allegation of Dalits' abuse of the Act may well be acting as a new form of discrimination, preventing Dalits from protecting themselves. Casteism as open abuse may be decreasing today but it resurfaces as a critique of those policies and laws that help Dalits.[14]

However, one positive thing that atrocity indicates is that despite angry resistance, Dalits' social position is changing for the better, and in some areas quite rapidly and radically (Chakraborty, Babu, and Chakravorty 2006). Two decades ago, Béteille predicted that '[c]losed status groups based upon birth are likely to yield increasingly

---

[13] So called after 'The Scheduled Caste and Scheduled Tribe (Prevention of Atrocities) Act', passed in 1989. See Human Rights Watch Report (1999) for more on this subject and Chalam (2007) for an analysis.

[14] I am grateful to Hugo Gorringe for this point and information about local conflicts over the Atrocities Act.

An Overview द 21

to relatively open status groups based upon education, income and occupation' (1991: 178). This may not have happened yet in India but it is true to say that for most Dalits, caste no longer *dictates* occupation, residence, marriage partner, social standing or life chances in the way it used to. A recent survey of Dalit households in rural UP documents massive changes in consumption patterns and social behaviours since 1990 (Kapur et al. 2010). The authors argue that although caste still exists, 'many practices that reflected social subordination and routine humiliation of dalits have declined considerably' (ibid.: 48). They continue, 'In a large majority of the villages in this survey, dalits no longer lift non-dalits' dead animals; dalit babies are often delivered by non-dalit midwives; dalits are rarely seated separately at weddings; and it is no longer uncommon for non-dalits to accept foods in dalit homes. Economically, there has been a rapid shift out of traditional dalit economic relationships into local occupations and professions, migration and changed agricultural practices' (ibid.).[15]

Similarly, in the city, anonymity prevents the free flow of caste-based behaviour in relationships insofar as one simply cannot know the caste of the owner of the grocery shop, the people who sit near you in restaurants, your colleagues at work, the manager of your bank, fellow diners at a social gathering, the man who serves you tea, your teacher at school, guests at a wedding, and so forth. One may hazard a guess, and the close correlation between class and caste means you might be right but it is not always possible for others to prevent Dalits making their way in the city. In some workplaces, colleagues who do know each other's caste identity may deliberately work and eat together anyway (although they may draw the line at eating beef); in others, managers deliberately attempt to instil a culture of equality through inter-caste dining (see Parry 1999) and ban the use of caste names (Gilbertson 2012). Inter-caste friendship is the norm rather than the exception in schools, hostels, campuses, offices, labour sites (Jeffrey 2010; Nisbett 2007), even if these friendships are 'fair-weather' and do not extend back into the

---

[15] Disappointingly, Kapur et al. (2010) shy away from commenting on the causes of these changes and if they have any link to liberalisation. They simply point out that major changes have occurred.

22 द *Clarinda Still*

natal home or villages. Although inter-caste marriage is uncommon, it is occurring nevertheless. Many people (admittedly usually non-Dalits) claim not even to know their caste, or if they do, declare its irrelevance. Moreover, as Fuller (1996) points out, discriminating on the basis of caste is now universally condemned in public life; it is unacceptable to publicly display negative caste-ist attitudes. The 'de-legitimation' of caste does not eliminate discrimination or prevent it from distorting into new forms, but it nevertheless marks a sea-change in favour of Dalits.

Conversion to egalitarian religions (neo-Buddhism, Christianity, Islam) and Hindu sects has for a long time enabled Dalits to reject Hinduism and has provided them with an alternative source of spiritual power, faith, status, self-respect and a ritual and religious infrastructure. In villages where Dalit subordination was enacted and produced through the degrading ritual roles they performed in festivals (such as drumming), this is especially important. Christian theology has challenged caste-ism in the church and attempted to create a theological stronghold for Dalits and address the specific concerns of Dalit Christians such as lack of reservation (Clarke 2003; Forrester 1980; Wyatt 2010). Dalits are renouncing humiliating services and roles or at least taking cash payment for them. They are refusing to toady at the feet of their employers; dress in low-status clothes or go barefoot or jewellery-less through upper-caste areas. The public practice of Untouchability has undoubtedly diminished: a tea shop operating on the two-tumbler system, a village prohibiting Dalits from using public water sources or debarring Dalits from upper-caste areas or the temple are now becoming newsworthy exceptions, not the rule. That is not to say that Dalits are anywhere near receiving the kind of treatment they desire. In their role as agricultural labourers and servants in villages, Dalits are still obliged to display the old forms of genuflection and they are still subject to multiple daily forms of humiliation.[16] But as systems of patronage, dependency, bonded labour, the practice of Untouchability and the legitimacy of the high-caste authority wane, Dalits are less reliant on others for their survival and well-being. They are gaining both the financial means and

---

[16] See Guru (2011) for a theorisation of Dalit humiliation.

An Overview   द   23

sense of entitlement necessary to acquire those symbols of status that confer dignity and honour.

All of this affects Dalits' view of themselves and means that acquiescent Dalits like Viramma[17] who accept their low position are probably the last of their kind, as the Racines (1998) say.[18] As commentators have repeatedly pointed out, Dalits today do not see their low social status as an unalterable fact of life. Life maybe characterised by deprivation but few, if any, accept this as a god-given state of affairs to be unquestioningly tolerated as *dharma*, if they ever did. Quite the contrary, most struggle hard to improve themselves and escape the ignominy which characterised their past. Indeed, negotiating an improved status for themselves is a project of vital importance to most Dalits today. As Béteille puts it, 'Among people who have been tied to social degradation for generations, the appeal of respectability is particularly urgent' (1991: 177).

In rare cases, Dalits have managed to become the dominant caste (see Mullard, this volume). However, as Mullard's case study shows, this may not stop them from instituting the same type of patronage relationships with their Dalit employees as other high castes do elsewhere. This, she argues, should not be seen as a replication or consensus of Brahmincal ideology (Moffatt 1979) but rather as a re-construction and manipulation of *jajmani* exchange practices in the context of economic crisis (the suspension of mining in the region). Nevertheless, it does remind us that idioms of dominance and subordination are often so entrenched that powerful Dalits may end up subordinating others as they themselves were subordinated. It also illustrates that Dalit mobility is not always revolutionary: there are always rewards in perpetuating a conservative system (Racine and Racine 1997: 10). In some cases, the inferior partner of the exchange may collude in this and similarly reinvigorate traditional relationships of hierarchy and patronage if they

---

[17] The extraordinary Tamil Dalit labourer, mother, singer and storyteller recorded and published by Jean Luc and Josiane Racine (1997).

[18] And even Viramma was not so acquiescent as to deny her children the opportunities afforded by education (I am grateful to Hugo Gorringe for this point).

24 द *Clarinda Still*

consider it in their interests. This is what Mosse called the 'trade-off' between security and respectability (Mosse 1994; see also Charsley 2010: 158).

This strategy of degrading others to advance oneself is not new (see Mosse 1994). There is plenty of evidence of jostling hierarchies among Dalit sub-castes, lineages, generations, and, of course, men and women. The gender hierarchy has been of particular interest to feminist scholars as there are signs that Dalit women are not only being left behind in Dalits' social advance but that social progress for Dalit men is premised on the degradation of Dalit women. Kapadia (1995, 2002), among others, argues that upward social mobility brings patriarchal practices that destroy the egalitarian nature of Dalit and non-Brahmin communities.

However, Judith Heyer (this volume) presents evidence that questions this view. Heyer's chapter shows that what may look retrograde to feminist observers, may in fact, be a mark of social advance for Dalit women themselves, not as 'false consciousness' but simply as the best of a very limited set of alternatives. For the Dalit women she has studied over three decades, becoming a housewife represents genuine progress. Compared to back-breaking, monotonous labour in the fields, the option of staying at home, looking after the house, the family and supporting the children's education is logically favoured when circumstances allow it. Heyer argues that 'housewification' goes hand- in-hand with substantial improvements in living conditions over three generations in her study villages. Whether this contributes to a growing patriarchy among traditionally egalitarian Dalit communities or enables unexpected forms of female empowerment is the question.

Dalit Political Mobility/ Marginalisation

Part of the reason for these social advances is Dalits' success in politics and the emergence of Dalits on to the political stage (Charsley and Karanth 2005; Omvedt 1994; Pai 2002; Shah 2001; Zelliot 1992). Much attention has been paid to the success of Mayawati and the BSP in north India who dominated the leadership of India's largest state for a decade. While the BSP's success is regionally inconsistent, today almost all Dalits are to some extent touched by the impact of Dalit politics, whether in or out of electoral politics. Gorringe's (2005) ethnographic study of the Dalit movement in Tamil Nadu documents the immense range of Dalit political groups and shows how Dalits are stridently challenging the bases of Dalit subordination. Indeed, the rise of Dalits in politics has led some scholars to argue that India is experi-encing an 'unfinished', 'democratic' or 'silent' Dalit revolution (Pai 2002; Omvedt 1994; Jaffrelot 2003, respectively). At the most basic level, the sheer size of the Dalit constituency means that no political party can afford to overlook the Dalit vote and that even the unlikeliest parties, such as the socially-conservative BJP, court Dalit support. Whilst the long-term significance of Dalit political success for India's democracy is unknown, there can be little doubt that Dalits are emerging as one of India's most potent and vocal forces of change.

In the last 10 years, Dalits have gone beyond national boundaries to campaign on an international stage against caste discrimination. From the bustling Indian city of Lucknow to the English town of Wolverhampton, Dalits are establishing their own global networks of activists and have made coalitions with allied campaigns for human rights, minority rights, global justice and even indigenous peoples. Hardtmann (2009) shows how Dalits' rejection of Hinduism and the Dalit 'counter public' are now becoming overt and how activists are becoming increasingly skilled at translating local concerns into international language. In 2001, Dalits made a strong impact in the UN World Conference against capital racism in Durban; in 2004, Dalits attracted international press attention at the World Social Forum in Mumbai; and in Britain, at the time of writing, groups are pressurising the government to recognise caste in the UK Equalities Bill (Waughray 2009). In all its various guises, activism against caste is now a veritable feature of a global rights landscape, heralding 'the internationalisation of the problem of Untouchability' (Rao 2009: 12). Dalits also have a significant presence in the NGO sector and in Christian organisations, sometimes with strong links to political parties and/or international sources of funding to help advance their visions (Mosse forthcoming). In this sense, globalisation (if not liberalisation) has opened up new possibilities for Dalits.

At the local level, Dalit political organisations can be extremely complex and idiosyncratic, often with a number of different political groups (with or without connections to parties) vying for supremacy. Saglio-Yatzimirsky (2010), for example, shows how Cambhar, Dhor and Holar slum dwellers in Dharavi, Mumbai use caste as a 'mobilizing agent, a community, a movement' (ibid.: 226). Caste loyalties are manipulated by political parties and Dalits themselves, sometimes to produce intense caste rivalry (ibid.). Representatives of these groups curry favour by helping slum Dalits with mundane things such as applying for caste certificates, accompanying Dalits to local government offices to file a complaint or register for state services. An important function of local level Dalit political groups is to offer support in case of grievances against employers, feuds with neighbours or in times of crisis such as atrocities, especially when the police and state representatives continually seem to fail them. Activities such as these reduce Dalits' vulnerability and give them recourse to justice when things go wrong. De Neve and Carswell (2011a, 2011b), for instance, have recently shown how Dalits activists in the Tirrupur region of Tamil Nadu have become skilled in using the Atrocities Act to protect and assert themselves, much to the chagrin of the dominant castes who have organised to counter them.

Through reservations, Dalits now occupy positions of power in local governance, sometimes simply as 'puppet sarpanches' but not always. When circumstances permit it, Dalits use their power in the panchayat to their own and their communities' advantage. Dalits' presence in local governance and politics is extremely important, not just because it enhances the honour and status of the individual and their community but also because it provides role models to younger Dalits and proves to sceptics that Dalits are as capable of leadership as anyone else. Whether in student unions, inner-city slums or rural hamlets, these local leaders, Dalit activists and Dalit organic intellectuals convince Dalits that subservience is no longer their preordained destiny. The spread of such ideas is fuelled not only by grassroots mobilisation, campaigning, speeches and everyday forms of activism but also by the production and dissemination of pamphlets and booklets, a process described and analysed for the first time by Narayan (this volume).

An Overview द 27

Dalit politics is in no small part a politics of culture. Influential activist scholars, such as V.T. Rajashekar and Kancha Ilaiah, and Dalit politicians such as the late Kanshi Ram express the view that first and foremost the consciousness and life-worlds of the oppressed must be revealed and celebrated in order to overthrow the dominant, 'Brahminical' view of the world. To this end, they promote a view of Dalit (or 'Dalit Bahujan', as Ilaiah calls it) culture that contrasts, conflicts and clashes with 'caste Hindu' culture (Ilaiah 2004). This 'culture' may be quite far from any empirical reality (see, for example, Ilaiah 1996) but the point is to encourage Dalits to celebrate aspects of 'difference' rather than hide, efface or change them. In line with this thinking, Dalits are successfully reversing the meanings of formerly shameful markers of Untouchability. Arun (2007) shows how the Dalit practice of drumming has been revived by the Dalit movement in South India. Similarly, Gundimeda (2009) discusses the demand for a beef stall at the Sukoon festival in the middle of the University of Hyderabad's campus. This politics of culture selectively seizes upon reviled Untouchable practices (drumming, beef-eating and leather work) and appropriates them as much-vaunted symbols of a Dalit identity. Rather than adopting upper-caste lifestyles, values and customs, Dalits are developing, asserting and celebrating their own 'counter-culture' (Hardtmann 2009). Ilaiah (1996) calls this the 'Dalitisation' of identity, a model of upward mobility which explicitly rejects 'caste Hindu' status criteria. This construction of identity can be seen as both the result of, but also the basis for, claims to resources and political power.

Dalit literature, art, storytelling, theatre and poetry are important parts of this cultural politics. Dalit intellectuals have established their own publishing houses, journals and poetry magazines. Racine and Racine (1998) also draw attention to the striking images that some of these publications carry in Tamil Nadu, including beef, blood, birth and death, arguing that, 'the use of such symbols clearly sends a new message: Dalits are not to be ashamed of the "polluted" images traditionally ascribed to them' (1998: 11). Satyanarayana and Tharu's (2011 and 2013) recent anthologies document some of the upsurge of Dalit writing in South India in the 1990s and bear witness to a ferment of Dalit creativity and social commentary. Written by authors from traditionally non-literate castes (and widely perceived as 'unintellectual' people)

28 द *Clarinda Still*

Dalit writing presents fresh, energetic, controversial perspectives that challenge conventional ideas of the literary. The relationship between Dalit politics and culture is also a dialectic one: politics nourishes cultural innovation but it also uses already-embedded, local ideas and practices and allows itself to be shaped by them. Narayan (2006), for example, shows how the BSP inventively linked Mayawati with grass-roots myths and memories of Dalit women heroes to cement Mayawati's popularity among Dalits in Uttar Pradesh. Now, as Mayawati's infamous statue construction projects attest, she is attempting to insert herself into this heritage of local myth to become part of the physical and imaginary landscape.

The flip side of this celebration of Dalit culture is a deep-seated anger against 'caste Hindu culture' and a ferocious determination to shatter its dominance. At its extreme edges, this manifests as a militantism which fuels violent confrontation. It is this aspect that alienates more moderate Dalits who seek integration rather than revolution, not to mention non-Dalit well-wishers. It should not be forgotten that many non-Dalits actively support Dalits' campaign for equality and dignity. Some of this may be in the Gandhian spirit of uplift but some is in the name of genuine transformation. Political alliances between Dalits and non-Dalits (such as the alliance between Brahmins and Dalits in the BSP in Uttar Pradesh or the alliance between Kammas and Dalits in the Communist Party in Andhra Pradesh) is often seen as pure strategy, but these alliances may also help to forge links between Dalits and others, as well as reflecting socio-economic commonalities that already exist. While activists fear ideological dilution, alliance may also curb the more violent polarising tendency of what Deliège (2010) calls 'Dalitism'.

But we must be wary of overstating the impact of Dalit politics. As Jeffrey, Jeffery and Jeffery (2008b) argue, Dalit political gains should not be exaggerated. The authors claim that Dalits in rural Uttar Pradesh have lost faith in Dalit politics and that 'the rise of lower-caste parties has not resulted in increased leverage and political power for Dalits on the ground' (ibid.: 1390). They relate this to educated un- and under-employment as well as rising expectations unmatched by increased incomes. Not only is there a 'standard of living paradox', then, but a

An Overview द 29

'political paradox' too. Despite the phenomenal rise of Dalit and low-caste politics, many ordinary Dalits are frustrated by disempowerment and exclusion from positions of authority. This, added to Babu's prediction (2004) that that political instability will increase if economic reforms proceed without social change should make us cautiously evaluate Dalits' success in politics.

Apart from what Dalit politics have or have not achieved for ordinary people, there is the wider issue of an 'impasse' in Dalit politics itself (Shah 2004). Using the case of the largest Dalit Party in Tamil Nadu (the *Viduthalai Chiruthaigal Katchi* [VCK]), Gorringe's chapter addresses this issue by exploring the VCK's entry into electoral politics. He assesses whether the VCK has been able to bring about change for Dalits and gain recognition (as well as change the nature of state politics itself) or whether entry into mainstream politics inevitability results in compromise, concession and corruption that distance the party from those it represents and leads to dissatisfaction and disempowerment.

These issues are all the more pertinent in light of the serious fragmentation of the Dalit movement that is occurring in several different parts of the country. This is largely due to the under-representation of two groups: Dalit women and the weaker Dalit sub-castes. Dalit women's 'triple' disadvantage is widely recognised (Dalit organisations often have a 'women's wing') but women's interests are often regarded as secondary and even divisive (Gorringe 2005: 236–40). More fundamental issues of patriarchy in the Dalit movement and caste-ism in the feminist movement have resulted in an upsurge of autonomous Dalit feminist groups across India.[19] At the same time, conflicts between Pallars, Pariayars and Arunthathiyars in Tamil Nadu; Mahars, Mangs and Charmakars in Maharashtra Madigas and Holeyas in Karnataka, Balmiki/Mazhabis and Ad Dharmis/Chamars in Punjab Jatavs, Balmikis and Pasis in Uttar Pradesh and Malas and Madigas in Andhra Pradesh have raised important questions about the ability of state- and national-level Dalit politics to respond democratically to the heterogeneity of

---

[19] See Baghel (2009); Dietrich (2003); Guru (1995); Kumar (2003); Malik (1999); Rao (2003); Rege (1995, 2000, 2003); Subramaniam (2006) for more on Dalit feminism and Dalit women's organisations.

30 ॡ *Clarinda Still*

their constituency.[20] It is this question that has effectively stymied a unified Dalit politics. This, added to the construction and celebration of individual caste identities and a firm rejection of the term 'Dalit' by some, would seem to signal the demise of a single Dalit identity as well as an increasing 'ethnicisation' of caste among Dalits.

And yet, as Charsley (2010) says, 'the resilience of *jatis* as major units of collective identity in the society generally means that, instead of 'Dalit' displacing those separate identities, it is something added to the available repertoire' (ibid.: 156). Indeed, some of the impetus of Dalit politics comes from the competing utility of the *jati* versus 'Dalit' identities, which may be drawn upon in different circumstances for different purposes. We find both centralising tugs towards a common 'Dalit' unity and fragmenting pulls away from it. But, as Charsley also asserts, the weaker and less organised castes who are the least able to assert a distinctive caste identity (and who are therefore more likely to rely on a common Dalit label) are at most risk of under-representation.

Furthermore, the reach of Dalit politics is very variable across India, and the ability of ordinary Dalits to express themselves is often highly contingent on local conditions. Dalits rightly fear jeopardising their livelihoods by antagonising their employers through involvement in oppositional politics. As Breman (2000) notes in reference to labourers' protest in Gujarat, 'Not only would the farmer sack the labourer concerned, but he would not hesitate to turn the other landowners against him' (ibid.: 306). Being blacklisted for employment is a blunt but effective tool against Dalit mobilisation. Whatever radical outlook is articulated at the top, empowerment is only possible when socio-economic conditions allow it. Focussed as it is on caste, Dalit politics has been charged with failing to respond adequately to the economic dimensions of a disenfranchised proletariat, whose needs are almost always subordinated to the interests of international corporations, Indian business, the state and the socially dominant classes. Indeed Dalit parties have been accused of forging advantageous pacts with businesses in Special Economic Zones, pacts that cut adrift the workers in those

---

[20] For more on sub-caste conflict and the subdivision of the reservation quota, see Balagopal (2000, 2005) in reference to Andhra Pradesh and Jodhka and Kumar (2007) in reference to Punjab.

'havens of liberalisation'.[21] New economic formations, this reminds us, may both reinforce as well as challenge relations of domination.[22]

The difficulty for anyone seeking to represent or describe Dalits (whether politicians or academics) is how to speak in generalised terms about the whole of this vast and diverse population. This brings us back to the concerns raised at the beginning. If Dalit-ness is indeed constituted by subordination, then can those who have managed to escape subordination genuinely be called Dalit? Are non-poor Dalits to be excluded from the classification to avoid them diluting the semantic force of the category 'Dalit'? After all, this word must refer to those who are 'broken' and ground down if it is to retain its true meaning. If not, then as Dalits' situation gradually improves, their very identity as *subordinates* must dissipate. This is a good thing for Dalits themselves but it will be a challenge to Dalit activists, whose political project rests on a premise of disadvantage (Deliège 2010).

But this has not happened yet and the work of Dalit politics is far from done. Extensive changes have occurred but most are still very far away from achieving the kind of status to which they aspire. It is safe to say that in relational terms, Dalit castes still occupy the lowest rungs of Indian society due to persistent exclusion and impoverishment. Dalit subordination may exist in an attenuated, transformed and less visible way but it is this, we would argue, that makes it as tenacious as ever. The challenge, then, is to find nuanced but robust strategies to respond to the ways in which Dalits are being marginalised anew in India's neoliberal era.

॥

References

Anandhi, S. and J. Jeyaranjan. 1999. 'Tamil Nadu: New Caste Equations', *Economic and Political Weekly*, 29 January: 15–16.

———. 2002. 'Work, Caste and Competing Masculinities: Notes from a Tamil Village', *Economic and Political Weekly*, 37(43): 4397–406.

---

[21] Personal communication with Gorringe, 31 January 2012.

[22] Personal communication with Gorringe, 31 January 2012.

32 ਰ *Clarinda Still*

Appadurai, Arjun. 1996. *Modernity at Large: Cultural Dimensions of Globalisation.* Minneapolis: University of Minnesota Press.

Arun, C. Joe. 2007. 'From Stigma to Self-Assertion: Paraiyars and the Symbolism of the Parai Drum', *Contributions to Indian Sociology*, 41(1): 81–104.

Babu, D. Shyam. 2004. 'India's Liberalisation and the Dalits'. Asia Programme Working Paper. London: Royal Institute of International Affairs (Asia Programme).

Baghel, Inda. 2009. *Dalit Women's Movement in Modern India.* New Delhi: Jnanada Prakashan (P and D).

Balagopal, K. 2000. 'A Tangled Web: Subdivision of SC Reservations in AP', *Economic and Political Weekly*, 35(13), 25 March: 1075–81.

———. 2005. 'Justice for Dalits among Dalits', *Economic and Political Weekly*, 40(29), 16 July: 3128–33.

Bayly, Susan. 1999. *Caste, Society and Politics in India from the Eighteenth Century to the Modern Age.* Cambridge: Cambridge University Press.

Béteille, André. 1965. *Class, Caste and Power: Changing Patterns of Stratification in a Tanjore Village.* Berkeley: University of California Press.

———. 1972. 'Pollution and Poverty', in J. M. Mahar (ed.), *The Untouchables in Contemporary India*, pp. 412–20. Tucson: University of Arizona Press.

———. 1991. *Society and Politics in India: Essays in Comparative Perspective.* London: Athlone.

———. 1992. *The Backward Classes in Contemporary India.* Delhi: Oxford University Press.

Bhaumik, Sumon Kumar and Manisha Chakrabarty. 2006. *Inter-Caste Differences in Formal Sector Earnings in India: Has the Rise of Caste-Based Politics Had an Impact?* Keele: Centre for Economic Research, Keele University.

Borooah, Vani. K. 2005. Caste, Inequality, and Poverty in India, *Review of Development Economics*, 9(3): 399–414.

———. 2010. 'Inequality in Health Outcomes in India: The Role of Caste and Religion', in Sukhadeo Thorat and Katherine Newman (eds), *Blocked by Caste: Economic Discrimination in Modern India.* New Delhi: Oxford University Press.

Bourdieu, Pierre. 1984. *Distinction: A Social Critique of the Judgement of Taste*, trans. R. Nice. Cambridge: Harvard University Press.

Breman, Jan. 2000. '"I am the Government Labour Officer...": State Protection for Rural Proletariat of South Gujarat', in Zoya Hasan (ed.), *Politics and the State in India.* New Delhi: Sage Publications.

An Overview द 33

Chakraborty, Debashis, D. Shyam Babu and Manashi Chakravorty. 2006. 'Atrocities on Dalits: What District Data Say about State-Society Complicity', *Economic and Political Weekly*, 41(24): 2478–81.

Chalam, K. S. 1990. 'Caste Reservations and Equality of Opportunity in Education', *Economic and Political Weekly*, 25(41): 2333–39.

———. 2007. *Caste-Based Reservations and Human Development in India*. New Delhi: Sage Publications.

Charsley, Simon. 1996. 'Untouchable: What Is in a Name?' *The Journal of the Royal Anthropological Institute*, 2(1): 1–23.

———. 2010. 'Untouchable Identity and Its Reconstruction', in Mikael Aktor and Robert Deliège (eds), *From Stigma to Assertion: Untouchability, Identity and Politics in Early and Modern India*, pp. 147–77. Copenhagen: Museum Tusculanum Press.

Charsley, Simon and G. K. Karanth (eds). 2005. *Challenging Untouchability: Dalit Initiative and Experience from Karnataka*. New Delhi: Sage Publications.

Chowdhry, Prem. 2009. '"First Our Jobs Then Our Girls". The Dominant Caste Perceptions on the "Rising" Dalits', *Modern Asian Studies*, 43(2): 437–79.

Ciotti, Manuela. 2006. 'In the Past We Were a Bit "Chamar": Education as a Self and Community Engineering Process in Northern India', *Journal of the Royal Anthropological Institute*, 12(4): 899–916.

Clarke, Sathianathan. 2003. 'Conversion to Christianity in Tamil Nadu: Conscious and Constitutive Community Mobilisation towards a Different Symbolic World Vision', in Rowena Robinson and Sathianathan Clarke (eds), *Religious Conversion in India: Modes, Motivations, and Meanings*, Oxford: Oxford University Press.

Cohen, Bernard. 1996. *Colonialism and Its Forms of Knowledge: The British in India*. Princeton: Princeton University Press.

Corbridge, Stuart, Glyn Williams, Manoj Srivastava and René Veron. 2005. *Seeing the State: Governance and Governmentality in India*. Cambridge: Cambridge University Press.

Das, S. 2010. 'Caste, Ethnicity, and Religion: Linkages with Unemployment and Poverty', in Sukhadeo Thorat and Katherine Newman (eds), *Blocked by Caste. Economic Discrimination in Modern India*, New Delhi: Oxford University Press.

Datt, Gaurav and Martin Ravallion. 2010. 'Shining for the Poor Too?' *Economic & Political Weekly*, 45(7): 55–60.

Debroy, Bibek and D. Shyam Babu (eds). 2004b. *The Dalit Question: Reforms and Social Justice*. New Delhi: Globus Books.

Deliège, Robert. 1992. 'Replication and Consensus: Untouchability, Caste and Ideology in India', *Man*, 27(1): 155–73.

———. 1994. 'Caste without a System: A Study of South Indian Harijans', in M. Searle-Chatterjee and U. Sharma (eds), *Contextualising Caste: Post-Dumontian Approaches*, pp. 122–46. Oxford: Blackwell Publishers.

———. 1999. *The Untouchables of India*. Oxford: Berg.

———. 2010. 'Introduction', in Mikael Aktor and Robert Deliège (eds), *From Stigma to Assertion: Untouchability, Identity and Politics in Early and Modern India*, pp. 13–30. Copenhagen: Museum Tusculanum Press, University of Copenhagen.

De Neve, Geert and Grace Carswell. 2011a. 'The Changing Face of Caste Politics in Western Tamil Nadu'. Paper presented in the Contemporary South Asia Seminar, University of Oxford, 13 October.

———. 2011b. 'From Field to Factory: Tracing Transformations in Bonded Labour in the Tiruppur Region, Tamil Nadu'. Manchester Working Papers in Political Economy, 1.

Desai, Sonalde, Cecily Darden Adams and Amaresh Dubey. 2010. 'Segmented Schooling: Inequalities in Primary Education', in Sukhadeo Thorat and Katherine Newman (eds), *Blocked by Caste. Economic Discrimination in Modern India*. New Delhi: Oxford University Press.

Deshpande, Ashwini. 2001. 'Caste at Birth? Redefining Disparity in India', *Review of Development Economics*, 5(1): 130–44.

———. 2011. *The Grammar of Caste: Economic Discrimination in Contemporary India*. New Delhi: Oxford University Press.

Deshpande, Ashwini and Katherine S. Newman. 2010. 'Where the Path Leads: The Role of Caste in Post-University Employment Expectations', in S. Thorat and K. Newman (eds), *Blocked by Caste: Economic Discrimination in Modern India*, New Delhi: Oxford University Press.

Deshpande, Satish and Yogendra Yadav. 'Redesigning Affirmative Action Castes and Benefits in Higher Education', *Economic and Political Weekly*, 41(24): 2419–24.

Dev, S. Mahendra and C. Ravi. 2007. 'Poverty and Inequality: All-India and States, 1983–2005', *Economic and Political Weekly*, 42(6): 509–21.

Dietrich, Gabriele. 2003. 'Dalit Movement and Women's Movements', in A. Rao (ed.), *Gender and Caste*, pp. 57–79. London, New York: Zed Books.

Dirks, Nicholas. 1992. 'Introduction: Colonialism and Centre', in *Colonialism and Culture*. Ann Arbor: University of Michigan Press.

———. 2001. *Castes of Mind: Colonialism and the Making of Modern India*. Princeton: Princeton University Press.

An Overview द 35

Dollar, David and Aart Kraay. 2002. 'Growth is Good for the Poor', *Journal of Economic Growth*, (7): 195–225.

Drèze, Jean and Amartya K. Sen. 1995. *India: Economic Development and Social Opportunity*. Oxford: Clarendon Press.

Dudley-Jenkins, L. 2003. *Identity and Identification in India: Defining the Disadvantaged*. London: Routledge.

Dumont, Louis. 1970. *Homo Hierarchicus: The Caste System and Its Implications*. London: Weidenfield and Nicolson.

Fitzgerald, Timothy. 1996. 'From Structure to Substance: Ambedkar, Dumont and Orientalism', *Contributions to Indian Sociology*, 30(2): 273–88.

Forrester, Duncan B. 1980. *Caste and Christianity: Attitudes and Policies on Caste of Anglo-Saxon Protestant Missions in India*. London: Curzon Press.

Froystad, Kathinka. 2010. 'Relegitimizing Caste Discrimination in Uttar Pradesh: Towards a Post-Mandal Untouchability?' in Mikael Aktor and Robert Deliège (eds), *From Stigma to Assertion: Untouchability, Identity and Politics in Early and Modern India*, pp. 178–200. Copenhagen: Museum Tusculanum Press.

Fuller, Christopher J. 1996. 'Introduction', in *Caste Today*. New Delhi, Oxford: Oxford University Press.

———. 2004. *The Camphor Flame: Popular Hinduism and Society in India*. Princeton: Princeton University Press.

Fuller. Christopher J. and Haripriya Narasimhan. 2007. 'Information Technology Professionals and the New-Rich Middle Class in Chennai (Madras)', *Modern Asian Studies*, 41(1): 121–50.

Galanter, Marc. 1971. 'The Abolition of Disabilities: Untouchability and the Law', in J. M. Mahar (ed.), *The Untouchables in Contemporary India*, pp. 228–316. Tucson: University of Arizona Press.

Gang, Ira, Kunal Sen and Myeong-SuYun. 2005. 'Poverty in Rural India: Ethnicity and Caste'. Departmental Working Papers. New Jersey: Department of Economics, Rutgers University. http://www.econstor. eu/bitstream/10419/31274/1/566327201.pdf (accessed 15 December 2013).

Ghosh, Jayati. 2007. 'Case for Caste-based Quotas in Higher Education', *Economic and Political Weekly*, 41(24), 17 June: 2428–31.

Gilbertson, Amanda. 2012. *Within the Limits of Respectability: Making Class and Gender in Hyderabad*. Unpublished DPhil Thesis, University of Oxford.

Gooptu, Nandini. 2009. 'Neoliberal Subjectivity, Enterprise Culture and New Workplaces: Organised Retail and Shopping Malls in India', *Economic and Political Weekly*, 44(22): 45–54.

36 ক Clarinda Still

Gorringe, Hugo. 2005. *Untouchable Citizens: Dalit Movements and Democratisation in Tamil Nadu.* London, New Delhi: Sage Publications.

Gundimeda, Sambaiah. 2009. 'Democratisation of the Public Sphere: The Beef Stall Case in Hyderabad's Sukoon Festival', *South Asia Research,* 29(2): 127–49.

Guru, Gopal. 1995. 'Dalit Women Talk Differently'. *Economic and Political Weekly,* 30(41), 14–21 October: 2548–50.

———. 2011. 'Theorizing Humiliation', in *Humiliation: Claims and Context,* pp. 1 –22. New Delhi: Oxford University Press.

Hardtmann, Eva-Maria. 2009. *The Dalit Movement in India: Local Practices, Global Connections.* New Delhi: Oxford University Press.

Harriss-White, Barbara. 1996. *A Political Economy of Agricultural Markets in South India: Masters of the Countryside.* New Delhi: Sage Publications.

———. 2003. *India Working: Essays on Society and Economy.* Cambridge: Cambridge University Press.

Harriss-White, Barbara and P. H. L. Nillesen. 2004. 'Life Chances: Development and Female Disadvantage', in Barbara Harriss-White and S. Janakarajan (eds), *Rural India Facing the 21st Century: Essays on Long term Village Change and Recent Development Policy: Policy Economy and International Relations,* pp. 328–48. London: Anthem Press.

Harriss-White, Barbara and Aseem Prakash. 2014. 'Globalisation, Economic Citizenship and India's Inclusive Development', in Jakub Zajączkowski, Jivanta Schöttli and Manish Thapa (eds), *India in the Contemporary World: Polity, Economy and International Relations,* pp. 127–59. New Delhi: Routledge.

Harriss-White, Barbara and S. Subramanian (eds). 1999. *Illfare in India: Essays on India's Social Sector in Honour of S. Guhan.* New Delhi: Sage Publications.

Heyer, Judith. 2000. 'The Changing Position of Agricultural Labourers in Villages in Rural Coimbatore, Tamil Nadu, between 1981/2 and 1996'. *QEH Working Papers Series 57.*

———. 2010. 'The Marginalisation of Dalits in a Modernising Economy', in Barbara Harris-White and Judith Heyer (eds), *The Comparative Political Economy of Development, Africa and South Asia.* London: Routledge.

———. Forthcoming. 'Dalits in Industrialising Villages near Coimbatore and Tirupur: 1981/2, 1996, and 2008/9', in V. K. Ramachandran (ed.), *Dalit Households in Village Economies.* New Delhi: Tulika.

Himanshu. 2007. 'Recent Trends in Poverty and Inequality: Some Preliminary Results', *Economic and Political Weekly,* 42(6): 497–508.

Human Rights Watch. 1999. *Broken People: Caste Violence against India's Untouchables.* New York, Washington, London, Brussels: Human Rights Watch.

An Overview द 37

Ilaiah, Kancha. 1996. *Why I Am Not A Hindu: A Sudra Critique of Hindutva, Philosophy, Culture and Political Economy*. Kolkata: Samya.

———. 2004. *Buffalo Nationalism: A Critique of Spiritual Fascism*. Kolkata: Samya.

———. 2006. 'Merits of Reservation', *Economic and Political Weekly*, 31(24), 17–23 June: 2447–49.

Inden, Ronald. 1990. *Imagining India*. Oxford: Blackwell.

Jaffrelot, Christophe. 2003. *India's Silent Revolution: The Rise of the Lower Castes in North India*. London: Hurst.

Jeffrey, Craig. 2010. *Timepass: Youth, Class and the Politics of Waiting in India*. Stanford: Stanford University Press.

Jeffrey, Craig, Roger Jeffery and Patricia Jeffery. 2004a. 'Degrees without Freedom: The Impact of Formal Education on Dalit Young Men in North India', *Development and Change*, 35(5): 963–86.

———. 2004b. '"A Useless Thing!" or "Nectar of the Gods?" The Cultural Production of Education and Young Men's Struggles for Respect in Liberalizing North India', *Annals of the Association of American Geographers*, 94(4): 961–81.

———. 2005. 'When Schooling Fails: Young Men, Education and Low–Caste Politics in Rural North India', *Contributions to Indian Sociology*, 39(1): 1–38.

———. 2008a. *Degrees without Freedom? Education, Masculinities, and Unemployment in North India*. Stanford: Stanford University Press.

———. 2008b. 'Dalit Revolution? New Politicians in Uttar Pradesh, India', *The Journal of Asian Studies*, 67: 1365–96.

Jodhka, Surinder S. 2010. 'Dalits in Business: Self-Employed Scheduled Castes in North-West India', *Economic and Political Weekly*, 45(11): 41–48.

Jodhka, Surinder S. and Avinash Kumar. 2007. 'Internal Classification of Scheduled Castes', *The Punjab Story Economic and Political Weekly*, 42(43), 27 October: 20–23.

Jodhka, Surinder S. and Katherine Newman. 2007. 'In the Name of Globalisation Meritocracy, Productivity and the Hidden Language of Caste', *Economic and Political Weekly*, 42(41), 13 October: 4125–32.

Jogdand, P. G. 2000. 'Introduction', in *New Economic Policy and Dalits*. Jaipur: Rawal Publications.

Kannabiran, Kalpana. 2002 'A Ravished Justice: Half a Century of Judicial Discourse on Rape', in K. Kannabiran and V. Kannabiran, *De-Eroticizing Assault: Essays on Modesty, Honour and Power*, pp. 104–69. Calcutta: Stree.

Kannabiran, Kalpana and Vasanth Kannabiran. 2002. *De-Eroticizing Assault: Essays on Modesty, Honour and Power*. Calcutta: Stree.

38 द *Clarinda Still*

Kannan, K. P. 2011. 'The Social Face of Poverty in a Fast Growing India: National and Regional Dimensions'. Paper presented at the 'Poverty in South Asia' conference. University of Oxford.

Kapadia, Karin. 1995. *Siva and Her Sisters: Gender, Caste and Class in Rural South India*. San Francisco, Oxford: Westview Press.

————. 2002. 'Introduction: The Politics of Identity, Social Inequalities and Economic Growth', in Karin Kapadia (ed.), *The Violence of Development: The Politics of Identity, Gender and Social Inequalities in India*, pp. 1–40. New Delhi: Kali for Women.

Kapur, Devesh, Chandraban Prasad, Lant Pritchett, and D. Shyam Babu. 2010. 'Rethinking Inequality: Dalits in Uttar Pradesh in the Market Reform Era', *Economic and Political Weekly*, 45(38), 28 August: 39–49.

Kijima, Yoko. 2006. 'Caste and Tribe Inequality: Evidence from India, 1983-1999', *Economic Development and Cultural Change*, 54(2): 369–404.

Kingdon, Geetha. 2001. 'The Gender Gap in Educational Attainment in India: How Much Can be Explained?', *Journal of Development Studies*, 39(2): 25–53.

Kingdon, Geetha and Mohd. Muzammil. 2001. 'A Political Economy of Education in India', *Economic and Political Weekly*, 36(32): 3052–63.

Klass, Morten. 1980. *Caste: The Emergence of the South Asian Social System*. Philadelphia: Institute for the Study of Human Issues.

Kothari, Rajni. 1994. *Politics in India*. New Delhi: Orient Longman.

Kumar, Vivek. 2003.'Dalit Movement and Dalit International Conferences', *Economic and Political Weekly*, 38(27), 5–11 July: 2799.

Malik, Bela. 1999.'Untouchability and Dalit Women's Oppression', *Economic and Political Weekly*, 34(6), 6 February: 323–24.

McCartney, Matthew. 2010. *Political Economy, Growth and Liberalisation in India, 1991–2008*. London, New York: Routledge.

Mehta, Aasha K. and Amita Shah. 2003. 'Chronic Poverty in India: Incidence, Causes and Policies', *World Development*, 31(3): 491–511.

Mendelsohn, Oliver and Marika Vicziany. 1998. *The Untouchables: Subordination, Poverty and the State in Modern India*. Cambridge: Cambridge University Press.

Michelutti, Lucia. 2008. *The Vernacularisation of Democracy: Politics, Caste and Religion in India*. Delhi, London: Routledge.

Moffatt, Michael. 1979. *An Untouchable Community in South India: Structure and Consensus*. Princeton: Princeton University Press.

Mohanty, M. 2006. 'Social Inequality, Labour Market Dynamics and Reservation', *Economic and Political Weekly*, 41(35), 2 September: 3777–91.

An Overview द 39

Mosse, David. 1994. 'Idioms of Subordination and Styles of Protest among Christian and Hindu Harijan Castes in Tamil Nadu', *Contributions to Indian Sociology*, 28: 67–106.

———. 1996. 'South Indian Christians, Purity/Impurity, and the Caste System: Death Ritual in a Tamil Roman Catholic Community', *Journal of the Royal Anthropological Institute*, 2: 1–22.

Mosse, David. 1999. 'Responding to Subordination: The Politics of Identity Change among South Indian Untouchable Castes', in John R. Campbell and Alan Rew (eds), *Identity and Affect: Experiences of Identity in a Globalising World*, pp. 64–104. London: Pluto Press.

———. Forthcoming. *The Saint in the Banyan Tree: Popular Christianity and Caste Society in South India*. Berkeley: University of California Press.

Nambissan, Geetha. 1996. 'Equity in Education? Schooling of Dalit Children in India', *Economic and Political Weekly*, 13(16): 1011–24.

———. 2010. 'Exclusion and Discrimination in Schools: Experiences of Dalit Children', in Sukhadeo Thorat and Katherine Newman (eds), *Blocked by Caste. Economic Discrimination in Modern India*. New Delhi: Oxford University Press.

Nancharaiah. G. 2000. 'New Economic Policy and Its Effects on Dalits', in P.G. Jogdand (ed.), *New Economic Policy and Dalits*. Jaipur: Rawat Publications.

Narayan, Badri. 2006. *Women Heroes and Dalit Assertion in North India: Culture, Identity and Politics*. New Delhi: Sage Publications.

Nisbett, Nicholas. 2007. 'Friendship, Consumption, Morality: Practising Identity, Negotiating Hierarchy in Middle-Class Bangalore', *Journal of the Royal Anthropological Institute*, 13(4): 935–50.

Omvedt, Gail. 1994. *Dalits and the Democratic Revolution: Dr Ambedkar and the Dalit Movement in Colonial India*. New Delhi: Sage Publications.

Oommen, T. K. 1990. *Protest & Change*. New Delhi: Sage Publications.

Pai, Sudha. 2002. *Dalit Assertion and the Unfinished Democratic Revolution: The Bahujan Samaj Party in Uttar Pradesh*. New Delhi: Sage Publications.

Paik, Shailaja. 2011. 'Mahar–Dalit–Buddhist: The History and Politics of Naming in Maharashtra', *Contributions to Indian Sociology*, 45(2): 217–41.

Parry, Jonathan. 1999. 'Two Cheers for Reservation: The Satnamis and the Steel Plant', in Ranajit Guha and Jonathan Parry (eds), *Institutions and Inequalities: Essays in Honour of André Béteille*, pp. 128–69. New Delhi: Oxford University Press.

———. 2001. 'Ankalu's Errant Wife: Sex, Marriage and Industry in Contemporary Chhattisgarh', *Modern Asian Studies*, 35(4): 783–820.

40 ॼ *Clarinda Still*

Parry, Jonathan. 2007. 'A Note on the Substantialisation of Caste and Its Hegemony', in Hiroshi Ishii, David. N. Gellner and Katsuo Nawa (eds), *Political and Social Transformations in North India and Nepal (Social Dynamics in Northern South Asia, Volume II)*, pp. 479–95. New Delhi: Manohar Publications.

Patnaik, Utsa. 2007. 'Neoliberalism and Rural Poverty in India', *Economic and Political Weekly*, 42(30), 28 July: 3132–50.

Prakash, Aseem. 2010. 'Dalit Entrepreneurs in Middle India', in Barbara Harris-White and Judith Heyer (eds), *The Comparative Political Economy of Development, Africa and South Asia*. London: Routledge.

Quigley, Declan. 1993. *The Interpretation of Caste*. Oxford: Oxford University Press.

Racine, Josiane, Jean-Luc Racine and Viramma. 1997. *Viramma: Life of an Untouchable*, trans. Will Hobson. London: Verso.

———. 1998. 'Dalit Identities and The Dialectics of Oppression and Emancipation in a Changing India: The Tamil Case and Beyond', *Comparative Studies of South Asia, Africa and the Middle East*, 18(1): 5–20.

Raheja, Gloria G. 1988a. *The Poison in the Gift: Ritual, Prestation and the Dominant Caste in a North Indian Village*. Chicago: Chicago University Press.

———. 1988b. 'India: Caste, Kingship, and Dominance Reconsidered', *Annual Review of Anthropology*, 17: 497–522.

Rao, Anupama. 2003. 'Introduction', in Anupama Rao (ed.), *Gender and Caste*, pp. 1–47, London, New York: Zed Books.

———. 2009. *The Caste Question Dalits and the Politics of Modern India*. Berkeley: University of California Press.

Reddy, D. N. 2012. 'Political Economy of Microfinance and Marginalised Groups: Implications of Alternative Institutional Strategies'. Unpublished paper presented at the conference, 'Capitalism and Development: South Asia in the 21st Century (in honour of Professor Barbara Harriss-White)', University of Oxford, 4–5 July.

Rege, Sharmila. 1995. 'Caste and Gender: The Violence against Dalit Women in India', in P. G. Jogdand (ed.), *Dalit Women in India: Issues and Perspectives*, pp. 18–36. New Delhi: Gyan Publishing House.

———. 2000. 'Real Feminism' and Dalit Women: Scripts of Denial and Accusation, *Economic and Political Weekly*, 35(6), 5 February: 492–95.

———. 2003. 'A Dalit Feminist Standpoint', in Anupama Rao (ed.), *Gender and Caste*, pp. 90–101. London, New York: Zed Books.

Rogers, Martin. 2008. 'Modernity, "Authenticity", and Ambivalence: Subaltern Masculinities on a South Indian College Campus', *Journal of the Royal Anthropological Institute*, 14(1): 79–95.

An Overview ॡ 41

Saglio-Yatzimirsky, Marie-Caroline. 2010. 'Caste as a Political Tool: The Case of the Camakars of Dharavi', in Mikael Aktor and Robert Deliège (eds), *From Stigma to Assertion: Untouchability, Identity and Politics in Early and Modern India*, pp. 201–31. Copenhagen: Museum Tusculanum Press, University of Copenhagen.

Satyanarayana, K. and Susie Tharu. 2011. *No Alphabet in Sight: New Dalit Writing from South India (Dossier 1: Tamil and Malayalam)*. New Delhi: Penguin Books.

——— (eds). 2013. *Steel Nibs are Sprouting: New Dalit Writing from South India (Dossier 2 Telugu and Kanada)*. New Delhi: Harper Collins Publihsers.

Searle-Chatterjee, Mary. 1981. *Reversible Sex Roles: The Special Case of the Benares Sweepers*. Oxford: Pergamon Press.

Seenarine, Moses. 2004. *Education and Empowerment among Dalit Untouchable Women: Voices from the Subaltern*. New York: The Edwin Mellen Press.

Sen, Amartya. 2000. *Development as Freedom*. New York: Anchor Books.

Shah, Ghanshyam (ed.). 2001. *Dalit Identity and Politics: Cultural Subordination and the Dalit Challenge, Volume 2*. New Delhi, London: Sage Publications.

——— (ed.). 2002. *Dalits and the State*. New Delhi: Concept Publishing Company.

———. 2004. *Social Movements in India*. New Delhi: Sage.

Shah, Ghanshyam, Harsh Mander, Sukhadeo Thorat, Satish Deshpande, and Amita Baviskar. 2006. *Untouchability in Rural India*. London, New Delhi: Sage Publications.

Shylendra, H. S. 2006. 'Microfinance Institutions in Andhra Pradesh: Crisis and Diagnosis', *Economic and Political Weekly*, 41(20), 20–26 May: 1959–63.

Srinivas, Mysore. Narasimhachar. 1966. *Social Change in Modern India*. Berkeley, Los Angeles: University of California Press.

Still, Clarinda. 2013. '"They Have It in Their Stomachs but They Can't Vomit It Up": Reservations and "Caste Feeling" among Dalits in Andhra Pradesh"', *Focaal — Journal of Global and Historical Anthropology (Special Issue)*, 65: 68–79.

Subramaniam, Mangala. 2006. *The Power of Women's Organising: Gender, Caste, and Class in India*. Oxford: Lexington Books.

Sundaram, K. and Suresh D. Tendulkar. 2003. 'Poverty in India in the 1990s: Revised Results for All-India and 15 Major States for 1993–94', *Economic and Political Weekly*, 38(46), 15 November: 4865–72.

Suri, K.C. 2002. 'Democratic Process and Electoral Politics in Andhra Pradesh, India'. *Working Paper 180*. London: Overseas Development Institute.

Teltumbde, Anand. 1997. Impact of New Economic Reforms on Dalits in India. Occasional Paper Sales 1. Pune.

42 द *Clarinda Still*

Teltumbde, Anand. 2008. *Khairlanji: A Strange and Bitter Crop*. New Delhi: Navayana.

Thorat, Sukhadeo. 2002. Oppression and Denial: Dalit Discrimination in the 1990s. *Economic and Political Weekly*, 37(6), 9 February: 572–78.

Thorat, Sukhadeo and Amaresh Dubey. 2012. 'Has Growth Been Socially Inclusive during 1993–94 — 2009–10?', *Economic and Political Weekly*, 47(10): 43–54.

Thorat, Sukhadeo, Aryama and Prashant Negi (eds). 2005. *Reservation and the Private Sector: Quest for Equal Opportunity and Growth*. New Delhi: Rawat Publications.

Thorat, Sukhadeo, Debolina Kundu and Nidhi Sadana. 2010. 'Caste and Own Enterprises: Consequences of Denial of Property Rights', in Katherine Newman (eds), *Blocked by Caste: Economic Discrimination in Modern India*. New Delhi: Oxford University Press.

Thorat, Sukhadeo and Katherine Newman. 2007.'Caste and Economic Discrimination: Causes, Consequences and Remedies', *Economic and Political Weekly*, 42(41): 4121–24.

———. 2010. 'Introduction: Economic Discrimination: Concept, Consequences, and Remedies', in Sukhadeo Thorat and Katherine Newman (eds), *Blocked by Caste: Economic Discrimination in Modern India*. New Delhi: Oxford University Press.

Thorat, Sukhadeo, M. Mahamallik and Nidhi Sadana. 2010. 'Caste System and Pattern of Discrimination in Rural Markets', in Sukhadeo Thorat and Katherine Newman (eds), *Blocked by Caste: Economic Discrimination in Modern India*. New Delhi: Oxford University Press.

Thorat, Sukhadeo and Paul Attewell. 2010. 'The Legacy of Social Exclusion: A Correspondence Study of Job Discrimination in India's Urban Private Sector', in S. Thorat and K. Newman (eds), *Blocked by Caste: Economic Discrimination in Modern India*. New Delhi: Oxford University Press.

Upadhya, Carol. 1988. 'The Farmer Capitalists of Coastal Andhra Pradesh', *Economic and Political Weekly*, 23(28), 9 July: 1433–42.

———. 1997. 'Social and Cultural Strategies of Class Formation in Coastal Andhra Pradesh', *Contributions to Indian Sociology*, 31(2): 169–93.

Upadhya, Carol and A. R. Vasavi. 2006. 'Work, Culture, and Sociality in the Indian IT Industry: A Sociological Study', *Final Report Submitted to Indo-Dutch Programme for Alternatives in Development*. http://www.uniglobalunion.org (accessed 10 January 2010).

Walker, Kathy Le Mons. 2008. 'Neoliberalism on the Ground in Rural India: Predatory Growth, Agrarian Crisis, Internal Colonisation, and the Intensification of Class Struggle', *Journal of Peasant Studies*, 35(4): 557–620.

An Overview द 43

Waughray, Annapurna. 2009. 'Caste Discrimination: A Twenty-First Century Challenge for UK Discrimination Law?' *The Modern Law Review*, 72(2): 182–219.

Weisskopf, Thomas. 2006 'Is Positive Discrimination a Good Way to Aid Disadvantaged Ethnic Communities', *Economic and Political Weekly*, 41(8), 25 February: 717–26.

Wood, Adrian and Michele Calandrino. 2000. 'When the Other Giant Awakens: Trade and Human Resources in India', *Economic and Political Weekly*, 35(52/53): 4677–94.

Wyatt, Andrew. 2010. 'Dalit Theology and the Politics of Untouchability', in Mikael Aktor and Robert Deliège, *From Stigma to Assertion: Untouchability, Identity and Poltics in Early and Modern India*, pp. 119–46. Copenhagen: Museum Tusculanum Press.

Zelliot, Eleanor. 1992. *From Untouchable to Dalit: Essays on the Ambedkar Movement*. New Delhi: Manohar Publications.

1

Dalit Entrepreneurs, Globalisation and the Supplier Diversity Experiment in Madhya Pradesh

Sudha Pai

A significant development during the 1990s has been the emergence of a small, but influential Dalit middle class. While many studies have focused in recent years on the rise of an Indian middle class in the context of globalisation (Fernandes 2007; Harriss 2007; Varma 1999); little attention has been paid to the emerging Dalit middle class, whose roots, needs and aspirations are arguably different.[1] This class is a product of state policies of protective discrimination (PD) or reservation that have provided education and employment, and democratisation, leading to high levels of political consciousness. As a consequence of these developments, the 1990s witnessed the emergence of a generation of young, educated, upwardly mobile and politically conscious middle class of Dalits. This new Dalit class reached a 'critical mass' precisely when the Indian polity experienced globalisation moving towards a market-oriented economy. More aggressive than the previous generation, this class argues that Dalits were excluded from the project of nation-building in the early years of independence; they question oppression and domination by the upper castes/classes and strongly feel that they should receive a fair share in the fruits of globalisation which has resulted in higher growth rates, a market economy, emergence of a strong private sector, high-paid professional occupations and business opportunities. They represent a different strand in the Dalit movement as it has evolved in the last two decades. While Dalit movements and

---

[1] A recent exception is Kapur et al. (2010).

Dalit Entrepreneurs in Madhya Pradesh 45

parties such as the Bahujan Samaj Party (BSP) have mobilised on issues of *socio-political empowerment* such as identity, dignity and self-respect, middle class Dalit intellectuals have emphasised the need for *economic empowerment* through variety of means, such as increased reservations in higher education for better educational attainments, professional jobs in the new and better paying sectors of the economy, and a share in business/industry through policies based on affirmative action in the private sector. It is on this last demand — the aspiration to create Dalit entrepreneurs — that this chapter primarily discusses.

A significant fallout of these developments has been the rise of a contentious debate since the mid-1990s — among both Dalit and non-Dalit scholars/activists — on the working of the policies of reservation in the post-independence period, the benefits that have accrued to them, and the new types of preferential policies that are required so that Dalits can also reap the benefits of globalisation. The contours of this debate are best encapsulated in the Bhopal Document (BD) discussed at the Bhopal Conference in January 2002 organised by Dalit intellectuals and activists with the support of the Congress government in Madhya Pradesh under the leadership of Digvijay Singh. This conference resulted in the adoption of the policy of Supplier Diversity (SD) in Madhya Pradesh in 2002 in order to create *Dalit entrepreneurs* who could enter into the arena of business/industry. The advocates of this policy argue that under the traditional policies of PD and state welfarism, Dalits have remained mere recipients of welfare, landless/asset-less, below the line of poverty, without a share in the capital in the economy and unable to improve their socio-economic status. While a tiny elite 'creamy layer' has emerged which has been able to enter into high paid jobs in the government, the professions and increasingly the private sector; the poorer sections have been unable to access education and avail the reservation policies. The educated sections that obtained 12 years of schooling or college degrees have been able to enter only into low paid government jobs. They have not been able to enter into areas which are becoming important in India's globalised economy, remaining on the fringes of the expanding professional market. Nor have many educated Dalits been able to enter into sectors such as the media, arts, academia, scientific establishment or business/industry. Some Dalit intellectuals/activists have criticised the demand for extension of reservation of jobs

46　द　*Sudha Pai*

to the private sector, arguing that they would help only a small number of Dalits. Instead, many have forcefully argued for 'democratisation' of control over 'capital' and the need of a strong Dalit business/industrial class, which could participate equally in the national economy. For this, policies such as SD based on affirmative action are needed with the help of the state and industrial sector, which are more in tune with the market economy that is emerging. They also hold that such a policy would be able to economically empower a large number of Dalits doing away with the need for reservations in the long run.

The chapter traces this debate by discussing the Bhopal Document and the scholarly debate on the subject. Against this backdrop, an attempt is made to examine the policy of SD introduced in 2002 by the Digvijay Singh government in Madhya Pradesh. An underlying argument is that this experiment is worthy of close examination, as it is both a policy supported/implemented by the state bureaucracy, and a market-based policy whose success depends on the entrepreneurial abilities of Dalits to supply high quality products within a price/time frame. This chapter discusses the elaborate framework of rules put into place by the Madhya Pradesh government for implementation of this policy and the number of SC/ST who have adopted it in the state between 2002 and 2007. Against this background, in-depth interviews of nine selected Dalit entrepreneurs in the Bhopal District Trade Centre (DTIC) were conducted to understand the actual working of the businesses established under this policy. The aim is to understand the reasons for success/failure of the selected entrepreneurs which could help locate the conditions required for the implementation of this policy in Madhya Pradesh, or elsewhere. The concluding section discusses the merits of the policy and the conditions needed to implement it on a larger scale, arguing that in an increasingly globalising economy, the policy if properly implemented has the potential to create, over time, a much needed business/industrial Dalit class.

Moving Beyond Protective Discrimination: The Contemporary Debate

Until the late 1980s scholarly attention was centred on the effectiveness of the policy of PD, more specifically reservations. These policies

Dalit Entrepreneurs in Madhya Pradesh 47

have encountered much criticism from various quarters in the post-independence period, ranging from poor implementation, jobs being only in the lower rungs of the bureaucracy, the policy not having the desired impact, only better-off urban-based groups benefiting, and encouragement to sub-caste divisions, to more fundamental issues of individual rights, justice, merit and efficiency. Many scholars still argue that reservations are the 'most workable method' to help remove long-standing discrimination (Ghosh 2007). Others point to continuing inequalities in education, employment and the labour market (Mohanty 2006) or that reservations should follow the democratic and rational path of change chartered by Ambedkar (Iliaih 2006). A recent study argues that the case for such policies remains still strong in India if 'the policies are carefully designed to maximize the benefits and minimize the costs' which it admits is not the case most of the time (Weisskopf 2006).

Until recently, this debate remained largely confined to the problems of implementation. But during the 1990s, mainly due to the rise of an educated middle class among Dalits and liberalisation of the economy; its usefulness has come to be debated and contested. Literacy levels and educational attainments among Dalits have risen faster during the 1980s and 1990s than the previous decades and thus they have become aware of the fact that liberalisation has led not only to shrinking of jobs in the state sector, but more importantly, provided greater room for the private sector. This has led to efforts by educated Dalits to demand the extension of reservation in the private sector (Thorat, Aryama and Negi 2005) and the adoption of SD based on affirmative action. Another reason has been the internationalisation of the debate on caste in the 2000s due the dismantling of Apartheid in South Africa and the World Conference Against Racism held in Durban in 2001 (Thorat and Umakant 2004).

The main source of the new debate on the need for programmes such as SD is the Dalit Agenda contained in the Bhopal Document (BD). Its immediate intellectual origin was the 'Dalit Millennium' (2000) — one of a number of *Millennium Supplements* — issued to mark the dawn of the millennium. This supplement edited by a Dalit bureaucrat Raja Sekhar Vundru brought together a number of Dalit intellectuals drawn from writers, academics and journalists and dealt

48 द Sudha Pai

with a wide range of issues such as problems with reservation policy, the controversial issue of merit, need for better educational attainments, caste atrocities and the need for a new 'Dalit Bourgeoisie' in the field of business and industry.[2]

Critical of both the excessive reliance on reservations and various forms of state welfarism by Dalits and the demand for extension of reservation to the private sector, the BD suggested a range of alternative policies of which SD is the most important.[3] One of the authors of the BD and leading advocate of SD, Chandrabhan Prasad does not recommend doing away with reservations, but points to the limits of this policy.[4] He argues that even if the existing job quota available in the government under reservations were to be filled, it would still leave as many as 18 crore Dalits seeking employment (The Bhopal Document 2002). Neither would extension of this model, i.e., of reservations into the private sector, Prasad points out, will be of much use. At a conservative estimate, low skilled, semi-skilled and unskilled workers make up more than three-fourths of the workforce. Therefore, even if the private sector was to religiously implement reservations, more than 17 crore Dalits would still be left unemployed; thereby illustrating the limits of reservations (ibid.).

Based on these arguments, the advocates of SD demand that both the state and the private sector practice diversity policies for Dalits. Pointing towards the need to 'democratise the ownership of capital' they argue that voluntary policies making use of the market, technology and skill development, rather than state-led policies of reservation based on caste-quotas, can play a determining role in ending the marginalisation of Dalits from the field of business/industry. This is particularly true with globalisation/liberalisation of the economy and emergence of a strong private sector. Rather than reservation in the

---

[2] Among those who wrote in the issue were Chandrabhan Prasad, Gail Omvedt, Tulsi Ram, Vimal Thorat, Sheoraj Bechain and journalists such as B. N. Uniyal. Prasad later has written extensively on the Supplier Diversity programme. I am grateful to Shyam Babu for giving me a copy of the 'Dalit Millenium' and discussing its importance on 30 October 2007.

[3] See Babu (2003).

[4] See also Prasad (2004).

Dalit Entrepreneurs in Madhya Pradesh   ᵟ   49

private sector, it is the business sector, which has not been explored yet, and which holds the greatest promise in the years to come with large number of the educated, unemployed population moving out of universities and colleges. The SD policy has features that borrow from both the PD policies of the past and from affirmative action. It is not only a state-supported policy implemented by the bureaucracy, but also a market-based voluntary policy, whose success depends upon the entrepreneurial skills and ability of Dalit entrepreneurs to supply goods and services in a time-bound manner in keeping with laid down standards and face caste-bias, competition and even monopoly from the traditional suppliers to the government belonging largely to the upper/middle castes. Such a policy will in the long run take the pressure off reservations for higher education with more and more Dalits attracted to the world of business and industry.

The advocates of the policy of SD draw on the American experience of affirmative action for 'minorities', i.e., African Americans and Asians. This is because they wanted to put forward a Dalit Agenda suited to a liberalised economy different from the state-supported PD policies of the past. The US experience is particularly useful because the American state since the 1970s has adopted a number of measures to bring in minorities into the area of business and industry that are of considerable relevance in any attempt to democratise capital in India such as: in all government purchases at least 5 per cent is set aside for purchase from minority suppliers; all government contractors are bound to have a certain percentage of their contract work sub-contracted to minority sub-contractors, obligatory by law; obligatory non-discrimination by law in any constructions contract where federal funds (grants or loans) or assistance (insurance, guarantee, contract) are involved such as buildings, bridges or involving real estate; non-discrimination obligations from all government contractors that they will not discriminate in their employment practices, etc. Not only the government but private industrial giants in the US are also practicing diversity by both employing and providing entrepreneurial opportunities to the minorities.[5]

The authors of the BD argue that Dalit entrepreneurs can be 'created' with state support even if the private sector is reluctant to participate

---

[5] For details see Pai (2010).

in this policy. Pointing out the fact that the Indian state has helped the industrial entrepreneur, both during the period of protection and the era of globalisation through various incentives such as lowering taxes, providing land at concessional rates etc., Prasad argues that the government's help now in the form of 'loans' and a share in government contracts/supplies can provide opportunities to Dalits to grow as new entrepreneurs and obtain a steady and assured market for their goods. Since breaking the 'monopoly' often held by established manufacturers or traders and obtaining financial stability is difficult, once established with support from the government over a period of time, Dalits might gravitate to become industrial entrepreneurs selling in the open market as well. State supported attempts could begin with SD policies in areas where little formal education or complex skills are required. For example, government departments buy a number of ordinary items such as stationery, furniture, office equipments, electrical gadgets from suppliers in the market in great bulk and give dealerships for petrol, diesel and kerosene and LPG, etc. If a percentage of these goods/supply contracts could be reserved, it would stimulate Dalit businesses and over time such entrepreneurs could graduate to becoming manufacturers (The Bhopal Document 2002). The private sector, Prasad argues could start by keeping aside 5 per cent or 10 per cent outsourced services for Dalits and making a conscious effort of 'integrating them in the supply chain' (ibid.). These ideas are supported by a growing cross-section of scholars who agree that rather than providing reservation in the private sector — which would yield only a meagre number of jobs — it is better to provide Dalits a share in the ownership of private capital (Vaidyanathan 2005). They agree there is need to provide a share in business opportunities of crores worth of public works, liquor licenses, numerous broadcasting licenses and so forth, awarded by the central/state government that could create 'Dalit capitalists' (Sachar 2006).

Supplier Diversity: Policy Framework and Adoption in Madhya Pradesh

Following the Bhopal Conference, the Digvijay Singh government decided to adopt the SD policy for Dalits and tribals. Beginning May 2002, the government framed the required government orders and by

August 2002, it began implementing two interrelated schemes: Thirty Percent scheme under which 30 per cent of all government supply orders were reserved for Dalits; and the Rani Durgawati Scheme (RDS) to provide credit to Dalit entrepreneurs to set up manufacturing enterprises.[6] Under the RDS a selected entrepreneur is given upto ₹50,000 as 'margin money'.[7] The amount could, in case of large industries, be more than ₹50,000 but in no circumstances more than 33 per cent of the total establishment cost. If the firm shows profits for the first three years then the margin money given under the RDS is free. The implementation of the policy was placed under the District Trade and Industry Centers (DTICs) with whom entrepreneurs would register as suppliers. This programme could be adopted mainly by urban-based Dalits and tribals as it required a minimum of educational attainments and entrepreneurial skill. However, it must be noted that the Digvijay Singh government also implemented two programmes for the rural-based groups in these communities: land redistribution — which was part of the BD — and the Education Guarantee Scheme which provided a school on demand for rural areas.[8] Thus, recognising that Dalits and tribals are not homogeneous groups, the government attempted to provide for all sections of disadvantaged groups in the state.

Prior to examining our Bhopal sample, the extent of adoption and spread of the policy in Madhya Pradesh is briefly examined. This allows us to locate the Bhopal sample within the larger context of the state. Table 1.1 provides data on the number of Dalits/tribals[9] who have adopted the 30 per cent SD policy in all the 51 districts.[10] Government

---

[6] See Government of Madhya Pradesh (2002).

[7] An entrepreneur who approaches a bank for credit to establish an industry has to put in a certain percentage of the loan he is requesting — described as margin money — before he can obtain the loan. Under the RDS a selected entrepreneur is given up to ₹50,000 as margin money, but in no circumstances more than 33 per cent of the total establishment cost.

[8] For details on these programmes see Pai (2010).

[9] In Madhya Pradesh the policy was meant for both Dalits and tribals.

[10] It is a continuously updated list maintained by the state government based on reports filed by the DTICs. The list given here is till October 2007. Three new districts were created in 2005: Ashok Nagar, Burhanpur and Annupur. Hence, data from 2005 to 2007 is for 51 districts.

52 द Sudha Pai

Table 1.1
Number of Dalit/Tribal Suppliers and Manufacturers
Who Have Adopted the 30 per cent SD Policy
in 50 Districts of Madhya Pradesh (2003–07)

No. of Suppliers	No. of Districts	No. of Manufacturers	No. of Districts	Total Entrepreneurs
875		57		932
None	7	None	31	
1–30	34	1–30	19	
30–50	5	30–50	–	
Above 50	4	Above 50	–	
Total Districts	50*	Total Districts	50*	

Source: Report compiled from the reports of all the DTIC in Madhya Pradesh, Bhopal, Government of MP.

Note: *51 districts between 2005–07.

reports do not maintain separate lists for Dalits and tribals for the 30 per cent scheme, but DTIC officials maintain that the large majority of the entrepreneurs are Dalits except in districts where tribals form majority of the population. It shows that a total of 932 entrepreneurs had made use of the SD policy over a period of about five years: 875 were suppliers to government departments and 57 were manufacturers. Out of 50 districts, only in seven no individual had adopted the 30 per cent supply scheme. In contrast, in 31 districts Dalits/tribals have not been able to take up manufacturing as this requires a high level of investment.

Official data collated from every DTICs on the spread of the 30 per cent policy shows that most of the entrepreneurs — both suppliers and manufacturers — are located in the more affluent districts such as Bhopal, Indore, Ujjain, Jhabua, Balaghat, Katni, and Damoh which had developed infrastructure, many government offices with a need for supplies and an educated Dalit class capable of responding to this demand. The increase in entrepreneurs over the last five years has been in these districts and has not spread to other districts. Even within these districts, almost all of them are located in the district headquarters or the bigger towns/cities in the district. About 70 per cent of the suppliers deal in four items: stationary, *kirana* or general provisions, furniture and electrical goods. A small number supply fertiliser, steel goods, cement, stone chips, electronic items and heavy machinery. The value of goods supplied/manufactured annually by each entrepreneur is small being between 0.1 to 1.5 million, except in the case of manufacturers. However, the items are supplied in bulk and therefore provide a reasonably good livelihood and an opening into the business and industrial sector.[11]

Table 1.2 gives the annual targets set and achieved for Dalit entrepreneurs who could apply for the RDS. Considering that Madhya Pradesh is a large state, the target set was not very high and therefore the response has been fairly good. A total of 5,174 Dalits applied for the scheme over a period of three years, which was 73.91 per cent of the target. The margin money provided had risen steadily, was doubled in 2006, and over 92 per cent has been used each year. Government data on the use of the RDS in all the districts[12] show a good spread across the state in utilisation of the margin money. This is because with the margin money provided entrepreneurs have set up small businesses such as shops in remote villages and small towns supplying goods urgently

Table 1.2
Targets Set and Achieved in the RDS for the State of Madhya Pradesh between 2004 and July 2007

Category Year	SC Target (in Nos)	Target Achieved (in Nos)	Target Achieved (in %)	Margin Money Earmarked (in ₹)	Margin Money Used (in ₹)	Margin Money Used (in %)
2004–05[#]	3,000	1,688	56.27	24,796,000	23,001,958	92.76
2005–06	1,000	1,349	134.9	42,927,000	42,874,921	99.88
2006–07	3,000	2,137	71.23	90,199,012	88,617,573	98.25
Total	7,000	5,174	73.91	157,922,012	154,494,452	97.82
Upto July 2007	2,000*	515	25.75	53,101,900	28,297,699	53.28

Source: Compiled from the reports on the RDS filed by each DTIC (2004–07), Bhopal, Government of MP.

Note: *Target set for the whole year.
[#]*Figures* for 2003–04 were not available.

---

[11] For details on each district, see Pai (2010).
[12] Compiled from the reports of all the DTIC, upto October 2007.

54 द *Sudha Pai*

required by students such as stationery and books through which they supply to both the government and the public. Once the entrepreneur is able to repay the loan by supplying to the government, he can continue to sell his product in the market. Dalits have adopted the scheme in all districts but there is considerable variation in the targets achieved being high in only a few. Moreover, government data[13] shows that the number of registrations per DTIC was 13 in 2003–04; 14 in 2004–05 and 17 in 2005–06, out of 51 DTICs in the state; all of which are the better off districts such as Bhopal, Ujjain, Hoshangabad, and Satna. Mostly simple items are being manufactured such as coolers, furniture, leather goods and clothes, but the percentage supplied is in many cases above 30 per cent annually since 2003, enabling many Dalits and tribals to enter into the business sector. The scheme has spread since 2003 but slowly adding just four districts between 2003 and 2007.

Creating Dalit Entrepreneurs: Bhopal Sample[14]

We move now to an analysis of the working of the policy of SD among our selected entrepreneurs in the DTIC in Bhopal. Bhopal was selected because of two reasons: one, it had the highest number of suppliers (105 entrepreneurs) among all the districts and two, Bhopal had a large number of educated Dalits who had heard about the SD programme and were enthusiastic to adopt it but faced many problems such as lack of contacts, corruption, lack of entrepreneurial ability and confidence. A first round of detailed interviews with the nine selected Dalits/tribal entrepreneurs in Bhopal district was conducted, held in January/February 2007 and a second round in August 2007.

Table 1.3 provides the number of entrepreneurs who have registered with the Bhopal DTIC. By 2007 a total of 105 entrepreneurs had registered, of whom 11 entrepreneurs already had enterprises of their own before 2002 and registered as suppliers to obtain contracts. Out of the 105 registered entrepreneurs, only six are manufacturers, the remaining are suppliers. Fifty-five entrepreneurs are proprietors while 49 are part-owners in keeping with the rule that a Dalit can join hands with a non-Dalit/tribal, provided 49 per cent of the profits

---

[13] Compiled from the reports of all the DTIC, upto October 2007.

[14] This section draws on Pai (2010).

Table 1.3
Dalit/Tribal Entrepreneurs Registered as Suppliers to the State Government
under the Thirty Percent Scheme in Bhopal DTIC (Up to 15 September 2006)

Total Entrepreneurs (in Nos)	Year of Establishment	Total No. of Businesses	Number of Suppliers	Number of Manufacturers	Proprietorship/ Partnerships	Orders Continuing since Registration	Orders Cancelled	Permanent Residents in Bhopal
105#	1999	4	98*/104	6	55/49	99^	4	52/104
	2000	1						
	2001	6						
	2002	5						
	2003	44						
	2004	19						
	2005	9						
	2006	9						
	2007 (September)	4						
	Total 101		98	6	104	99	4	52

Source: Bhopal District Trade Centre, Bhopal, Government of Madhya Pradesh.

Note: *One supplier is also a manufacturer.

#*The* details of one entrepreneur was not available.

^*One* order was only upto 2005 and Year of Establishment was not available for three entrepreneurs.

56   व   *Sudha Pai*

are given to the former. The largest number was registered in 2003, by which time the scheme was well known due to the government's efforts to disseminate information and began to drop after the defeat of the Digvijay Singh government.

Table 1.4 provides the initial capital invested and the annual production of the 105 entrepreneurs registered with the DTIC Bhopal. Out of the total 104 entrepreneurs for whom information was available, large number were small businessmen and medium-sized businessmen who supplied simple to more expensive goods depending on the amount invested. Only seven entrepreneurs had invested above ₹20 lakhs (2 million) and supplied highly-specialised goods such as medicines, hospital supplies, civil construction material, cement, computers, mobiles, etc. When we come to production, as Table 1.4 shows, although 36 entrepreneurs had invested less than ₹2 lakhs, only 10 have shown an annual turnover of less than ₹2 lakhs (0.2 million), others are therefore performing much better. Similarly, of the 31 entrepreneurs who invested ₹2–5 (0.2 –0.5 million) lakhs only 21 have shown this figure in their annual production. A number of entrepreneurs have performed well in the bracket of ₹5–20 lakhs. Similarly, although only seven entrepreneurs invested over ₹20 lakhs, as many as 39 have shown a turnover of that amount annually. Thus, the big and medium entrepreneurs have done well; the smaller ones have tended to do worse. DTIC officials point out that the rate of success is 50 per cent[15] with failure high among small investors. But they argue that this success rate is high compared to most government programmes, which in most cases perform much worse.

Against this background we turn to analysis of our interviews with the nine selected entrepreneurs in order to understand the reasons for their success/failure.[16] The interviews with the selected entrepreneurs covered broadly four aspects. First, the social aspects: family background, educational attainments, business contacts, membership of caste/community associations and political organisations. Second, in order to understand the viability of the business, we asked about the

---

[15] This estimate was mentioned by R. L. Tiwari, General Manager, DTIC Bhopal, during a discussion in November 2007.

[16] Family members of the entrepreneur were also questioned during the interviews.

Dalit Entrepreneurs in Madhya Pradesh द 57

Table 1.4
Capital Invested and Annual Production by Dalit/Tribal Entrepreneurs under the Supplier Diversity Policy with DTIC Bhopal (Up to 15 September 2007)

Initial Capital Invested (in Lakhs)	Number of Entrepreneurs	Annual Production (in Lakhs)	Number of Entrepreneurs
Less than 2 lakhs	36	Less than 2	10
2–5 Lakhs	31	2–5	21
5–10 Lakhs	17	5–10	22
10–20 Lakhs	13	10–20	12
Above 20 Lakhs	7	Above 20	39
	104*		104*

Source: Bhopal District Trade Centre, Bhopal, Government of Madhya Pradesh.
Note: *Information about one entrepreneur was not available.

financial aspects of the enterprise such as the initial investment, annual income, expenditure and value of goods supplied. Third, we asked about the ability of the entrepreneurs to compete and whether there were instances of caste discrimination in the market, particularly from trading castes who have traditionally enjoyed a monopoly as suppliers, wholesalers and retailers. And fourth, we asked about the relationship with bureaucrats.

Of the nine entrepreneurs selected from the list of Dalit entrepreneurs registered with the Bhopal DTIC, five are supplying goods under the 30 per cent supplier scheme to government departments and four have made use of the Rani Durgawati Scheme (RDS), introduced by the state government to start a business. Six of them are suppliers and only three can be described as 'producers' of the material they supply. There are no large-scale Dalit and tribal manufacturers in Bhopal, i.e., those who both manufacture and supply as the expertise needed and the initial cost is too high. The RDS introduced in 2003 was designed to address this problem but soon afterwards the Congress government was defeated in the election and was replaced by the government of the Bhartiya Janata Party and it introduced new rules which made the implementation of RDS more difficult. There are few tribal entrepreneurs in Bhopal district; one of the selected entrepreneurs in the sample is a tribal woman. One example of failure was selected to understand the reasons for his inability to continue supply of items to the government.

58 ड़ *Sudha Pai*

Table 1.5 provides the socio-economic background of the nine selected Dalit/tribal entrepreneurs registered with the Bhopal DTIC.[17] The data provided and our interaction with them suggests that they represent a new class of young, educated Dalits found in many of the bigger cities in Madhya Pradesh who have moved in recent years — or earlier with their parents — from smaller towns/villages to Bhopal, prepared to take the risk of starting a business/industry. Table 1.6 provides the financial details of the entrepreneurs: the initial amount of capital invested, time taken to start the business, products supplied, turnover, annual production, persons employed and success or failure in supplying goods to the government. Three entrepreneurs (number 7, 8 and 9 in Tables 1.3 and 1.4) have formed partnerships with non-Dalits: one is a Saini (OBC) while the caste of the other two could not be ascertained.[18] Our study suggested that family background and education in combination with other factors play a significant role in the success/failure of the entrepreneurial venture undertaken. Accordingly they are placed in three groups: lower middle class entrepreneurs, upper middle class entrepreneurs and partnership firms with non-Dalits.

Lower Middle Class Entrepreneur

Four of our selected entrepreneurs (1–4 in Tables 1.5 and 1.6) can be described as belonging to the lower middle class in terms of family background, education and savings and share certain characteristics which have helped three of them in achieving a modicum of success. Belonging to 'first generation' educated families, recent migrants from rural areas, they are an upwardly mobile group keen to provide financial security to their families. Used to struggle in their early years in order to obtain education, with middle class values of thrift and determination, they are prepared to work hard and make a success of the opportunity

---

[17] No names have been used in Tables 1.5 and 1.6 in order to conceal the identity of the entrepreneurs and of their firms.

[18] The figures in Table 1.6 regarding turnover, average yearly income and value of total sales of the various firms are for the year 2005–06 brought up to January 2007 when the interviews were conducted.

Table 1.5
Socio-Economic Background of the Selected Dalit/Tribal Entrepreneurs in Bhopal

Caste/Tribe	Age	Education	Migrant to Bhopal	Earlier Occupation	Father's Education	Father's Occupation	Spouse Education
1. Chamar (Male)	37	Class 10	Harda, 1992	Typesetter, Salesman Duplicating Machines	Illiterate	Agricultural Labourer	Class 3
2. Ahirwar (Male)	31	Class 10 Fail	Vidisha, 1991	Flexo Printing Press Operator	High School	Military Service	Class 10
3. Ahirwar (Male)	36	Post-Graduation (LLB)	Raisen, 1992	Computer Operator Salesman	Illiterate	Farmer	Class 10
4. Mahar (Male)	27	Class 10	Hoshangabad, a generation ago	Shopkeeper	Class 10	Class IV Employee	Unmarried
5. Gond tribal (Female)	33	Post-Graduation	Shivani, 1974	Housewife	Graduate	Not Alive	Post-Graduate
6. Bairawa (Male)	31	B.E. (Mechanical Engineering)	Tonk, 1974	Assistant Manager in Public Sector	Graduate	IAS Officer (Serving)	L.L.B.
7. Ahirwar (Father–Son Partnership)	31	Post-Graduation L.L.B.	Raisen, 1995	Lawyer	Intermediate	Retired Police officer	Unmarried
8. Balahi (Three Male Partners)	29/30 34	Post-Graduation	Khandwa, 1993	Tutor	Graduate	Teacher	Graduate
9. Chamar (Two Male Partners)	29/34	Class 12	Indore, 2000	Salesman	Class 6	Labourer	B.Com

Source: Interview of entrepreneurs in January/Februrary 2006 and August 2007 in Bhopal. Only the Dalit partner of the firm could be interviewed in the case of nos. 8 and 9.

Table 1.6

Investment and Income Gained from Business by Entrepreneurs Registered with the Bhopal DTIC

Firm/Year of Registration	Time in Obtaining Registration	Getting Supply Order	Initial Investment	Annual Turnover	Average Yearly Income of Firm*	Value of Total Sales*	Articles Supplied	Taxes Paid	Number of Employees	Annual Personal Expenditure	Progress in Supply to Govt.
1. Chamar Proprietary/ 2005	15 Days	1 and 1/2 months	2,00,000 (Bank)	75,00,000	17,10,000	90,45,000	Stationery, Furniture Electricals	1,50,000	3	1,09,000	Successful, wants to manufacture.
2. Ahirwar Proprietary/ 2006	3 Months	3 months	21,00,000 (Bank, RDS)	48,85,000	11,06,000	48,85,000	Flexo (Printed Articles on Self-owned Press	NA	6	75000	Still Facing Financial Hurdles as Firm is New.
3. Ahirwar Proprietary/ 2005	4 Months	2 months	35,000 (Bank)	65,50,000	9,11,500	10,50,000	Sprinklers, Agricultural Implements, Seeds	2,15,000	3	63,880	Successful, Wants to Manufacture.
4. Mahar Proprietary/ 2003	1 Month	1 month	60,000 (Family)	10,000,000	6,96,000	NA	Stationery	NA	1	92,600	Failure, Stopped Supply to Govt.
5. Gond 2003, 2004#	2 Months, 3 Weeks	3 weeks	20,00,000 (Bank)	5,00,00,000	3,686,000	5,00,00,000	Computer, Supply of Software and Hardware	3,35,000	4	2,195,60	Successful but Fluctuations in Business.

Firm / Year							Products				Outcome
6. Bairawa Proprietary/ 2006	2 Months	2 months	50,00,000 (Bank, RDS)	35,00,000	18,75,000	5,50,000	Horticulture Nursery, Supply of Plants	NA	7	70,000	Successful Business, Well-established.
7. Ahirwar Partnership 2003, 2006	2½ Months + 2 Months	1 Month + 1 Month	(1) 1,50,000 (2) 8,00,000 (Bank)	59,95,600 from Both Firms	14,07,575 from Both Firms	59,95,600 from Both Firms	Lunch Supply, Furniture, Uniforms, Electrical Goods	1,42,799	6 and 12	3,50,080	Successful, Started Second Firm.
8. Balahi Partnership, 2004	2 Months	1 Month	2,60,000 (Bank, RDS)	2,58,00,000	57,59,500	2,58,00,000	Furniture, Fans, Steel Sheets, Sanitary and Surgical Items	1,50,000	7	87000	Initial success, Now Facing Problems due to BJP Order.
9. Chamar Partnership, 2005	3 months	3 months	20,00,000 (Bank, RDS)	3,50,48,750	93,81,783	3,50,48,750	Manufacture and Supply of Bread, Snacks, Midday Meals	12,45,000	21	1,34,300	Successful.

Source: Prepared by the author based on interviews with the nine respondents.

Note: *For the year 2005–06 brought up to January 2007, all figures are in lakhs;

#Proprietorship working of only this firm has been analysed.

62 ड Sudha Pai

provided. In all cases the mother is illiterate and the father has little education and worked as a class IV government employee, agricultural labourer or in the military while some close family members still work as landless labourers.

Typically, the respondent would describe a visit to relatives in Bhopal, having struggled to gain an education in a small town or village. They would then subsequently decide to stay in Bhopal and try their fortune. Working their way through various jobs such as salesmen, office boys, typesetters, printing press operators etc., they gained some enterprise and marketing skills. All of them adopted the SD/RDS programme on hearing about it from a friend, relative, Dalit MLA or bureaucrat, but some also mention Brahmin or Jain friends who helped them establish the business. Generally they have worked hard to establish their enterprises, which are family firms run with the help of fathers, brothers or wives. Most of them have made good use of contacts with influential members of their caste or community organisations to help overcome teething problems and emerge as successful small businessmen, which have considerably improved the financial position of their families as Table 1.6 shows. Despite an increase in income, their personal expenditure remains modest, with most of it spent on education of their children. The major hurdles faced have been: payment of bribes to officials, caste bias, market discrimination and competition from vaishya and upper caste traders who have long held a monopoly over government contracts.

Entrepreneur 1 has achieved considerable success in his venture as the figures in Table 1.6 show and is keen to start manufacturing of some products supplied by his firm. The success of the second entrepreneur stems from linkages developed with the wider market, in addition to supplying the government, as there is a substantial demand for the products. The third entrepreneur experienced a phase of considerable struggle to achieve success and is keen that his children take up professional jobs as he feels surviving in business is difficult for Dalits due to the strong position of the Baniya community, which he argues is close to the BJP government and is able to obtain government contracts easily. Despite these problems one of them described the SD policy as 'a ray of hope and development for Dalit people in a caste ridden society'. In case of entrepreneur 4, the reasons for his failure seem to lie in the

Dalit Entrepreneurs in Madhya Pradesh ॼ 63

lack of entrepreneurship and experience to face market competition, and inability to establish contacts within the market, officialdom or caste/community organisations that could have helped him. He feels that family reluctance to pay bribes and collective opposition from the trading community were important reasons. Our interviews suggest that it is this class consisting of rapidly increasing high school educated, unemployed Dalits and tribals migrating into cities in constant search of employment, for whom the SD policy could prove to be a stepping stone into the business sector. Given their high level of commitment and desire to succeed, with experience and time they could gravitate to bigger business and even industry. This class is similar to the 'Harijan elite' as identified by Oliver Mendelsohn who due to some advantages such as ownership of a piece of land, or father's government or military service were able to rise out of poverty and break fresh ground, setting them apart from the vast majority of their poorer brethren (Mendelsohn, 1986).

Upper Middle Class Entrepreneur

The second group consists of two entrepreneurs; a tribal and a Dalit (rows 5 and 6 in Tables 1.5 and 1.6) who are well educated and economically well-off (read upper middle class), and were already economically well-off prior to adopting the SD policy. Entrepreneurs belonging this category have a number of advantages that enable them to successfully use the SD policy — a good job prior to entering the business arena, the required knowledge and professional skills, contacts with political leaders and senior bureaucrats — which makes overcoming difficulties in obtaining credit, receiving supply orders, overcoming price competition and monopoly in the market and caste bias relatively easier than those belonging to the other categories. But such linkages can be affected by change in the political regime. For instance, entrepreneur 5 lost all her contracts when the Congress party lost power. However, some of their success is also due to their high educational attainments, which makes them more capable in dealing with banks and the bureaucracy. In fact, entrepreneur 5 as Table 1.6 shows was able to start a second firm in 2004 with her husband. She is also member of many organisations in Bhopal city, including women and tribal organisations. Yet they did encounter corruption and caste discrimination in the market and

64 ॅ *Sudha Pai*

strongly argued that the SD policy is required as Dalits are unable to set up business establishments of their own. As one of them remarked, it was required to 'break the *bania* monopoly'.

It can be argued that this category of Dalit and tribal entrepreneurs should not be provided special protection under the SD policy as they already possess the skills and contacts required to establish a business or industry. However, advocates of the policy would argue that the entry of such persons would lead to the growth of a formidable business class which can form the vanguard that poorer yet educated sections of their community would want to emulate.

Entrepreneurial Partnerships with Non-Dalits

A third route by which three Dalit entrepreneurs (rows 7, 8 and 9 in Tables 1.5 and 1.6) have made use of the policy of SD, is partnerships with non-Dalits belonging to either the Jain trading caste or OBCs. This shows that it is possible for Dalits to reach out and enter into business with a non-Dalit person. Under the rules, 50 per cent of the profits of both supplier and manufacturing partnership firms must be given to the Dalit partner. Two of these firms have made use of the RDS facility. Compared to the first category, these Dalit entrepreneurs, as Table 1.5 shows, belong to middle class, second-generation educated families that have received the benefits of reservation in both education and employment. Over two generations their families through struggle have risen from agricultural to government employment. At the same time though not as highly educated, or economically as well off as the second category, unable to enter into well-paid professional jobs, they have decided to use the opportunity provided by the SD policy.

In contrast to their lower middle caste brethren, with a better education, as Table 1.6 shows, they are ambitious and have established large partnership firms. As two persons are involved the investments are relatively high. These are not family firms which operate out of home but rather are professionally managed businesses with a relatively large number of employees; entrepreneur 9 uses as many as 21. They provide more sophisticated goods such as electrical goods, medicines, steel items, computers, etc. They do not have bureaucratic or political connections, but they are aware of the importance of networking that they have managed to establish helpful contacts. Some are members

Dalit Entrepreneurs in Madhya Pradesh व 65

of scheduled caste organisations that help them maintain contacts with officials belonging to their own community. Consequently, their sales and income is higher and some are keen to shift to manufacturing. They have also faced corruption and caste bias within the bureaucracy, to a lesser extent banks and competition and monopoly from traditional suppliers and retailers; but have been able to deal better with these problems due to help from non-Dalit partners. Hence, they emphasise the need for reservation in the business/trading sector, as disadvantaged sectors require 'protection' for their fledgling business. Among our categories they constitute an upwardly mobile, entrepreneurial and industrial middle class in the making.

Conclusion

This chapter attempts to understand the significant socio-political changes taking place in recent years within the Dalit community in the context of the globalisation of the Indian economy. By the 1990s a small, but educated, politically-conscious Dalit middle class has emerged, which is the product of state policy and social movements. This new class is deeply influenced by internationalisation of the caste question, models of preferential programmes based on affirmative action in other countries and the emergence of a market-oriented economy with better employment and business opportunities. Some of them, even critical of the PD policies adopted at independence have become vocal in demanding alternative preferential policies that will help Dalits achieve greater equality in the new economy. These developments have triggered a contentious debate that was reflected in the Bhopal Document, drafted at the Bhopal Conference by the Dalit intellectuals with the support of the then Congress chief minister of Madhya Pradesh, Digvijay Singh. This document put forward, as the paper shows, two innovative proposals: policies based on diversity and the need for democratisation of capital. These policies are part of their larger project of creating a Dalit middle class with a presence in all sectors of the post-reform society, polity and the economy, which they feel will provide this community voice, equality of status and opportunity.

Based on this document, Madhya Pradesh became the first state to adopt the policy of SD to help Dalits enter into the field of business

66 द *Sudha Pai*

and industry.[19] It can be described as a bold, new *initiative* or *experiment* for the upliftment of Dalits and tribals by the Digvijay Singh government. Its adoption marked a shift in the approach used in addressing the concerns of these disadvantaged groups from rights and entitlements, to a stake in the economy. Official data on adoption and spread of the SD policy reveals that it is at present limited to a small Dalit/tribal class based mainly in the better-off districts and cities such as Bhopal, Gwalior, Indore, Jhabua, etc. Considering that Dalits and tribals together constitute almost a quarter of the total population of Madhya Pradesh, the number that has adopted the policy is as yet small. Moreover, so far the items being supplied are few and limited largely to simple items such as stationery, uniforms and plants, the number of Dalits/tribals who have taken to supply of more specialised goods or manufacturing under this policy are also few.

Critics of the policy have held that it will benefit only the educated urban-based Dalit/tribal groups and lead to further divisions within these communities. The poorer sections — arguing that the better-off, educated sections have cornered the major share of the gains of PD — are demanding in many states specific quotas or shares within the existing policy of reservation. However, its advocates point out that reservation policies can be better implemented and separate programmes can be designed for the poorer sections in the rural areas, as seen from the attempt to redistribute land and set up schools in rural areas by the Digvijay Singh government. They strongly argue for the need to 'create' a Dalit and tribal business class that will both participate in economic decision making, obtain a share in the benefits of the new economy and most importantly provide the required leadership to the poorer sections of these communities. Against the backdrop of this debate, our interviews of nine selected entrepreneurs from the Bhopal DTIC indicate that the SD policy in Madhya Pradesh is moving in a *positive direction*. Our analysis suggests that Dalit/tribal entrepreneurs in the state have welcomed the SD policy and shown keenness to adopt it as it has provided them an opportunity to improve their socio-economic

---

[19] On 2 November 2011, the central government has decided that 4 per cent of all purchases will be sourced from Dalits (*The Times of India* 2011).

Dalit Entrepreneurs in Madhya Pradesh द 67

position. Despite problems faced by them, eight entrepreneurs have been fairly successful in their business venture and hope in future to do even better. They can be described as a vanguard that has set an example that others in the community could emulate.

But certain conditions are required if these policies are to benefit larger number of Dalits and tribals in Madhya Pradesh and elsewhere in the country: a sizeable educated class capable and willing to take entrepreneurial risks; a growing industrial sector that could provide opportunities to Dalits/tribals to become part of the supplier/dealer chain of the government or the private sector; a sympathetic political class and committed senior bureaucracy willing to help struggling entrepreneurs deal with corruption, caste bias and monopoly practices of the traditional suppliers. In Madhya Pradesh the first two — a class of educated Dalits/tribals and an industrial economy — are as yet, too small. Such a policy arguably might have greater chances of being adopted on a larger scale in states such as Tamil Nadu or Punjab. However, the presence of a government with political leaders and bureaucrats who were supportive during the regime of Digvijay Singh helped launch the policy. The BJP government since 2003, though it continued the policy, has shown little interest in advancing this and on the contrary has brought in new rules which have made it more difficult for disadvantaged groups to adapt. This has helped the trading castes who traditionally had links with the bureaucracy and controlled the market to regain the monopoly they have long enjoyed. With greater support the policy could have perhaps been more successful.

Despite these problems it can be argued that in the prevailing globalising economy, the policy of SD has great potential in helping Dalits and tribals develop entrepreneurship. It offers latent possibilities for economic advancement and upliftment of at least the educated section within these communities which would also help democratise capital in the Indian economy. Though a state-supported policy, it is at the same time voluntary, competitive, market-based, depends on individual ability and is therefore, less contentious. Its voluntary nature might also persuade the private sector to adopt it. The policy has the prospect of making entrepreneurial Dalits/tribals part of the 'supply chain' and thereby gradually over time bringing them into the business/industrial sector. In recent years Dalits and to a much lesser extent tribals, have

68 द *Sudha Pai*

entered the political arena in large numbers; the former have formed political parties and governments, but both remain conspicuously absent in the business/industrial sector. Policies such as SD would end the marginalisation and exclusion that these disadvantaged sectors face in the economic arena and provide them economic empowerment. It can be seen as a second stage in PD, a policy suited to the shift from a socialist welfare state to a neoliberal state that is still expected in a democratic society to look after the welfare of the disadvantaged sections. It has the potential to introduce substantial change in the socio-economic position of Dalits, even though so far the results have not been up to the expectations voiced by Dalit intellectuals and activists when the programme was inaugurated.

४

References

Babu, Shyam. 2003. 'Dalits and the New Economic Order: Some Prognostications and Prescriptions from the Bhopal Conference'. RGICS Working Paper Series, 44, October. New Delhi: Rajiv Gandhi Institute for Contemporary Studies.

Dalit Millennium. 2000. *The Pioneer*, 30 January.

Elayaperumal Committee. 1969. 1979. 'Report of the Commission for SC and ST', July 1978 to March 1979 (1st Report). New Delhi: Government of India.

Fernandes, Leela. 2007. *India's New Middle Class Democratic Politics in an Era of Economic Reform*. New Delhi: Oxford University Press.

Ghosh, Jayati. 2007. 'Case for Caste-based Quotas in Higher Education', *Economic and Political Weekly*, 41(24), 17 June: 2428–31.

Government of Madhya Pradesh. 2002. 'The Bhopal Document: Charting a New Course for Dalits for the 21st Century', January.

———. Government Order 6-7/2002/11 A. 2002. 30 May and 11 June. Bhopal.

Harriss, John. 2007. 'The Onward March of the New "Great Indian Middle Class"', *The Hindu*, 15 August.

Iliaih, Kancha. 2006. 'Merits of Reservations', *Economic and Political Weekly*, 41(24), 17–23 June: 2447–49.

Kapur, Devesh, Chandra Bhan Prasad, Lant Pritchett, and D. Shyam Babu. 2010. 'Rethinking Inequality: Dalits in Uttar Pradesh in the Market Reform Era', *Economic and Political Weekly*, 28 August, 45(35): 39–49.

Mendelsohn, Oliver. 1986. 'A Harijan Elite? The Lives of Some Untouchable Politicians', *Economic and Political Weekly*, 21(12), 22 March: 501–09.

Mohanty, Mritunjoy. 2006. 'Social Inequality, Labour Market Dynamics and Reservation', *Economic and Political Weekly*, 41(35), 2 September: 3777–91.

Pai, Sudha. 2010. *Developmental State and the Dalit Question in Madhya Pradesh: Congress Response*. New Delhi: Routledge.

Prasad, Chandrabhan. 2004. *Dalit Diary: 1999–2003 Reflections on Apartheid in India*. Chennai: Navayana.

Sachar, Rajindar. 2006. 'Towards Dalit Capitalism'. *The Times of India*, 12 July.

The Times of India. 2011. 4 November.

Thorat, Sukhadeo, Aryama and Prashant Negi (eds). 2005. *Reservation and the Private Sector Quest For Equal Opportunity and Growth*. New Delhi: Rawat Publications.

Thorat, Sukhdeo and Umakant (eds). 2004. *Caste Race and Discrimination Discourses in International Context*. New Delhi: Rawat Publications.

Vaidyanathan, R. 2005 'Make Them Entrepreneurs Instead', in Sukhadeo Thorat, Aryama and Prashant Negi (eds), *Reservation in the Private Sector Quest For Equal Opportunity and Growth*, pp. 356–60. New Delhi: Rawat Publications.

Varma, Pavan K. 1999. *The Great Indian Middle Class*. New Delhi: Penguin Books.

Weisskopf, Thomas. 2006. 'Is Positive Discrimination a Good Way to Aid Disadvantaged Ethnic Communities', *Economic and Political Weekly*, 25 February: 717–26.

II

Trajectories of Dalits' Incorporation into the Indian Neoliberal Business Economy

Kaushal K. Vidyarthee

Dalits form 16 per cent of the total population and are labelled 'backward groups' in India. The Indian state has made many provisions to improve the situation of Dalits including a constitutional framework which includes protective arrangements, compensatory discrimination and the promotion of development; and policies such as 'Special Component Plan'[1] that reinforce their formal constitutional protection (National Human Rights Commission 2004: 48). However, even after six decades of India's independence the literature continues to record discrimination against Dalits in many settings including employment, housing, services, credit, and land markets. Tanning, scavenging, sweeping, and cleaning jobs remain largely Dalit occupations in modern India and the majority of Dalits work as landless or near-landless labourers in agricultural production or in the lowest paid kinds of manual labour (Thorat 2002 ; Thorat and Mallick 2004; Thorat and Umakant 2004). Marginalisation has been central to the existence of Dalits in India. It has not only permeated their social life but also their economic lives (Shah 2001).

My interest in this chapter lies in a hitherto neglected area: the analysis of Dalits' incorporation in India's private business economy.

---

[1] Special Component Plan (SCP) for SCs has been an important strategy used in the planning process for quite some time in order to ensure that outlays and benefits from the general sectors of the plans flow to SCs at least in proportion to their population both in physical and financial terms.

Trajectories of Dalits' Incorporation **द** 71

This area is a neglected area of study, both empirically and theoretically. The private business economy has grown rapidly in the post-reform period and there are very few studies analysing the relationship between caste and business ownership. And yet, an understanding of Dalits' incorporation into the business economy is crucial from the perspective of equity and inclusive development in contemporary India. This is because the issue of inclusive development has come to centre stage in light of the failure of economic growth to bring about holistic improvements in the living conditions of the vast majority of marginalised people.

Understanding the marginalisation of Dalits in business enterprises is the central concern of this chapter. The objective is to analyse the spatial and sectoral variation of Dalit participation in the business economy. Specifically, I analyse the geographic and regional variation of economic incorporation of Dalits for different economic sectors and their nature and dynamics during the period 1990–2005. In the second section, I situate the research objectives within wider theoretical literature and Dalit studies with a specific reference to the economic incorporation of Dalits in the post-liberalisation era. The third section details out the quantitative methods and data used in this research. The fourth section outlines the trajectory of Dalits' incorporation, both temporal and spatial. Here, I offer explanations for the differential incorporation across regions and the last section summarises the findings.

Caste, Dalit Occupations and Liberalisation

It is important to examine how Dalit occupations can be situated within the context of caste and liberalisation. The criterion for inclusion of castes into the schedule were based on indicators of social, educational and economic backwardness arising out of the 'traditional' customs related to the practice of untouchability (Webster 2007). The caste has been subjected to a lot of theorisation focusing on the principle of natural superiority, the notion of purity and pollution, bodily connotations of untouchability and in terms of terms of indignity, stigma, prejudice, humiliation and social disdain among others (Béteille 1966; Dumont 1988; Gupta 1980, 1992; Srinivas 1962).

72 द *Kaushal K. Vidyarthee*

However, despite this vast literature on caste, there are few economic analyses of caste. Akerlof's formal model of the caste system attempted to apply the neo-classical economic theory to the institution of caste (Akerlof 1976). He argued that the persistence of caste may be due to the fact that the caste represents a voluntary stable equilibrium and this equilibrium has been allowed to persist for centuries. In a system in which occupation is hereditary, compulsory and endogamous, any transaction that breaks the caste code changes the subsequent behaviours leading to economic disincentives. This feature results in an inherent immobility of labour between caste occupations, and creates caste-based segmentation in the labour markets. The consequence is a lack of competition. Expanding upon the Akerlof model, James Scoville argues that through a system of social and economic ostracism, the caste system creates enormous and virtually insurmountable transition costs to break the restrictions on labour or occupational mobility (Scoville 2003). Discrimination and social exclusion are thus manifested in the social as well as the economic lives of marginalised groups (Shah 2001). Room establishes that 'where citizens are unable to secure their social rights, they will tend to suffer processes of generalised and persistent disadvantage and their social and occupational participation will be undermined' (1995: 5).

Much of the social–economic theorising in the last century together with the observations made by the founding fathers of modern Indian sociology and the work of anthropologists suggest that capitalist modernity would destroy archaic forms of exchange and economic regulation (Harriss-White and Sinha 2007).[2] However the condition of Dalits in the contemporary context would seem to contradict this. Instead of accelerating the destruction of old forms of exchange, India's liberalisation has increased the tension between forces which dissolves social forms of regulation and forces which intensify them or create new forms (Harriss-White 2003; World Bank 2006: 179). Aspects of identity such as caste and religion are transformed and resurface not only in the liberalised economy but also inside the state apparatus. Contradictory social and economic relations based on identity also

---

[2] See the review in the introductory chapter (Harriss-White and Sinha 2007).

Trajectories of Dalits' Incorporation द 73

develop in close physical proximity in the same social space (Mhaskar 2012). This process is socially and spatially uneven. Recent literature on Dalits and liberalisation has argued different points of view. For instance Teltumbde in his study on the examination of the magnitude and direction of the impact of liberalisation policies on the Dalits has found that Dalits have been negatively impacted in absolute as well as relative terms (Teltumbde 2001). He further argues that Dalits' social disabilities, largely reinforced by and sustained on the economic deprivations, is accentuated with liberalisation policies. Chandra Bhan and colleagues, on the other hand, have argued that liberalisation has broken down caste barriers especially in terms of consumption patterns and has led to 'very substantial shifts in Dalits' lives, consistent with a growing sense of empowerment and opportunity and declining ability of others to impose social inequalities' (Kapur et al. 2010: 48). Sudha Pai (2010) has argued that the absence of an upsurge from below limits the ability of the state-sponsored economic upliftment aimed to help Dalits in the market reforms era.

At the start of the 21st century, Dalits were roughly twice as likely to be poor, unemployed and illiterate than non-Dalits (Gang, Sen and Yun 2008; Sen 2002). Dalits are still largely confined to casual agricultural labour, construction, and sanitary work, or to petty production and trade.[3] However, perhaps the worst traditional occupations of Dalits is the practice of manual scavenging which employs up to one million Dalits, most of them women (Narula and Macwan 2001). Furthermore, there are noted caste-based differences in the terms and conditions of contracts, prices, and the services in education, housing, health, access to common property resources, to public space and to other infrastructure; and wages in the labour market (Banerjee et al. 2009; Das and Dutta 2007; Heyer 2009; Iversen et al. 2010b; Thorat 2002; Thorat and Newman 2007). India has a poor record of recruitment of Dalits relative to non-Dalits in the organised sector and Dalits are under-represented in the informal economy (Thorat, Aryama and Negi 2005).

---

[3] This has been recorded by the National Commission for Scheduled Castes and Scheduled Tribes in their sixth report in 2000–01 as well as 11th Five-year Plan document.

74   ठ   *Kaushal K. Vidyarthee*

Most empirical research in India has focussed on discrimination within the labour market (Banerjee and Knight 1985; Iversen and Raghavendra 2003; Kingdon 1998; Thorat and Attewell 2007). These studies show that Dalits are disadvantaged in terms of lower wages higher propensity to be stuck in jobs with low opportunities (Banerjee and Knight 1985), and inferior employment terms (such as casual employment) (Das and Dutta 2007; Dutta 2006). Recent research also indicates that caste-based prejudice also operates in high status urban jobs and occupations (Deshpande and Newman 2007; Madeshwaran and Attewell 2007). Very recently, a limited number of studies (Harriss-White and Vidyarthee 2009; Jodhka 2010; Prakash 2009) have examined the economic incorporation of marginalised groups in the liberalised business economy. Two studies are of direct relevance to the material presented in this chapter: Jodhka's study (2010), which showed that caste powerfully affects Dalit entrepreneurs in the contemporary market economy, and Prakash's (2009) analysis of 90 life histories of Dalit entrepreneurs, which showed that market outcomes are embedded in existing social structures. However, neither of these studies told us about regional or sectoral variation in Dalits' participation in the business economy. Using the Economic Census data (1990 and 1998), Harriss-White and Vidyarthee (2009) analysed Dalits' and Adivasis' participation in the business economy in the 1990s trying to locate their participation according to regional variation and in the context of stigma attached to their work. The present work looks at the period between 1990–2005 using the latest data. My research fills these gaps by analysing the spatial and sectoral dynamics of the structures of economic incorporation of Dalits.

India's incorporation into the global capitalist system accelerated in the 1990s with the introduction of 'New Economic Policy', which was implemented in India in 1991 at the behest of international donor agencies (Nair 2008). The expansion of private capital in India during the post-1991 period marked the state's retreat from the economy (Jodhka 2010). Private enterprise was allowed and encouraged to expand into areas of economic activity that were hitherto unavailable. In the first 15 years of the reform period, the absolute number of private enterprise in India increased by more than two-thirds (Harriss-White et al. 2013b). Most of the enterprises were small with a family labour force, employing wage workers ad hoc according to

Trajectories of Dalits' Incorporation द 75

their growth (ibid.). The growth in the business economy of India in the neoliberal era has been self-employment driven, with a thrust on small enterprises. Technology intensive growth under this regime led to a decrease in the number of jobs in the organised sector, an informalisation of the organised sector and an expansion of the unorganised sector (Nair 2008). Until now research has primarily focussed on the differential participation of marginalised groups in the formal sectors (i.e., wage employment in the public and private sector) (Thakur and Thakur 2008; Thorat 2002; Thorat, Attewell and Rizvi 2009; Thorat and Newman 2009). My research attempts to analyse the nature and dynamics of sectoral structures of incorporation from the perspectives of micro-entrepreneurship and self-employment.

However, the increased opportunity for micro-entrepreneurship and ownership of private small enterprises in neoliberal India holds the potential to expand areas of the economy detached from the still existing traditional caste occupation structure. In recognition of this, the government initiated few measures to encourage Dalit ownership of private enterprises. These policies mainly include preferential allocation of sites for business, supply of capital to Dalit business people, training in entrepreneurship skill and incentives for market development (Thorat and Sadana 2009). During this time, the agenda of inclusive development came to dominate development discourses in India as the earlier agenda of single point focus one conomic growth had failed. Consequently, the Government of India has aimed to distribute the benefits from accelerated economic growth to all citizens, especially marginalised groups of the society.[4] Thus, the incorporation of Dalits into the business economy is not only an important research issue, it also has clear policy significance from the perspectives of equity and inclusive development.

---

[4] In the context of promoting sustained high economic growth, Spence (2008) outlines 'inclusiveness' in terms of equity of outcomes, equality of opportunities and the protection of people in transition. Economists at the Asian Development Bank argue that inclusive development should focus on two specific areas: extreme poverty and rising inequalities; and creating economic opportunities and broadening access to opportunities to support social inclusion (see Ali and Zhuang 2007).

76 ᵈ *Kaushal K. Vidyarthee*

Spatial and sectoral analysis of Dalits' enterprise ownership can therefore act as a tool to measure the inclusiveness of the private business economy in general and the degree of incorporation of Dalits in particular. The spatial dimension of the participation is of significance in its own right for four main reasons. First, it shows a concern with the maintenance and promotion of national cohesion and social and political stability, and second, it shows a concern with the impact of a regional concentration of discrimination and exclusionary processes, in turn limiting the agenda of inclusive development (Cook 2006). Third, it demonstrates a critical concern of the issue of ignorance of the spatiality and degree of variation within the frameworks of discrimination and social exclusion. The geographical variation of inequality and development in India have long been of interest to anthropologists, sociologists, public health specialists, political scientists and economists (see Harvey 1996; Henderson, Shalizi and Venables 2001; Kanbur and Venables 2007; Krugman 1997, 1999; Lobao, Hooks and Tickamyer 2007; Porter and Sölvell 1998). However, the way in which exclusion and discrimination vary from region to region, and persist or change over time have not been analysed. So forth, in an era of liberalisation and regional configuration, it is very important to self-consciously situate social processes in spatial context. This paper therefore aims to examine the spatial variation and regional patterns of economic incorporation at the state level.

Data and Methodology

Studying a trajectory can involve multiple approaches. A trajectory refers to tracing the course of evolution of a certain phenomenon, in this case, the extent to which Dalits have been incorporated into the economy as owners of enterprises. In this paper, I analyse patterns and trajectories from a spatial perspective at three different points in time. I then aggregate these spatial analyses of the Dalits' incorporation to view patterns at the state level. This masks geographical variations within the states and it undermines the complexity, dynamism and specificity of different Dalit castes.

This research relies on secondary data. The Government of India has several economic statistics programmes for the enumeration of

Trajectories of Dalits' Incorporation ७ 77

enterprises: the Annual Survey of Industries (ASI), the National Sample Surveys (NSS), the Economic Census, and Census of Registered Small Scale Industries (now termed micro, small and medium enterprises [MSMEs]) (Government of India 2008 and 2009). ASI primarily estimates the contribution of different industry groups to national income and analyses various factors influencing industry. It covers the entire country except three states and one Union Territory (UT). The NSS makes enterprise surveys for particular groups of sectors every five or 10 years. Its design follows a stratified multi-stage sampling scheme which makes substantial number of sub-areas thereby making the sample sizes too small. The All India Census of MSMEs however only enumerates all *registered* enterprises. Unregistered enterprises — the vast majority — are only covered through a sample survey. The Economic Census includes economic activities except those involved in crop production and plantation on a full enumeration basis and covers all states and UTs.

In this research, I use the Economic Censuses, which provide statewise data on the number of private, overwhelmingly 'own account' enterprises (OAEs), owned and operated by Dalits, Adivasis and other castes. I analyse 10 sectors of the economy for the year 1990 and I look at 14 sectors in 1998 and 2005. Enterprises in this context are economic undertakings not for the sole purpose of own consumption. Rather than discuss the classification of 'enterprise', in this paper I have simply adopted the definitions of the Economic Census. In addition, the population censuses have been used to provide data for Dalits and total populations by each Indian state for the years 1991 and 2001. It should be noted that there are three difficulties with these data: first, matching business data for 1990, 1998 and 2005 with demographic data for 1991 and 2001; second, it is difficult to aggregate the changes in sectoral classifications over the 'short decade' of 1990–98; and third, the territories of the states (which were also reclassified over this period) produce distortions to India's agro-ecological regions. In 1990, the sectors were livestock, agriculture and forestry, mining, manufacturing, utilities (electricity, gas and water), construction, trade, hotels and restaurants, transport, storage and communications, finance and real estate, and health, education community and personal services. In 1998 and 2005, they were livestock, agricultural services, mining, manufacturing, utilities, construction, wholesale trade, retail trade, restaurants

78 ᘯ *Kaushal K. Vidyarthee*

and hotels, transport, storage, communication, finance and real estate, and community, social and personal services. With due caution these data may be used to produce indices of participation (PI):

[SC enterprises (SCE) in sector i, state x/total enterprises in sector i, state x]/[SC Population (SCP) in state x/total population in state x],

$$\frac{SCE_{ix}}{\sum E_{ix}} \Big/ \frac{SCP_x}{\sum P_x}$$

A value of 1.0 represents absence of bias or a state of parity: i.e., the proportion of Dalit enterprises equals the proportion of Dalits in the state. A rank of <1 denotes disproportionately low participation in the market, and a rank of >1 disproportionately high participation (Harriss-White and Vidyarthee 2009).

These indices were then mapped, using the Geographical Information System (GIS), to produce a series of maps showing the differential incorporation of Dalits as owners of capital in the Indian business economy in 1990–2005 across states and economic sectors. GIS choropleth mapping techniques are useful in analyzing statistical data aggregated over defined regions and it provides an easy way to visualise how a measurement varies across a geographic area, allowing us to identify trends (Andrienko and Andrienko 1999). It must be noted that this mapping method is limited in three ways: first, mapping achieves a smoothing out of data by suppressing the variation in an attribute through reclassifying values into just a few categories; second, the patterns of a map depend substantially on the analyst's choice of both classification method and the number of data classes; and third, this technique assumes a relatively even distribution of the measured phenomenon within each spatial unit (Grengs 2007; Haining 2003). The data for mapping has been classified using the method of statistically optimal classification rather than classification into equal intervals or classification with equal frequencies of objects in the classes since the statistical distribution of a mapped variable is not uniform. Keeping these limitations in mind, this research uses mapping to depict the indicators and attributes of the spatiality of Dalits' incorporation at the aggregated level.

Trajectory of Dalits' Incorporation

General Trends in the period 1990–2005

In the first 15 years of the reform period, 1990–2005, the absolute number of private enterprise in India increased by more than two thirds (i.e., from 22 million to 38 million). While during 1990–98, it increased by a quarter; in the subsequent seven years, 1998–2005, it increased by more than a third. Even though the total number of Dalit enterprises increased from 2.18 million to 3.69 million, the proportion of all private enterprises owned by Dalits remained stable at 9.8 per cent (see Figure 2.1). This is disproportionately low, given that Dalits constitute roughly 16 per cent of the general population. This persistent inequality in the ownership of firms during the first 15 years of liberalisation. Here, it is important to note that during 1990–98, the proportion of enterprises owned by Dalits actually *declined* by 15 per cent and between 1998–2005, the proportion only increased by a very small amount (17 per cent). The annual growth rate of Dalit enterprise

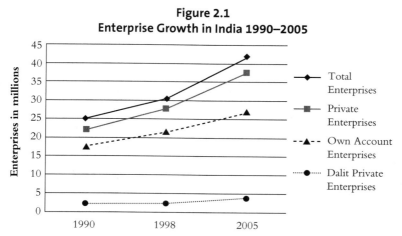

**Figure 2.1
Enterprise Growth in India 1990–2005**

Source: Economic Censuses of 1990, 1998 and 2005.

80   द   *Kaushal K. Vidyarthee*

was comparatively low during 1990–98 (0.42 per cent per annum) in comparison to the period of 1998–2005 (6.77 per cent per annum). The increase in the growth rate has been observed both in own-account enterprises and enterprises with hired workers.

The average employment per enterprise at an all-India level reduced from 2.88 employees in 1990 to 2.75 in 1998, and 2.41 in 2005. The proportion of own-account enterprises marginally decreased during 1990–2005 but it still accounts for almost two-thirds of all enterprises. However, the proportion of enterprises with more than 10 workers reduced by more than 50 per cent. In 2005, more than 95 per cent of enterprises have been employing less than five workers (see Table 2.1). This clearly shows that growth and capital accumulation in the neo-liberal business economy has been driven by small enterprises in the informal sector. The point to note here is that formal sector jobs constitute merely 8 per cent of the total employment available in the country.

Table 2.1
Distribution of Enterprises by Size, Employment and Enterprise Type (in per cent)

Employment Size	1990	1998	2005
1–5	93.41	94.00	95.07
6–9	3.46	3.30	3.42
10 and Above	3.13	2.80	1.51
Enterprise Type			
Own-account Enterprises	70.73	70.43	64.41
Enterprises with Hired Workers	29.27	29.57	35.59

Source: Economic Censuses of 1990, 1998 and 2005.

From a sectoral perspective, the most important category of enterprise — in the range of 42 to 46 per cent in 1990, 1998 and 2005 — is wholesale and retail trade, hotels and restaurants. While health, education, community, and personal services declined relatively from 19 to 8 per cent in the first 15 years, firms in agriculture and allied sector rose from 10 to 16 per cent (see Table 2.2). Together, by the turn of the century, trade and services constituted 56 per cent of the GDP but 67 per cent of enterprises. Manufacturing firms accounted for 20

Table 2.2
Distribution across Sectors of Private Enterprises in India

	Sectors	1990 Total Private Enterprise	%	1998 Total Private Enterprise	%	2005 Total Private Enterprise	%
1	Agricultural and Allied	2,243,042	10.13	3,438,010	12.41	5,887,783	15.66
2	Mining and Quarrying	47,143	0.21	34,072	0.12	80,179	0.21
3	Manufacturing	5,131,524	23.18	5,481,722	19.78	7,968,435	21.20
4	Electricity, Gas and Water Supply	10,557	0.05	12,159	0.04	28,348	0.08
5	Construction	221,162	1.00	283,200	1.02	314,520	0.84
6	Wholesale and Retail Trade, Hotels and Restaurants	9,373,327	42.34	12,407,036	44.77	17,264,756	45.93
7	Transport, Storage and Communication	628,054	2.84	1,120,313	4.05	2,043,795	5.44
8	Finance, Real Estate, Business and Others	351,806	1.59	597,711	2.16	1,120,791	2.98
9	Health, Education, Community and Personal Services, etc.	4,125,573	18.63	4,334,534	15.64	2,878,250	7.66
10	Others (n.a.d.)	8,645	0.04	5,648	0.02	1,294	0.00
	Total	22,140,833	100.00	27,717,190	100.00	37,588,151	100.00

Source: Economic Census 1990, 1998 and 2005.

82 द *Kaushal K. Vidyarthee*

to 23 per cent of the total number of firms (and about 22 per cent of GDP, proportionate to their share of total enterprises) (Harriss-White and Vidyarthee 2009).

The sectoral trends for Dalits are striking. During 1990–98, the absolute number of Dalit firm owners in the agricultural, manufacturing, and mining and quarrying sectors declined by 3.8 per cent, 63.6 per cent and 16 per cent respectively. In wholesale retail trade, hotels and restaurants sectors, the number of Dalit owners of firms increased by 47.2 per cent. However, during the period of 1998–2005, the absolute number of Dalit enterprises saw a significant increase in all sectors, except a notable decline of 33 per cent in the sector of health, education, community and personal services, etc. It is clear that the sectoral unevenness increased during the first 15 years of reforms.

Spatial Variation

The size of the Dalit population varies significantly from state to state in India. The proportion of Dalits in relation to the total population is greatest in the North and South-east (SE) India and smallest in West India, the North-eastern states (NE) and Kerala in the south. The proportion of Dalit enterprises takes a somewhat different spatial expression from enterprises in general (see Maps 2.1 and 2.2).

State-wise enterprise growth during 1990–2005 is very uneven. During 1990–98, the central belt (i.e., including Bihar, Madhya Pradesh, Haryana, Gujarat, and Rajasthan), Karnataka in the South and Mizoram in the NE saw negative growth rate in terms of the absolute number of Dalit enterprises. Yet, between 1998–2005 these states reversed this trend and reported positive growth rates. Himachal Pradesh and Goa were the only states with negative growth rates (see Maps 2.3–2.5).

Strong regional patterns emerge. Dalit enterprises are proportionally most abundant in the NE. While between 1991 and 2001 there was no change in the demographic regions, maps of the participation index (PI) for all private enterprises show that during 1990–98, the apparent effects of 'negative discrimination' against Dalits spread throughout the south and intensified in the area between Rajasthan and Gujarat, through to UP, Bihar and Chhattisgarh. From 1998 to 2005, Dalits' relative participation increased in most of the southern states and UP.

Map 2.1
Proportion of SC Population, 2001 Census (in per cent)

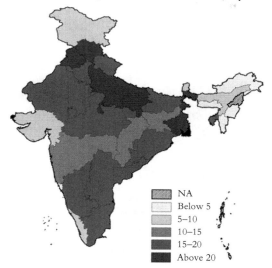

Source: All maps in this chapter are prepared by the author. Maps are not to scale.

Map 2.2
Proportion of SC Enterprises, 2005 Census (in per cent)

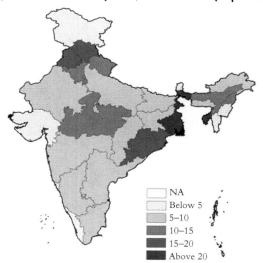

Map 2.3
Enterprise Growth, 1990–98 (in per cent)

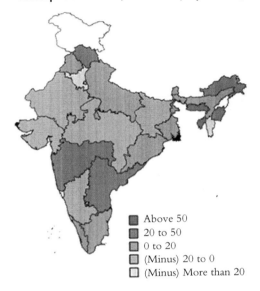

- Above 50
- 20 to 50
- 0 to 20
- (Minus) 20 to 0
- (Minus) More than 20

Map 2.4
Enterprise Growth, 1998–2005 (in per cent)

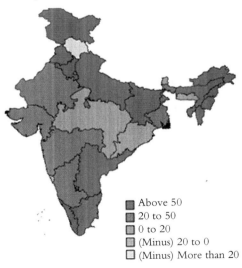

- Above 50
- 20 to 50
- 0 to 20
- (Minus) 20 to 0
- (Minus) More than 20

**Map 2.5
Enterprise Growth, 1990–2005 (in per cent)**

It decreased in Orissa and remained unchanged in the rest of India (see Maps 2.6 to 2.8).

Harriss-White et al. (2013a) have suggested that, although there is considerable internal variation and state-level idiosyncrasy, there are four regional patterns of incorporation. It is possible to discern commonalities in two polar compass directions — South and North — and across a swathe of states from the centre-east of India and a set of small tribal states in the extreme NE (see Table 2.3). The western states are anomalous in various ways.

Sectoral Spatiality of Dalits' Incorporation

Despite the limitations of the data, different sectors show different patterns of regional distribution, which intensify both positively and negatively during 1990–2005.

**Map 2.6
PI for 1990**

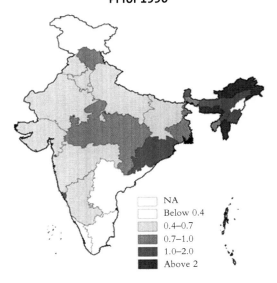

**Map 2.7
PI for 1998**

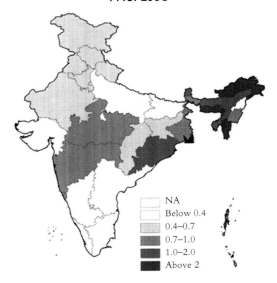

Map 2.8
PI for 2005

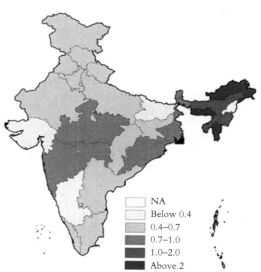

Agricultural and Livestock Businesses: In 1990 Dalits were disproportionately prominent in agricultural business in the NE and under-represented in the western India. By 2005, however, negative PIs spread throughout the country except Orissa, West Bengal and NE states (see Maps 2.9 to 2.11).

Non-agricultural Business in General: In 1990, SCs were strongly under-represented in the south and relatively over-represented in Himachal Pradesh, MP and the NE states. By 2005, disproportionately low participation had spread from the south to NW making a solid region of low participation throughout southern India and in UP, Bihar and the NW (see Maps 2.12 to 2.14).

Mining, Quarrying and Construction: In 1990, Dalits were disproportionately active in these sectors in large parts of India. By 1998 'positive discrimination' had spread to a belt in the centre and north but the whole of south India had negative discrimination. Even in 2005, the South was starting to see the effects of 'negative discrimination'.

Table 2.3
Regional Patterns of Economic Incorporation of Dalits

	Regions	SC Population (in %)	Total Enterprises	Enterprise Ratio (Firm vs People)	Structure of the Enterprises	Participation Indices	Discrimination against Dalits
1	Southern Region (Andhra Pradesh, Tamil Nadu, Kerala and Karnataka)	10–20	9m (High Absolute No.)	1:40	Relatively Well Developed Non-agricultural Economy	0.37–0.3 (unusually low)	Strong Negative Discrimination
2	Central-eastern Swathe (Madhya Pradesh, Maharashtra, Orissa, West Bengal and Assam)	16–28 (Higher than Average Proportion)	10m	1:30	Well Developed Non-farm Economy	0.8 and over 1	Weak, Moving into Positive in the East
3	Northern States (Bihar, UP, Punjab, Haryana, HP, Delhi, Chandigarh)	15–28 (Above Average Incidence)	7.5m (Relatively Low Total Incidence of Firms)	1:46	Very Low Wage Labour Base	0.3–0.6 (generally low participation indices)	Strong Negative Discrimination
4	Western States (Gujarat and Goa)	2–7 (Low Incidence of SC — Distinguishing Feature of This Region)	2.6 m	1:20	Flourishing Non-farm Economies		Strong Negative Discrimination
5	North-eastern Tribal States: Arunachal, Meghalaya, Mizoram, Nagaland, Sikkim, Tripura		0.2	1:62	High Frequency and High Wage Labour Base		Positive Discrimination

Source: Harriss-White et al. 2013b.

Map 2.9
PI (Agriculture and Livestock) for 1990

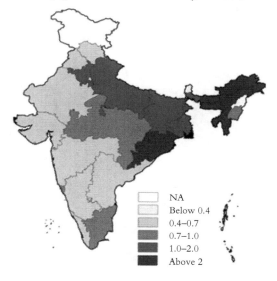

Map 2.10
PI (Agriculture and Livestock) for 1998

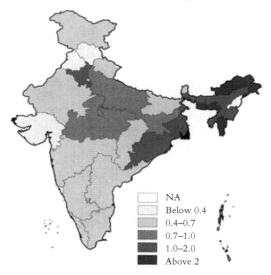

**Map 2.11
PI (Agriculture and Livestock) for 2005**

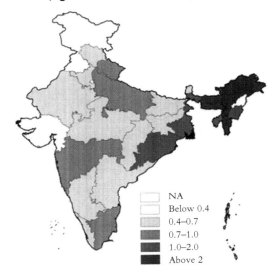

**Map 2.12
PI (Non-agricultural Business) for 1990**

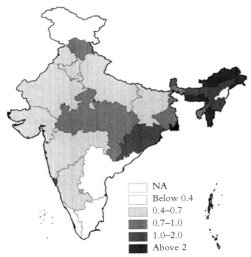

Map 2.13
PI (Non-agricultural Business) for 1998

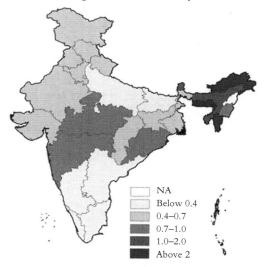

Map 2.14
PI (Non-agricultural Business) for 2005

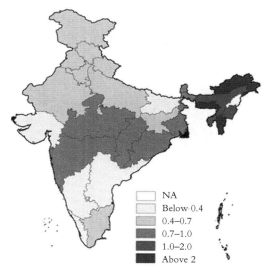

Manufacturing: In 1990, Dalit participation was positive in central India and relatively low in the so-called 'cow belt', SE and NW. However, by 1998 relative disadvantage had spread to Karnataka in the south and to Gujarat and Rajasthan in the North-west while positive advantage was starting to emerge in central and northern parts of central India. By 2005, there was a disproportionate increase in participation in the NE and a relative decrease in the West (see Maps 2.15 to 2.17).

Trade, Hotels, etc: In 1990, Dalits were conspicuous for their low levels of participation, except in Orissa and the NE tribal states. It seems that here above all there are powerful entry barriers at work. By 1998, when these categories are disaggregated, the pattern persisted. However, by 2005 Maharashtra and West Bengal had observed a relative increase in participation (see Maps 2.18 to 2.20).

Transport, Storage, Communications, Finance, Real Estate: There is persistently low participation in these sectors throughout India, except in the NE states. However, by 2005 a relative increase in participation has started emerging in a belt in the SW and East.

**Map 2.15
PI (Manufacturing) for 1990**

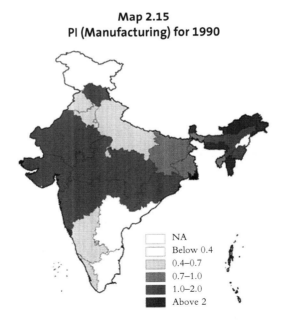

Map 2.16
PI (Manufacturing) for 1998

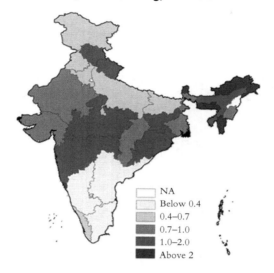

Map 2.17
PI (Manufacturing) for 2005

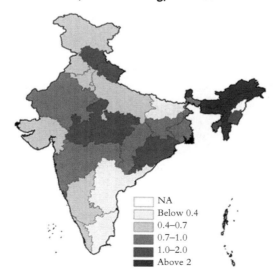

**Map 2.18
PI (Trade, Hotel & Restaurants) for 1990**

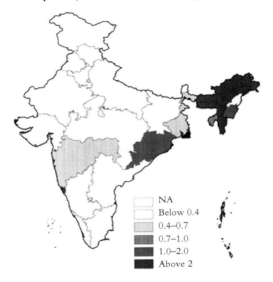

**Map 2.19
PI (Wholesale Trade) for 1998**

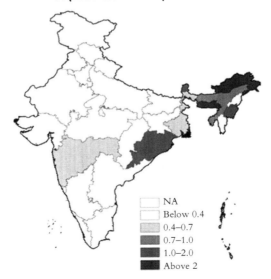

Map 2.20
PI (Trade — Wholesale & Retail) for 2005

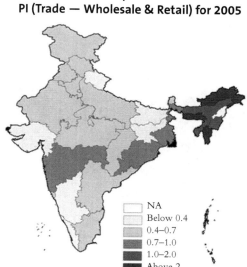

Personal and Community Services (Health and Education): These are sectors in which it might be expected that the impact of reservations in education and the public sector would be most obvious. But in general, the participation of Dalits is disproportionately low, intensifying throughout the decade except in a belt in the SW and East, and the NE states (see Maps 2.21 to 2.23).

Thus, the regionalisation of the economic participation of Dalits and their entry barriers are highly differentiated in sector-specific ways (see Table 2.4).

The all-India analysis of the Economic Census of 2005, disaggregated by states, shows that India has a series of regions of relative advantage and disadvantage for Dalits in various sectors of the business economy. Dalits are 'relatively advantaged' in the construction sector and consistently disadvantaged in those sectors that are driving Indian growth: trade, transport, food, hospitality and service sectors. Over time, Dalit disadvantage has *intensified* in southern India. However, it is notable that there is a relatively high Dalit participation in NE tribal states where there is a very low absolute number of Dalits.

**Map 2.21
PI (Education) for 1990**

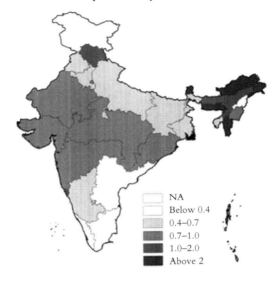

**Map 2.22
PI (Education) for 1998**

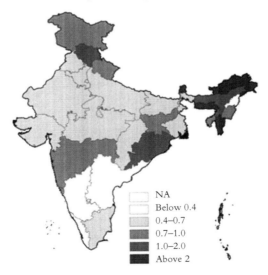

Trajectories of Dalits' Incorporation द 97

Map 2.23
PI (Education) for 2005

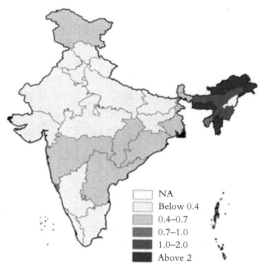

Table 2.4
Regions of Differential Incorporation for Various Sectors

East Advantaged West Disadvantaged Agriculture	Central Belt (E-W) Advantaged Rest Disadvantaged Non-agriculture in General; Manufacturing	Relative Advantage Everywhere Construction	Relative Disadvantage Everywhere except the NE States Trade; Mining; Quarrying; Transport; Storage; Finance; Real Estate; Services

Explaining the Unevenness of Differential Incorporation and its Persistence

In this section, I explore some explanations that may help us understand the differential incorporation of Dalits across regions and sectors.

First, this research showed that the discriminatory and exclusionary economic practices of the traditional caste system have not weakened markedly with the process of liberalisation and modernisation. This

98 � *Kaushal K. Vidyarthee*

substantiates Prakash (2009) and Jodhka's (2010) work which has also shown how market outcomes are embedded in the existing social structures. A deeper institutional analysis of this phenomenon can generate ideas which might critique theories of institutional change and help us understand why, with liberalisation, certain social institutions are perpetuated and reproduced as well as destroyed and created (Schumpeter 1994). It is clear that some practices adapt to become forces that regulate the social economy (Meagher 2010) while others persist practically unchanged (Harriss-White 2003).

The persistence of economic exclusion and discrimination has been highlighted in numerous studies including Government of India's plan documents and government commissioned reports (Prakash and Harriss-White 2009). Yet none of these analyses tell us how these processes are allowed to persist. I would argue that in order to understand this phenomenon, the policies designed to improve the economic incorporation of Dalits need to be scrutinised. There is a need to look at the roles played by the various stakeholders and levels of the bureaucracy, NGOs, political representatives in the policy processes at a local level. Here, Schaffer's work on the inseparability of policy and implementation (Schaffer 1984), Long and Long's framework (1992) of policy makers' motivations, interests and negotiations; and Sabatier's (2007) treatment of policy change as a result of interaction between actors would be pertinent.

Second, this research showed that economic incorporation of Dalits is very uneven across sectors as well as region. Explaining several types of uneven participation is difficult using the normal principle of parsimony. Harriss-White and Vidyarthee (2009) did not offer any conclusive theoretical or empirically verifiable explanations for regional or sectoral unevenness. However, these findings highlight the need for a more refined form of investigation, using other kinds of evidence and different levels of aggregation. It also shows the need for new micro-level research on the modes of 'political' incorporation of Dalits and on the relation between these processes and their entry into business.

Here, I argue that in order to understand the spatial unevenness in the economic incorporation of Dalits, we first have to understand the process of incorporation and the ways in which this process is socially constructed. We also need to know how these processes interrelate and why they vary regionally and by sector. This can be done using different levels of aggregation for regions (i.e., state, district and selected local-level case studies) for spatial and statistical analyses. Even though states are the appropriate administrative unit to study regional variations in many aspects, economic incorporation can differ widely within a state. Therefore, it is important to understand the local factors that may inhibit Dalits from entering business. The underlying intuition is that district level spatial and sectoral analyses will provide additional insights apart from the more aggregate ones we have already got from the state-level analysis. This is because districts are more ecologically homogeneous (affecting rural social structure) (Palmer-Jones and Sen 2003), politically distinctive, being the focus of the local administrative system and more representative of disaggregated social and economic relations. Case studies at local level would help identify those local factors, processes and mechanisms such as the extent of occupational status hierarchy, social differentiation among Dalits, the role of elites and so which may affect Dalits' entry into business. Moreover, different geographic scales in spatial analysis of social processes can generate different sets of patterns and explanations (Anselin 1992 and 1999; Fouillet 2009; Gough 2004). I would argue that in the era of liberalisation and regional reconfiguration, it is very important to self-consciously situate social processes in spatial context at different levels.

Third, the social dynamics between the Dalits and the upper castes are also at play. Some scholars have argued that the upper castes do not allow Dalits to progress as they feel that Dalits are already getting an advantage through reservations in various public sector jobs (Deliege 2001; Froystad 2005; Somanathan 2006; Still forthcoming). Froystad (2005) argues that the upper castes have adjusted to the reality of the Dalit power without really giving up on their differences with the Dalits. Dalits' inclusion in the business economy has been further exacerbated by the fact that they have received little government support (apart from some states — like MP and UP) for easing transactions in the market. Pai (2010) highlights the limited impact of the supplier diversity programme in Madhya Pradesh due to the absence of Dalits' mobilised group at the receiving end.

Fourth, the marginalisation of Dalits from business entrepreneurship can perhaps be explained in terms of their lacks. Dalits already start

100 ਰ Kaushal K. Vidyarthee

at a disadvantaged level in the levels of physical and human capital to enter the entrepreneurial sphere. They lack human capital in terms of education. Lack of access to education has plagued Dalits since a long time and overcoming such historical barriers has proved to be extremely difficult. A recent study on the relationship between social background and different dimensions of well-being suggests continued persistence of caste disparities in education, income and social networks and Dalits being the most disadvantaged (Desai and Dubey 2011). Dalits usually rely on their own small community networks which are not strong and thus not particularly helpful for any form of assistance for capital, contacts or managing regulatory barriers (Jeffrey, Jeffery and Jeffery 2004; Mosse 2006; Vanneman et al. 2006). Moreover, physical capital in terms of land and money are also not usually available to the Dalits. Iversen et al. (2010) have argued that land redistribution holds the key to neutralising disparities attributable to upper caste dominance and found that in terms of land ownership Dalits remained the worst off and fell further behind Adivasis and other backward castes in the post reform years (Iversen et al. 2010a). There is, of course, regional variation in these lacks which may have differential impacts across business sectors.

Conclusion

This paper enriches our understanding about the spatiality of differential economic incorporation, and the maps provide both a scientific basis as well as a dynamic framework for analysing the impacts of structural shifts in policy, such as liberalisation. As these maps show both the regions of economic discrimination against Dalits as well as regional success stories, they can be used to inform the overall strategy of inclusive development in India.

This paper also shows that the participation of Dalits has followed an uneven path and there are large differences between geographic regions across the country. Clearly, the post-1991 economic growth has not been inclusive. The proportional participation of Dalits as owners of enterprises has not changed. The data also indicates that Dalits in the northern and southern states persistently face strong negative discrimination in almost all sectors of the economy. The spatial pattern across sectors is neither uniform, nor are there uniquely distinct patterns of spatial concentration. This implies that both micro and macro factors and processes affecting economic incorporation are unfolding in sector-specific ways.

ॣ

References

Akerlof, George. 1976. 'The Economics of Caste and of the Rat Race and Other Woeful Tales', *The Quarterly Journal of Economics*, 90(4): 599–617.

Ali, Ifzal and Juzhong Zhuang. 2007. *Inclusive Growth toward a Prosperous Asia: Policy Implications*. Manila: Asian Development Bank.

Andrienko, Gennady L. and Natalia V. Andrienko. 1999. 'Interactive Maps for Visual Data Exploration', *International Journal of Geographical Information Science*, 13(4): 355–74.

Anselin, Luc. 1992. 'Spatial Data Analysis with GIS: An Introduction to Application in the Social Sciences'. Technical Report 92–10. Santa Barbara: National Center for Geographic Information and Analysis.

———. 1999. 'The Future of Spatial Analysis in the Social Sciences', *Annals of Geographic Information Sciences*, 5(2): 67–76.

Banerjee, Abhijit, Marianne Bertrand, Saugato Datta, and Sendhil Mullainathan. 2009. 'Labor Market Discrimination in Delhi: Evidence from a Field Experiment', *Journal of Comparative Economics*, 37: 14–27.

Banerjee, Biswajit and John B. Knight. 1985. 'Caste Discrimination in the Indian Labour Market', *Journal of Development Economics*, 17: 277–307.

Béteille, Andre. 1966. *Caste, Class and Power: Changing Social Stratification in a Tanjore Village*. Delhi: Oxford University Press.

Cook, S. 2006. 'Asian Paths to Poverty Reduction and Inclusive Development', Asia 2015: Promoting Growth, Ending Poverty: 6–7 March 2006 Conference Report, Institute of Development Studies and Overseas Development Institute.

Das, Maitreyi Bordia and Puja Vasudeva Dutta. 2007. 'Does Caste Matter for Wages in the Indian Labor Market?', *Mimeo*. New Delhi: World Bank.

Deliege, Robert. 2001. *The Untouchables of India*. Oxford: Berg Publishers.

Desai, S. and A. Dubey. 2011. 'Caste in 21st Century India: Competing Narratives', *Economic and Political Weekly*, 46(11): 41.

Deshpande, A. and K. Newman. 2007. 'Where the Path Leads — the Role of Caste in Post-University Employment Expectations', *Economic and Political Weekly*, 13 October: 4122–40.

102 ব় *Kaushal K. Vidyarthee*

Dumont, Louis. 1988. *Homo Hierarchicus: The Caste System and Its Implications*. Delhi: Oxford University Press.

Dutta, P. V. 2006. 'Returns to Education: New Evidence for India, 1983–1999', *Education Economics*, 14(4): 435–55.

Fouillet, Cyril. 2009. 'The Spatial Construction of Microfinance in India', *Centre Européen de Recherche en Microfinance*. Bruxelles: Universite Libre De Bruxelles (ULB).

Froystad, Kathinka. 2005. *Blended Boundaries: Caste, Class and Shifting Faces of 'Hinduness' in a North Indian City*. Delhi: Oxford University Press.

Gang, Ira N., Kunal Sen and Myeong-Su Yun. 2008. 'Poverty in Rural India: Caste and Tribe', *Review of Income and Wealth*, 54(1): 50–70.

Gough, Jamie. 2004. 'Changing Scale as Changing Class Relations: Variety and Contradiction in the Politics of Scale', *Political Geography*, 23(2): 185–211.

Government of India. 2008. *Economic Census 2005 — All India Report*. New Delhi: Ministry of Statistics and Programme Implementation.

———. 2009. *Quick Results: Fourth All India Census of Micro, Small & Medium Enterprises 2006–2007*. New Delhi: Development Commissioner, Ministry of Micro, Small & Medium Enterprises.

Grengs, Joe. 2007. 'Reevaluating Poverty Concentration with Spatial Analysis: Detroit in the 1990s 1', *Urban Geography*, 28(4): 340–60.

Gupta, Dipankar. 1980. 'From Varna to Jati: The Indian Caste System from the Asiatic to the Feudal Model of Production', *Journal of Contemporary Asia*, 10: 249–71.

———. 1992. *Social Stratification*. Delhi, New York: Oxford University Press.

Haining, Robert P. 2003. *Spatial Data Analysis: Theory and Practice*. New York: Cambridge University Press.

Harriss-White, Barbara. 2003. *India Working: Essays on Society and Economy*. Cambridge: Cambridge University Press.

Harriss-White, Barbara and Anushree Sinha (eds). 2007. *Trade Liberalisation and India's Informal Economy*. New Delhi: Oxford University Press.

Harriss-White, Barbara and Kaushal Vidyarthee. 2009. 'Stigma and Regions of Accumulation: Mapping Dalit and Adivasi Capital in the 1990s', in Barbara Harriss-White and Judith Heyer (eds), *The Comparative Political Economy of Development: Africa and South Asia*. London: Routledge.

Harriss-White, Barbara, Kaushal Vidyarthee, Anita Dixit, and Pinaki Joddar. 2013a. *An Atlas of Dalit and Adivasi Participation in the Indian Business Economy*. New Delhi: Three Essays Press.

Harriss-White, Barbara, E. Basile, Anita Dixit, Pinaki Joddar, A. Prakash, and Kaushal Vidyarthee. 2013b. *Dalits and Adivasis in India's Business Economy: Three Essays and an Atlas*. New Delhi: Three Essays Collective.

Harvey, David. 1996. *Justice, Nature and the Geography of Difference*. Oxford: Basil Blackwell.

Henderson, J. Vernon, Zmarak Shalizi and Anthony J. Venables. 2001. 'Geography and Development', *Journal of Economic Geography*, 1(1): 81.

Heyer, Judith. 2009. 'The Marginalisation of Dalits in a Modernising Economy', in Barbara Harriss-White and Judith Heyer (eds), *The Comparative Political Economy of Development: Africa and South Asia*. London: Routledge.

Iversen, Vegard, Adriaan Kalwij, Arjan Verschoor, and Amaresh Dubey. 2010. 'Caste Dominance and Economic Performance in Rural India', Discussion Paper 10–01. Delhi: Planning Unit, Indian Statistical Institute.

Iversen, Vegard and P. S. Raghavendra. 2003. 'What the Signboard Hides: Food, Caste and Employability in Small South Indian Eating Places', *Contributions to Indian Sociology*, 40(3): 311.

Jeffrey, C., R. Jeffery and P. Jeffery. 2004. 'Degrees without Freedom: The Impact of Formal Education on Dalit Young Men in North India', *Development and Change*, 35(5): 963–86.

Jodhka, Surinder S. 2010. 'Dalits in Business: Self-Employed Scheduled Castes in North-West India', *Economic & Political Weekly*, 45(11): 41–48.

Kanbur, R. and Anthony J. Venables. 2007. 'Spatial Disparities and Economic Development', in David Held and Ayse Kaya (eds), *Global Inequality: Patterns and Explanations*, p. 204. Cambridge: Polity.

Kapur, D., C. B. Prasad, L. Pritchett, and D.S. Babu. 2010. 'Rethinking Inequality: Dalits in Uttar Pradesh in the Market Reform Era', *Economic and Political Weekly*, 45(35): 39.

Kingdon, Geeta Gandhi. 1998. 'Does the Labour Market Explain Lower Female Schooling in India?', *Journal of Development Studies*, 35(1): 39–65.

Krugman, Paul. 1997. *Development, Geography, and Economic Theory*. Cambridge: The MIT Press.

Lobao, Linda M., Gregory Hooks and Ann R. Tickamyer.1999. 'The Role of Geography in Development', *International Regional Science Review*, 22(2): 142.

———. 2007. *The Sociology of Spatial Inequality*. Albany: State University of New York Press.

Long, N. and A. Long. 1992. *Battlefields of Knowledge: The Interlocking of Theory and Practice in Social Research and Development*. London: Routledge.

104 ᵭ *Kaushal K. Vidyarthee*

Madeshwaran, S. and Paul Attewell. 2007. 'Caste Discrimination in the Indian Urban Labour Market: Evidence from the National Sample Survey', *Economic and Political Weekly*, 13 October: 4146–53.

Meagher, Kate. 2010. *Identity Economics: Social Networks & the Informal Economy in Nigeria.* Woodbridge: James Currey.

Mhaskar, S. 2012. 'The Unmaking of the Worker-self in Post-industrial Mumbai: A Study of Ex-Millworkers' Responses to the Closure of Textile Mills in Girangaon'. Unpublished DPhil Thesis. University of Oxford.

Mosse, D. 2006. 'Collective Action, Common Property, and Social Capital in South India: An Anthropological Commentary', *Economic Development and Cultural Change*, 54(3): 695–724.

Nair, G. S. 2008. 'Post-reform Labour Market Paradoxes in India', *International Review of Business Research Papers*, 4(4): 396–405.

Narula, Smita and Martin Macwan. 2001. 'Untouchability: The Economic Exclusion of the Dalits in India', Seminar on the Economics of Racism, 24–25 January. Geneva: International Council on Human Rights Policy.

National Human Rights Commission. 2004. *Report on Prevention of Atrocities against Scheduled Castes: Policy and Performance: Suggested Interventions and Initiatives for NHRC.* New Delhi: NHRC.

Pai, Sudha. 2010. *Developmental State and the Dalit Question in Madhya Pradesh: Congress Response.* New Delhi: Routledge.

Palmer-Jones, Richard and Kunal Sen. 2003.'What Has Luck Got to Do with It? A Regional Analysis of Poverty and Agricultural Growth in Rural India', *Journal of Development Studies*, 40(1):1–31.

Porter, M. E. and Ö Sölvell. 1998. 'The Role of Geography in the Process of Innovation and the Sustainable Competitive Advantage of Firms', in Alfred D. Chandler, Peter Hagstrom and Orjan Solvell (eds), *The Dynamic Firm: The Role of Technology, Strategy, Organization, and Regions*, pp. 440–57. Oxford, New York: Oxford University Press.

Prakash, Aseem. 2009. 'Dalit Entrepreneurs in Middle India', in Barbara Harriss-White and Judith Heyer (eds), *The Comparative Political Economy of Development: Africa and South Asia.* London: Routledge.

Prakash, A. and Barbara Harriss-White. 2009. 'Social Discrimination: A Case for Economic Citizenship'. National Workshop on Policies and Strategies for Inclusive Development in India, New Delhi.

Room, Graham. 1995. *Beyond the Threshold: The Measurement and Analysis of Social Exclusion.* Bristol: The Policy Press.

Sabatier, P. A. 2007. 'Fostering the Development of Policy Theory', in P. A. Sabatier (ed.), *Theories of the Policy Process.* Colorado: Westview Press.

Trajectories of Dalits' Incorporation द 105

Schaffer, B. 1984.'Towards Responsibility: Public Policy in Concept and Practice', in Edward J Clay (ed.), *Room for Manoeuvre: An Exploration of Public Policy Planning in Agricultural and Rural Development*, pp. 142–90. London: Heinemann Educational Books.

Schumpeter, J.A. 1994. *Capitalism, Socialism and Democracy*. London and New York: Routledge.

Scoville, James. 2003. 'Discarding Facts: The Economics of Caste', *Review of Development Economics*, 7(3): 378–91.

Sen, Abhijit. 2002. *Agriculture, Employment and Poverty: Recent Trends in Rural India*. New Delhi: Tulika Print Communication Limited.

Shah, Ghanshyam (ed.). 2001. *Dalit Identity and Politics*. New Delhi: Sage Publications.

Somanathan, R. 2006. 'Assumptions and Arithmetic of Caste-based Reservations', *Economic and Political Weekly*: 2436–38.

Spence, M. 2008. 'The Growth Report: Strategies for Sustained Growth and Inclusive Development', in *IPS Nobel Laureate Lecture Series*. Singapore: National University of Singapore.

Srinivas, Mysore Narasimhachar. 1962. 'Varna and Caste', in *Caste in Modern India and Other Essays*. Bombay: Asia Publishing House.

Still, Clarinda. Forthcoming. '"They Have It in Their Stomachs but They Can't Vomit It Up": Reservations and "Caste Feeling" among Dalits in Andhra Pradesh', *Journal of Global and Historical Anthropology*.

Teltumbde, Anand. 2001. *Globalisation and the Dalits*. Nagpur: Sanket Prakashan.

Thakur, Anil Kumar and R. N. Thakur (eds). 2008. *Impact of Economic Reform Policies on Dalit and Weaker Sections*. New Delhi: Deep & Deep Publications Pvt Ltd.

Thorat, Sukhadeo. 2002. 'Oppression and Denial: Dalit Discrimination in the 1990s', *Economic and Political Weekly*, 37(6).

Thorat, Sukhadeo Aryama, Prashant Negi and Indian Institute of Dalit Studies. 2005. *Reservation and Private Sector: Quest for Equal Opportunity and Growth*, Jaipur: Rawat Publications.

Thorat, Sukhadeo and Katherine Newman. 2007. 'Caste and Economic Discrimination: Causes, Consequences and Remedies', *Economic & Political Weekly*, October 13: 4121–24.

———. 2009. *Blocked by Caste: Economic Discrimination and Social Exclusion in Modern India*. Delhi: Oxford University Press.

Thorat, Sukhadeo and Mallick. 2004. 'Labour and Occupation Discrimination in Rural Areas', Working Paper. New Delhi: Indian Institute of Dalit Studies.

Thorat, Sukhadeo and Nidhi Sadana. 2009. 'Caste and Ownership of Private Enterprises', *Economic & Political Weekly*, 44(23): 13–16.

Thorat, Sukhadeo and Paul Attewell. 2007. 'The Legacy of Social Exclusion: A Correspondence Study of Job Discrimination in India', *Economic and Political Weekly*, October 13, 4141–45.

Thorat, Sukhadeo, Paul Attewell and Firdaus F. Rizvi. 2009. 'Urban Labour Market Discrimination', Working Paper Series, 3(1).

Thorat, Sukhadeo and Umakant. 2004. *Caste, Race, and Discrimination: Discourses in International Context*. Jaipur: Rawat Publications.

Vanneman, R., J. Noon, M. Sen, S. Desai, and A. Shariff. 2006. 'Social Networks in India: Caste, Tribe, and Religious Variations', *Proceedings of the Annual Meeting of the Population Association of America*, University of Maryland College Park, March–April.

Webster, John C.B. 2007. 'Who Is a Dalit?', in S. M. Michael (ed.), *Dalits in Modern India*. New Delhi: Sage Publications.

World Bank. 2006. *World Development Report*. Washington: International Bank for Reconstruction and Development.

III

Locating Caste in a Globalising Indian City

A Study of Dalit Ex-millworkers' Occupational Choices in Post-industrial Mumbai

*Sumeet Mhaskar**

$\mathbf{M}$umbai[1] is envisioned to be a 'world class' city, 'the city of the future' by the Maharashtra State Government and powerful business groups (Government of Maharashtra 2004: 2; Bombay First and McKinsey 2003). Central to this transformation of Mumbai is the cotton textile

---

*This paper is based on my doctoral research (Mhaskar 2012). I would like to thank Anthony Heath and Nandini Gooptu for their suggestions. It has benefited from discussions at the following conferences and seminars where I had presented an earlier draft of this paper: Mobility or Marginalisation? Dalits in Neo-liberal India Conference, University of Oxford; Department of Society and Globalisation, Roskilde University; CISCA, Aarhus University; Department of Sociology, Harvard University; Sciences Po and South Asia DPhil Colloquium, University of Oxford. I would like to thank Barbara Harriss-White and Clarinda Still for their comments on the earlier draft of this paper. Conversations with Subodh More, Ashit Mhaskar, Prabodhan Pol, Harish Wankhede, Suhas Bhasme, and Rahul Tiwrekar were useful sources of information in writing this paper. I would also like to thank Christine Polzin, Juta Kawalerowicz and Christian Lund for their suggestions on the earlier drafts. All errors are mine.

[1] The city of Mumbai has always been known by three different names — Bombay in English, Mumbai in Marathi and Bambai in Hindi. In November 1995, the then ruling Shiv Sena–Bharatiya Janata Party government dropped the English and Hindi language usages and retained its Marathi name, Mumbai, for all official purposes. In this paper the name 'Mumbai' will be used in most places, except for the occasional use of 'Bombay' when deemed necessary.

108 द Sumeet Mhaskar

industry, which employed 250,000 workers in the early 1980s (Wersch 1992: 78). The textile industry underwent a major decline during the last two decades leading to the closure of textile mills in *Girangaon* (meaning village of textile mills), the working class district of Mumbai. These closures resulted in the retrenchment about 100,000 workers. The retrenched textile workforce had to face the challenge of finding new employment due to the transformation of Mumbai into a service sector economy. The service sector economy demanded a workforce with altogether new skills and knowledge in comparison to the textile industry. As a result, ex-millworkers, whether skilled or unskilled, had to rely on the informal sector for their livelihood. Whilst scholars have documented ex-millworkers' movement into the informal sector (Breman 2004; Joshi 2002), little is known whether social institutions such as caste, religion and gender played any role in deciding their occupational choices.

In the context of India's changing political economy scholars have argued the link between caste and occupation is eroding because of economic liberalisation (e.g., Panini 1996: 60). Panini (ibid.) has argued that economic liberalisation will enhance economic competition and employers will give importance to efficiency and skill while recruiting a worker rather than their caste identity. Contending these assumptions, recent research on the formal urban labour market has demonstrated how even highly-qualified Dalits and Muslims face discrimination (Thorat and Newman 2010: 23). Using the methodology of correspondence study of job applicants Thorat and Attewell (2010: 46) found that 'job applicants with a Dalit or Muslim name were on average significantly less likely to have a positive outcome than equivalently qualified persons with an [high caste] Hindu name'. Similarly, using qualitative interviews conducted amongst Human Resource Managers, Jodhka and Newman (2010) show that while the employers use the language of meritocracy and efficiency, prejudice against the low-caste candidates create barriers during the recruitment process. These empirical findings suggest that India's move towards economic reforms is not contributing to the dissolution of social institutions such as caste and religion in the labour processes.

While both the views discussed here refer to the formal labour market, little information is available on the informal economy where most of the Indian workforce is located.[2] This paper aims to fill this gap by examining the occupational choices of Mumbai's ex-millworkers, and by analysing the case of Dalits vis-à-vis other caste groups. This paper examines the following questions. Does caste as a social institution influence ex-millworkers' occupational choices? How significant is caste in the informal economy? How are Dalits coping with the challenges posed by the changes in Mumbai's political economy? To answer these questions, this paper will rely on qualitative and quantitative data collected between August 2008 until August 2009 and December 2010 until January 2011. As for the qualitative data, 80 in-depth interviews were conducted amongst Mumbai's ex-millworkers who lost their jobs since the late 1990s. In addition, semi-structured interviews were conducted with major trade union leaders and government officials. Besides, informal discussions were carried out with political activists, social workers and others engaged in varied ways with the issues of Mumbai millworkers. In terms of the survey data, information on 924 ex-millworkers' households that have stayed back in Mumbai, and 113 households that have migrated back to their villages, was collected.

This chapter is structured in the following way. First, I outline the context of Mumbai and the case of Dalits with reference to the cotton textile industry. After this, I examine the occupational choices of Mumbai's ex-millworkers with a particular focus on the Dalits. The findings presented in this paper suggest that caste has a weaker influence on the wage labour occupations but plays a significant role in the small businesses. In wage labour occupations, I argue, the fast growing service sector economy and flexible working conditions make these jobs open to individuals irrespective of caste. The entry of high-caste groups into the cleaning occupations, I argue, is due to the change in the nature of work as well as the nomenclature from *safai kam* (meaning cleaning work) to housekeeping work. In self-employed occupations, I argue that the lack of political patronage creates barriers for Dalits to engage in small businesses. Furthermore, since caste-based networks

---

[2] According to the National Sample Survey of Employment and Unemployment carried out in 2004–05, the Indian workforce constitutes about 457 million workers. Of the total workforce, more than 92 per cent work in the informal sector.

110 ठ *Sumeet Mhaskar*

control the newer opportunities it becomes difficult for other groups to enter those businesses. I conclude the paper by arguing that while the service sector economy opens up fewer opportunities for the Dalits, self-employed occupations continue to create barriers.

The Context of Mumbai

Mumbai, India's commercial and finance capital and the capital of the state of Maharashtra, serves as an interesting case to examine the issue of caste in the modern urban context. According to the 2011 census (provisional), Greater Mumbai is the largest metropolis of India with a population of 18.4 million people, and Dalits constitute about 10 per cent of the city's population. Mumbai accounts for about 40 per cent (US$ 15 billion) of the total size of Maharashtra state's economy (Municipal Corporation of Greater Mumbai 2005.). Greater Mumbai alone contributes about US$ 10 billion to the state's economy. The city also contributes around 33 per cent of all India income tax collections, 60 per cent of all India customs duty collections, 20 per cent of all India central excise tax collections, and 40 per cent of India's foreign trade and significant quantum of corporate taxes (ibid.). From the colonial days to the present, Mumbai remains an important economic centre. It is one of the first Indian cities to undergo the raft of economic, technological, and social change associated with the growth of capitalism.

In addition to its economic importance, Mumbai is politically significant, especially in terms of caste, religion, language, nation and class. In the early twentieth century, the Communists gained a stronghold over Mumbai's working class movement, which persisted until the late 1960s and early 1970s. Mumbai is also the birthplace of a nativist political party called the Shiv Sena,[3] which sought to mobilise the 'sons of the soil' during the mid-1960s (Gupta 1982; Katzenstein 1973). Beginning with the under-representation of Maharashtrians in clerical employment (public sector offices, banking, insurance, etc.) they championed the interests of Marathi-speaking job seekers and campaigned for preferential treatment. However, since the 1980s, Shiv Sena has moved towards

---

[3] Shiv Sena literally means the 'Army of Shiva', derived from the name of Shivaji *Maharaj* (King), the legendary warrior king of 17th-century western India and founder of Maratha Empire (Katzenstein 1973: 387).

Locating Caste in a Globalising Indian City द 111

the Hindutva rhetoric (Heuze 1999), although it continues to evoke the 'sons of the soil' rhetoric. Shiv Sena's nativist agenda is considered as one of the crucial factors in weakening the Mumbai labour movement. The employers as well as the Congress-led state connived with the Shiv Sena to keep the working classes fragmented. In the recent years, Mumbai has witnessed the re-emergence of nativist politics with the formation of Maharashtra Navanirman Sena (MNS) — a breakaway group from the Shiv Sena. Similar to its parent organisation, the MNS also espouses preferential treatment for Marathi *Manus* (meaning people)[4] in employment and entrepreneurship.

Mumbai has also witnessed a vibrant Dalit assertion, initially under the leadership of B. R. Ambedkar, whose Independent Labour Party was successful in the 1937 elections,[5] and later under the leadership of the Dalit Panthers in the early 1970s (Dangle 1992). The intervention by the Dalit Panthers sparked off a pan-Indian wave of Dalit movement whose influence was visible in several arenas of social life, especially literature and politics. Although a short-lived phenomenon, the Dalit Panthers influence spread not only across Maharashtra but also in India and internationally too. Indeed, the ubiquity of the word Dalit across South Asia today, can be attributed to the Dalit Panthers.

The political-economic developments, since the last two decades, constitute a watershed in the city's history and inaugurate a new beginning for Mumbai. The manufacturing industrial units in the city dominated by the textile industry and ancillary industries have been closed down. The mill owners sold the manufacturing units in 'scrap' rates to transfer the production process to the powerloom units. The mill owners took advantage of the 18 month strike that took place during 1982–83 period to shut down their mills citing the 'losses' they incurred during this period, and the 'sickness' that had begun to ail this industry, making the mills 'unviable'. D'Monte (2002) analyses

---

[4] MNS defines Marathi *Manus* 'to be the person living in the State and born to Marathi parents, or one, though of a different linguistic origin, born in Maharashtra, who speaks Marathi and loves Maharashtra. See http://www.manase.org (accessed 4 April 2011).

[5] Of the 18 seats (14 reserved and four general seats) the Independent Labour Party contested in the 1937 Bombay Provincial Assembly elections, and secured 14 (11 reserved and 3 general) (Zelliot 2013).

112 ਫ਼ *Sumeet Mhaskar*

the nexus between organised crime syndicates, the state, political parties, the mill owners and real estate developers during the textile mill closures and mill land sale. It should also be noted that there were no attempts made by the mill owners to modernise the mills even when they had made huge profits, and when various schemes were launched by the government to 'revive' them (D'Monte 2002; Krishnan 2000).

The mill owners pursued short-term gains by diverting their profits to other industries and shifting cloth production to powerlooms in the outskirts of the city, in places such as Bhiwandi. When the mill land acquired enormous value in the real estate market, they were ready to sell the land, and the state facilitated by amending various land use laws such as Development Control Regulations, 1991 and 2001. These changes resulted in new avenues of profiteering for mill owners, and to a diffusion of the organised workforce. This led to the informalisation of the workforce, leading to an increase in informal sector workers from 35 per cent in 1961 to 65 per cent in 1991 (Bhowmik and More 2001: 4822). The number of formal sector workers further came down with the closure of the textile mills.

Globalisation and liberalisation also affected Mumbai in a significant way. The city is now expected to adapt itself to the role of a 'world class city' where international businesses could locate themselves and link Indian economy with the global economy (Weinstein 2008: 33). As a result, the state placed more emphasis on the 'environment friendly' industries such as banking, insurance and information technology-enabled services. In the name of establishing these 'environment free' industries, the state and employers were complicit in the dispersal of the manufacturing units from the city. This process further affected the textile workers' neighbourhood. In fact, the restructuring of spaces once occupied by the textile industry, and by the working class neighbourhoods is central to Mumbai's current transformation.

Dalits and Mumbai's Textile Industry

The labour migration to Mumbai took place with the caste, kinship and village networks (Chandavarkar 1994: 168). Caste, religion, and since last few decades, language, have been deployed in Mumbai to gain access to scarce employment and now entrepreneurial opportunities. Since the late 19th century, but more specifically from early

Locating Caste in a Globalising Indian City द 113

20th century onwards Dalits[6] migrated to the Mumbai city (Morris 1965: 74). Among Dalits, the Mahars (village servants doing all types of manual and low-paid work) were the first to leave their villages and migrate to various cities. The changes brought about by the British regime in the areas of communication and systems of law resulted in the loss of Mahar's traditional jobs[7] (Zelliot 2013: 34). Thus, Mahars without any specialised craft or skill, which could survive the economic and administrative changes under the British regime, were forced out of their traditional occupations 'to a greater degree than were other untouchable castes such as Chambhars and Mangs' (ibid.: 38). Mang/ Matang (basket and rope makers and village musicians) and Chambhars (leather workers) were able to hold on to their traditional occupations, as their services were still required, and thus migrated to the cities in relatively less numbers. Although the 1921 census shows that only 13 per cent Mahars were engaged in traditional occupations compared to one-third of Mangs, and more than half of the Chambhars, it would be incorrect 'to picture a widespread movement of Mahars to cities and urban occupations' (ibid.). The 1961 census shows overall untouchable castes were less urbanised in Maharashtra and Mahars, in comparison Chambhars, were less urbanised (ibid.).

In Mumbai, the Dalits worked in the textile mills, the Municipal Corporation, railways and as dock labourers.[8] As for the Mumbai textile mills, Dalits constituted about 9 per cent of the total millworkers

---

[6] There are 59 SCs in Maharashtra of which *Mahar, Mang, Bhambi* (synonymous with *Chambhar*) and *Bhangi* together constitute 92 per cent of the SC population of the state. See *Maharashtra, Data Highlights: The Scheduled Castes, Census of India* (2001).

[7] The following is the list of jobs Mahars were traditionally engaged in: 'acting as village watchman, arbitrating in boundary disputes, serving as guide and messenger to government servants, calling landowners to pay revenue, escorting the government treasury, tracking thieves, repairing the *caudi* (village wall) and village hall, sweeping the village roads, carrying messages (particularly those of deaths) to other villages, removing the carcasses of dead cattle from the village, bringing fuel to the burning ground' (Zelliot 2013).

[8] About 21,305 Mahars and 5,645 Chamars worked in the Bombay Municipal Corporation in 1911. By 1931 their numbers increased to 67,360 and 7,097 respectively (Solanki 2011: 179).

114　द　*Sumeet Mhaskar*

in 1911 (Morris 1965: 74).[9] By 1941, the proportion of Dalits rose to about 14 per cent of the total textile workforce (ibid.). About 73 per cent of the Dalit men worked in the ring-spinning department according to the Bombay Mill Owners Association (BMOA) survey conducted in 1941 (Gokhale 1957: 116).[10] Dalit men constituted nearly 40 per cent of the total millworkers in the ring-spinning department and constituted a major workforce followed by the Marathas. Similar is the case of Dalit women. Of the total women mill workers inside the ring-spinning department, nearly 78 per cent were Dalits (ibid.). However, of the total Dalit women workforce only 13 per cent worked in the ring-spinning department. A major bulk of the Dalit women, nearly 74 per cent, worked in the winding and reeling department.

In contrast to the ring-spinning department, Dalit men constituted merely 0.6 per cent of the total workforce in the weaving shed. Among Dalits, only 2.2 per cent worked in the weaving department. This low proportion of Dalit workers in the weaving section was due to the exclusionary practices by the Maratha weavers (Chandavarkar 1994: 226). While the weavers were the highest paid skilled workers in the textile mills, the exclusion of Dalits from the weaving department must not be seen merely as 'a scramble for jobs' (ibid.). But as Chandavarkar has rightly argued, it should be seen as 'an expression of caste consciousness which extended beyond the workplace' (ibid.).

Caste, religion and gender were reinforced in the Mumbai textile mills, through the division of work, and in the working class neighbourhoods, by way of segregated housing. The recruitment in the textile mills was done through the jobbers (ibid.: 168), who were entrusted with extensive powers of hiring and firing workers. The jobbers too relied on caste, kinship and village networks for hiring labourers. Therefore, caste was reproduced due to the strategies employed by the capital for recruitment, labour supply and labour control. According to

---

[9] Among Dalits, Mahars dominated the workforce (Pradhan 1938: 8).

[10] The study conducted by Pradhan (1938) on the untouchable workers shows that the percentage of Dalits working in the ring and spinning department as 82 per cent. This means of the various occupations that the Dalits were engaged in the Mumbai city this is where most of them were concentrated.

Locating Caste in a Globalising Indian City ठ 115

the 1921 census, '59.9 per cent of the jobbers came from the Maratha and allied castes, 22.2 per cent from the Kolis and backward classes and 9.1 per cent from the Muslims' (Newman 1981: 53). Since jobbers were responsible for hiring labourers and allocation of work, it was bound to affect the social composition of the workforce. This also explains why Marathas and Muslims dominated the highest-paid weaving department and Dalits were concentrated in the unskilled and 'unclean' occupations inside the textile mills.

The weavers successfully continued with their exclusionary practices even during the peak of the 'rationalisation' process, which started during the 1930s and accelerated in the 1940s. These practices also helped the mill owners to keep the working classes fragmented. For instance, in the aftermath of the 1928 strike, the Bombay Mill Owners Association attempted to recruit Dalits in the weaving sheds in order to divide the most militant workers and to break their carefully constructed barriers of skill (Chandavarkar 1994: 427–28). However, mill owners' attempts failed because workers resisted its implementation. Moreover, as experienced weavers returned to work they complained that the Dalits 'lacked the necessary skills and aptitude for weaving' (ibid.: 428). There were other reasons too. The millowners also realised that recruitment of the Dalits in the weaving shed could potentially result in the unification of the Dalit workers and the Communists supporters. The Communists were indifferent towards Dalits exclusion from the weaving section. It is over this issue that Ambedkar remained critical of the Communists and in fact urged the Dalits to resume their work during 1929 strike (Omvedt 1994: 154–55).

After the BMOA 1941 survey (Gokhale 1957: 116), very little information is available on the social composition of the textile workforce. Even Patel's study (1963) on the Ratnagiri labour migrants that has *jati* specific information on 500 millworkers, do not tell us much about the social composition of the workforce. The only study that has information on the social composition of the workforce was conducted by Deshpande in the late 1970s and has a sample of 208 millworkers (see Holmstrom 1984: 40–41). Although the study by Deshpande has jati and religion specific information, it only provides evidence for two departments, weaving shed (weavers) and spinning (doffer boy). To the best of my knowledge, then, my own survey conducted in 2009 among

116 ॐ *Sumeet Mhaskar*

ex-millworkers is the only other large-sample effort to collect this kind of data. Of course, by this time all the textile mills had closed down.

The findings from my survey data inform us that Dalits constituted nearly 10 per cent of the entire workforce. A significant decline is seen in the proportion of Dalits working in the ring-spinning department. Whilst 73 per cent of the Dalit men worked in the ring-spinning department in the 1940s the proportion came down to merely 12 per cent when the mills closed down. The Dalits now constituted only 15 per cent of the total workers in the ring-spinning department in contrast to 40 per cent as per BMOA 1941 survey (Gokhale 1957: 116). Although there has been an overall decline in the number of workers in the ring-spinning department, Marathas, with 56 per cent, continued their dominance.

About 21 per cent of the Dalit men worked in the reeling and winding department, which was historically dominated by women millworkers. However, this pattern of male millworkers' movement into the reeling and winding department is witnessed across caste groups. Since the 1950s, women millworkers were gradually retrenched from the mills and were replaced by the men (James 1962). The presence of Dalit men in the weaving shed increased marginally but the dominant castes continued their exclusionary practices, this time by not co-operating with them. As a result, they had to learn to operate the machines on their own or had to join the 'upper caste lobby' inside the department.

What explain this decline of Dalits inside the textile mills? One of the significant factors is of course the political nature of the Dalit (particularly Mahar) millworkers who had become vocal about their rights, particularly after the victory of Independent Labour Party in the 1937 elections. This probably prompted the mill owners as well as the unions to get rid of this militant workforce. Following independence, reservation for SCs and STs had come into place. Therefore, Dalits preferred government jobs, as they are permanent in nature and most importantly provided social security benefits.

Since the late 1970s, there was a growth in the better-paid employment opportunities in the municipality, hospitals, hotels and BEST (Brihanmumbai Electric Supply and Transport). Besides, the provision of housing was an important consideration. As Burnett-Hurst (1925: 20)

Locating Caste in a Globalising Indian City ॡ 117

noted, Dalits (Mahars, Chambhars[11] and Dheds) had a great difficulty in obtaining an accommodation. Since, the hospitals, the railways and the municipality jobs provided accommodation to its employees it is likely that preference was given to these occupations. Younger generation Dalits who grew up in Mumbai wanted to disassociate with the 'unclean' occupations. As one of my Dalit informants stated that his father was not pleased to hear that even he was going to join the same 'unclean' occupation in the textile mill.[12] While Dalits diversified into non-textile occupations, they, along with women and Muslim millworkers, did face the major brunt of rationalisation.[13] It is against this backdrop that I examine the occupational choices of Dalit ex-millworkers.

Occupational Choices in Post-Industrial Mumbai

Before I analyse the survey data, a note about the occupational classification is necessary. While I have adopted the occupational categorisation according to Patel's study (1988, cited in Breman 2004: 195–200) on Ahmedabad millworkers, I have also created new occupational groups. I have classified eight occupations as self-employed in traditional caste-based businesses. They include leatherwork, carpenters, barbers, goldsmiths, handloom, washerman, fishing, and religious preachers. The creation of a separate category for traditional caste-based occupations helps to examine whether caste or religion plays any role in other non-caste self-employed occupations. I have also created a new occupational category: self-employed in fast food, tea and juice, which is included in trade category in Patel's study (1988). The other two occupational

---

[11] 'Chambhars' refers to leather workers in Western India, particularly Maharashtra state. The nomenclature Charmakar is a Sanskrit term and encompasses various castes engaged in leather-related occupations. In my survey, most of them reported their caste as Charmakar.

[12] In this case the ex-millworkers' father (also a millworker) was under the impression that he was going to join Ring department but on hearing that he was going to work as a weaver he was quite pleased.

[13] The rationalisation of the workforce also took place along gender and religion resulting in the retrenchment of women millworkers since the 1950s, and Muslim millworkers since the 1960s.

Table 3.1
Distribution of Ex-Millworkers by Caste, Religion and Post-textile Mill Closure Occupation, Frequency

	SE in Traditional Caste-based Business	SE in Industry, Repair or Processing	SE in Trade — Daily Products	SE in Fast Food, Tea & Juice	SE in Service	WL in Industry, Repair or Processing	WL in Cleaning and Manual Work	WL in Security, Counter & Shops	WL in Service	WL in Clerical, Supervision and Marketing	Total
High Caste Hindus	1	10	30	6	15	27	23	102	7	2	223
Hindu OBCs	13	24	17	11	10	28	20	91	11	6	231
Dalits	3	–	9	–	2	6	3	23	3	1	50
Muslims	–	10	5	–	2	7	5	6	2	1	38
Miscellaneous	1	3	4	2	1	4	5	14	–	1	35
Total	18	47	65	19	30	72	56	236	23	11	577

Source: Mumbai Ex-millworkers Survey (Mhaskar 2012).

Note: SE = Self-employed and WL = Wage Labour. While the total survey sample is 924 ex-millworkers, this table includes only those ex-millworkers who were engaged in some economic activity. In the table, 40 ex-millworkers are engaged in two occupations. I have included both the responses, as my sample size gets too small if I remove either of their response.

Figure 3.1
Distribution of Ex-millworkers by Caste, Religion and Post-textile Mill Closure Occupation, Row Percentages

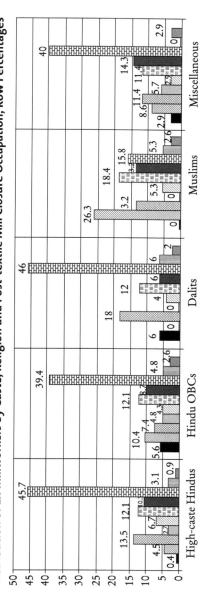

Source: Mumbai Ex-millworkers Survey (Mhaskar 2009).

Note: SE = Self-employed and WL = Wage Labour. While the total survey sample is 924 ex-millworkers this graph is based on the above table which includes those only ex-millworkers who were engaged in some economic activity.

120 ढ *Sumeet Mhaskar*

categories that I have created are wage labour in cleaning and manual work and wage labour in clerical, supervision and marketing. Besides, I am treating wage labour and self-employed separately because labour in the urban informal economy is presumed to be 'self-employed', which often disguises the sundry forms of wage labour.

I now examine the occupational choices of the ex-millworkers and see whether social institutions such as caste played any role. Of the total sample of 924 ex-millworkers who have stayed back in the city, more than 60 per cent are engaged in some economic activity. Of those engaged in some economic activity, nearly 70 per cent are engaged in wage labour, while the remaining 30 per cent are self-employed. I will examine those engaged in wage labour first and then the ones in self-employed category.

Trends in Employment

The survey results suggest that about 40 per cent of ex-millworkers engaged in some economic activity are incorporated in the wage labour security, courier and shops occupational category. It is in this occupational category that ex-millworkers from most caste groups have found employment. For instance, 46 per cent of the high caste Hindus, 39 per cent of the OBC Hindus and 46 per cent of the Dalits are employed in this occupational category (see Figure 3.1). The only exception to this is Muslims as only 16 per cent of them are employed in this occupational category. This is because Muslim ex-millworkers, especially the ones in their 30s and early 40s whom I interviewed, perceived discrimination in the labour market. Thus, except for Muslims, employment opportunities in the 'Security, Courier, and Shops' occupational category are open to most individuals irrespective of castes. The concentration of ex-millworkers in this occupational groups, and particularly security guards is a reflection of the demand for such a workforce in Mumbai. As Dattatray Atyalkar, General Secretary of the *Suraksha Rakshak Aghadi* (Security Guard Union) informed that for 'every one hour a security guard is born in Mumbai'.

I argue that openness of the jobs such as security guards, courier boy or working in shops and establishments to various caste groups is due to the non-concentration of the workforce and flexible working

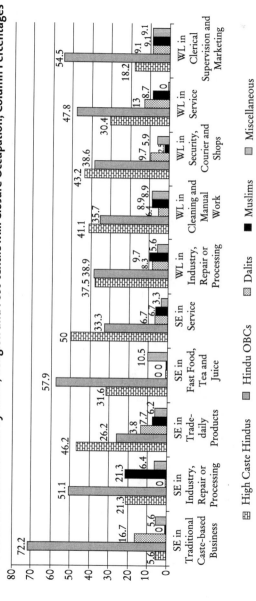

Figure 3.2
Distribution of Ex-millworkers by Caste, Religion and Post-textile Mill Closure Occupation, Column Percentages

Source: Mumbai Ex-millworkers Survey (Mhaskar 2009).
Note: SE = Self-employed and WL = Wage Labour. While the total survey sample is 924 ex-millworkers this graph is based on the above table which includes those only ex-millworkers who were engaged in some economic activity.

conditions. The workforce is scattered all over the city in various offices and establishments and all these jobs involve working on a contractual basis, long working hours and low wages. Most importantly, the service sector is the fastest growing sector that needs a continuous flow of labour supply. This explains why occupations associated with the service sector remains open to people of most castes. However, the working conditions in the 'industry, repair or processing' occupational group are similar and even here one can see ex-millworkers from most caste groups. How can we explain this situation? Is it because of the flexible working conditions in the industry that there is less caste clustering? If the answer to this question can be given in the affirmative, then, it means that flexible employment conditions (such as long working hours and low wages) make some jobs open to individuals from all social groups.

Thus, in terms of the employment taken up by the ex-millworkers there is no clear-cut relationship between caste and occupations. In fact, in occupations such as cleaning and manual work (where Dalits are known to be in a majority) one can see non-Dalits as well. The movement of non-Dalits, particularly high-caste Hindus, in manual and cleaning occupations is due to changed nature of work as stated by Datta Iswalkar, leader of *Girni Kamgar Sangharsh Samiti* (Mill Workers Struggle Committee). Iswalkar stated that earlier the ones who did the cleaning job inside the textile mills or factories were not well-dressed and had to deal with the actual dirt. In the service sector, cleaners are well-dressed and use sophisticated equipment for cleaning. While this is an important change, I argue that the change in the nomenclature of these jobs explains the entry of non-Dalits in cleaning occupations. While in the textile mills and factories it was known as *safai kam*, in the service sector the cleaning work fall under the nomenclature housekeeping.

Dalit male ex-millworkers appear to have not perceived direct discrimination in the labour market. This is due to the new recruitment practices that have emerged in the service sector economy. Dalit ex-millworkers reported that they obtained jobs by applying to a newspaper advertisement or through some recruitment agency. In the case of the recruitment agency, since their efficiency and business depends on how quickly they supply the labour demanded by the company, they could not afford to discriminate based on an individual's caste

Locating Caste in a Globalising Indian City द 123

background. Second, companies providing services are increasingly competing for cost and business, which makes it less likely to have any forms of barriers. The change in the recruitment system from jobber to the recruitment agency, which is not caste-based, has opened up some opportunities for the Dalits.

One of the Human Resource managers stated that when the 'attrition rate', understood in terms of how many employees leave that particular company over a period of time, is high then the chances of discrimination are less and vice-versa. That is, higher the attrition rate the lower is the chance of discrimination. The higher rate is usually associated with the service sector economy, where the nature of demand fluctuates. By the same logic, lower the attrition rate, higher the chances of discrimination. Thus, when the company is in a dire need of the workforce, the chances of being discriminated are less. However, it also means that when the attrition rate is low is it very likely that discrimination might take place. The 'attrition rate' thus provides a key to understand how some Dalits have managed to enter into new occupations in the service sector economy.

Trends in Self-Employment

When I analyse self-employed ex-millworkers, there is a trend towards a relationship between caste and occupation. In terms of self-employment 179 ex-millworkers (30 per cent of the total ex-millworkers engaged in some economic activity), reported to have been 'self-employed'. In traditional caste-based occupations, OBC Hindus are dominant, many of whom belong to the Nhavi (barber) caste. Millworkers from Nhavi caste have been engaged in hair cutting work in addition to their work in the textile mills. One of my respondents from the Nhavi caste has two sons (also ex-millworkers), who work as barbers since the mill closure. While the man in question has been doing the hair cutting work while he was working in the mill, his sons had newly taken up the profession.

I also came across one of the barbershop that belonged to the relative of the Nhavi ex-millworker. From a little shop with a few chairs, in the midst of Girangaon, this shop is now a fully air-conditioned saloon with high-tech equipment, gels and creams. Of the three brothers running

124 द *Sumeet Mhaskar*

this shop, one of them has been trained at the L'Oreal Institute who after finishing his training passed on the knowledge to his other siblings. This shop has now become popular amongst young men and college students. This example shows ex-millworkers from Nhavi caste could rely on their caste-based occupation because there is a demand for their services. Since the Nhavis have adapted to the demands of a new class, they can continue with their traditional caste-based occupation.

One of the changes that could be seen in the barber profession is the entry of females across castes into this profession. Beauty parlours mostly run by female hair dressers have grown in large number since the early 1990s. Across castes and religion, girls have entered this profession. There has also been a growth in female hairdressers for men in the high-end saloons. This, however, is one side of the urban India, as not all Nhavis across the city are transforming in similar ways. Contrary to this, things have remained more or less unchanged if one looks at the lower end of the urban economy. Barber businesses in the slums and in the lower middle-class areas of Mumbai is completely dominated by the male members of Nhavi castes. Similarly, in the rural areas there has been little change as the male members of Nhavi castes carry out most hairdressing work.

Although, lack of skills might create barriers for individuals to rely on their caste-based businesses, caste networks helps its fellows to set up related businesses. For instance, one of my Charmakar respondents had never learned his traditional caste occupation and so could not engage in footwear repair. However, his caste fellows helped him establish a small shop where he could sell the footwear. Interestingly, after he started this work, people in his locality got to know his caste identity. This tells us at least two things. First, in small business such as leather-related work, caste networks still control the traditional businesses. Even the newer opportunities, such as opening a footwear stall, are dependent on such networks. Second, engaging in leather-related occupations is still not an option for the non-Charmakars.

Similarly, Brahmins are engaged in the religious preaching work after the closure of mills. One of the former mill employees mentioned that Brahmins, in most cases north Indians, did religious preacher work along with their textile mill job. The religious preachers have many clients in the corporate offices and in some cases, they use numerology to guide the 'new' middle class in choosing a 'better' Multinational Corporation. Most particularly, religious preachers are consulted while joining a new company to see whether that particular starting date is appropriate according to numerology. The religious preachers were also quite 'popular' during the financial crisis as many employees were laid off during this period. The uncertainty of jobs due to the policy of 'hiring and firing' makes the preachers valuable.

In analysing non-caste businesses, one can see a relationship between caste and occupations. Dalits are absent from the industry, repair and processing occupational category which has many skilled jobs like repairing stoves, bicycles, bags, welding and lamp making. Here Muslims are present in substantial numbers. In terms of fast food business, both Dalits and Muslims do not figure in this occupational category. This occupation is dominated by OBC Hindus followed by High Caste Hindus. What explains this? In his study on Ahmedabad millworkers Breman (2004: 173) has noted that if Dalits carried out such businesses it will not be patronised by the caste Hindus. Therefore, Dalits did not enter such businesses. The only possibility was to go to unknown places, something that was impractical for carrying out a small business. In addition, if someone in the new area gets to know their caste identity they might get in trouble (ibid.). Thus, social relationship between the business and its clientele is a crucial aspect that can determine whether an individual engages in a particular occupation. While the client base is certainly important, I argue, that the access to political patronage is crucial in understanding which sections of ex-millworkers can enter certain kinds of businesses.

Most fast food businesses are carried out without any license from the Municipal Corporation. Of the total number of street vendors in Mumbai (around 200,000) only 14,000 have a license to carry out their business (Bhowmik 2001: 9). Since more than 90 per cent of the street vendors are un-licensed, it means they must pay 'rents' to various authorities (police, municipal officials, local political units and in some cases the mafia). Having a license was not an issue until 1998 as the Municipal Corporation, under the *pauti* (receipt) system, charged ₹5 to 10 from the non-licensed hawker — a charge for the 'unauthorised occupation cum refusal removal charges' (Anjaria 2006:

126　ढ　Sumeet Mhaskar

2140). By paying this daily charge, the hawkers could carry out their business. In 1998, however, the *pauti* system was discontinued due to interventions by the judiciary (ibid.: 2141).[14] Since then, non-licensed street vendors, in order to carry out their businesses, have to pay rents to one or various authorities (police, municipal officials, local political units, and in some cases the mafia).

The rule of Shiv Sena, thus, explains the dominance of OBC and high-caste Hindus in small businesses. Two of my respondents (one Maratha and one OBC Hindu) faced municipal raids, which resulted in their confiscation of their products. Both of them told me that they went to their respective local municipal councillors and explained their job loss from the textile mill. In both cases, the local municipal councillor intervened and since then they ceased to have any problem in carrying out their business without a licence. Since political patronage is extended in accordance with electoral calculations, it is likely that non-Shiv Sena supporters would find it difficult to carry out such businesses. This also explains why, despite Shiv Sena's anti-Muslim image, during municipal corporation elections Muslim hawkers in the Nehru Nagar, Kurla area campaigned for the Shiv Sena candidates and participated in their victory processions.

The trade in daily products occupational group is the one where most caste groups are represented. Most are engaged in selling daily products such as milk, vegetable and fruits. Many of my Dalit respondents informed that they have been engaged in this occupation for three generations. In the bigger street market, Dalits argued that it is relatively easier to preserve anonymity. In some cases Dalits' caste identity was not a barrier since business was carried out in the locality dominated

---

[14] In the mid-1980s, the Supreme Court in its judgement on the Delhi hawkers' case suggested to regulate hawking by creating hawking and non-hawking zones. Until the mid-1990s, however, few efforts were made by the BMC as it continued with the *pauti* system. Later, in 1998, a petition was filed by the Citizens' Forum for the Protection of Public Spaces (CFPPS) (later to change its name to CitiSpace) in the Bombay High Court, claiming that the BMC was taking no action on the 1985 Supreme Court ruling. The petitioners cited the *pauti* system as an illegal practice carried out by the BMC, which the High Court ordered to discontinue (Anjaria 2006: 2141).

by their caste groups. These findings resonate with Bhowmik's study (2001: 21) on the street vendors in Mumbai, which noted that 51 per cent vendors are OBCs and 40 per cent are middle and upper castes.[15] The study notes that the percentage of Dalits in street vending is very low (ibid.). This means that Dalits engage in small businesses in the locality dominated either by their caste members or in places that are highly vulnerable for municipal raids. This suggests that except for the areas where Dalits are numerically dominant, they are unable to carry out such a business in non-Dalit areas.

Thus, in post-industrial Mumbai while some employment opportunities are open to the Dalits, small businesses continue to exclude them. The fast growing nature of the service sector economy requires continuous supply of workforce. This gives the agencies less possibilities to discriminate based on caste identity. The jobs too are neither stable as the employers can 'hire and fire' at their will and wages are low and employees have to work long hours. These conditions also provide employees the opportunity to move to other agencies if they find jobs with 'better' working conditions. The new ways of recruitment such as newspapers and recruitment agency have opened up opportunities for the Dalits, as these ways recruitment are not caste specific. The change in the nature of cleaning work as well as the nomenclature from *safai kam* to housekeeping has led high-caste Hindus to shed their hesitation to these jobs.

In case of self-employed occupations, the influence of caste is more obvious. There are occupations such as scrap metal collection, leather related work, which the OBCs and the high caste Hindus would not engage in due to the low social status and meagre earnings.[16] Then, there are fast food occupations where Dalits (and Muslims) are entirely

---

[15] By middle castes, the said study is referring to the castes that are higher than OBC but lower than high-caste Hindus, such as Brahmins and Marathas.

[16] It is true that in small businesses and employments related to leather high-caste Hindus are rare. However, in Dharavi (an important centre for leather export), Brahmins have entered the leather business mainly in distribution and not at the level of production.

128 द *Sumeet Mhaskar*

absent and they are present in low numbers in other businesses. Here, while the client base is a very important factor, I argue that the political patronage is more important in deciding whether someone engages in the small businesses. Lastly, lack of skills might create barriers for individuals to run their caste-based businesses but caste networks help them to set up new businesses.

Conclusion

This paper has examined Mumbai's ex-millworkers' occupational choices with a special focus on the Dalits. Caste shows a weaker influence on wage labour occupations while it remains a crucial factor in self-employed occupations. In post-industrial Mumbai, employment opportunities at the lower end have grown in three occupations: security guards, courier work and work in shops. These occupations appear to be open to ex-millworkers from most caste groups. I have argued that the higher demand for labour in the fast-growing service sector provides the labour supplying agencies with little scope for discriminating based on caste identity. In addition, no particular caste is able to control these occupations because they are not concentrated in one place. The recruitment agencies too are not caste specific. Most importantly, these jobs are not permanent, they involve working for long hours, and wages are low. The entry of non-Dalits, particularly high-caste Hindus, into cleaning and manual work, I have argued, is due to the changed nature of work and nomenclature from *safai kam* to housekeeping work.

Rather than providing alternative employment, the state's policy in the era of liberalisation has been to encourage the retrenched workforce to become 'self-employed'. It is here that one can say that traditional caste-based occupations became the safest if not the easiest route. At least a few ex-millworkers have chosen to rely on their caste-based occupation rather than venturing out into new businesses that the state had attempted to train them. For ex-millworkers too, it was possible to engage in traditional caste-based occupations as there was still demand for such services in the service sector economy.

Not all ex-millworkers could rely upon their traditional occupations. For instance, the caste-based occupation of Mang Dalits has historically been rope and basket makers. This caste group continued with their caste profession even in the urban settings. However, with the arrival of plastic ropes, basket, and *chatai* (mats) this community faced a major challenge in terms of declining demand for their products in the market. The community, therefore, had to diversify into other occupations because of the changes in the economy. With regard to neo-Buddhist/Mahar Dalits, their political mobilisation resulted in the deliberate repudiation of their traditional caste-based occupation now regarded as lowly and demeaning.

In the self-employed occupations, OBC and high-caste Hindus are cornering the opportunities. While the social relationship between the business and the clientele is a crucial factor in deciding who can engage in those particular businesses, I have argued that access to political patronage is more significant. Since caste decides electoral behaviours it is not surprising that certain castes tend to accrue more benefits than others do. The role of political patronage in small businesses is crucial to understand how caste-based hierarchies are reproduced. Lack of political patronage leaves Dalits with little option to engage in small businesses. Therefore, Dalits' engagement in the small businesses takes place in the locality dominated by their caste fellows or the places that are highly vulnerable for municipal raids.

I conclude this paper by arguing that India's move towards economic reforms and Mumbai's transformation into a service sector economy has not resulted in the dissolution of social institutions such as caste and religion. While fewer job opportunities are open to the Dalits, they remain at the margins in self-employed occupations. Small businesses, in addition to the client base, rely on the political patronage and caste-based networks. Local politics combined with the social institutions of caste and religion continues to shape ex-millworkers livelihood opportunities in the context of wider urban economic transformations. These together continue to exclude the Dalits.

४

130 द *Sumeet Mhaskar*

References

Anjaria, Jonathan Shapiro. 2006. 'Street Hawkers and Public Space in Mumbai', *Economic and Political Weekly*, 41(21): 2140–46.

Bhowmik, Sharit K. 2001. 'Hawkers and the Urban Informal Sector: A Study of Street Vending in Seven Cities'. National Alliance of Street Vendors in India (NASVI). http://www.nasvinet.org/userfiles/file/A%20study%20of%20street%20vending%20in%20seven%20cities.pdf (accessed 4 April 2011).

Bhowmik, Sharit K. and Nitin More. 2001. 'Coping with Urban Poverty: Ex-Textile Mill Workers in Central Mumbai', *Economic and Political Weekly*, 36(52): 4822–27.

Bombay First and McKinsey. 2003. 'Vision Mumbai: Transforming Mumbai into a World-class City. A Bombay First-McKinsey Report'. New Delhi. http://www.bombayfirst.org/McKinseyReport.pdf (accessed 3 April 2011).

Breman, Jan. 2004. *The Making and Unmaking of an Industrial Working Class: Sliding Down to the Bottom of the Labour Hierarchy in Ahmedabad, India*. Amsterdam: Amsterdam University Press.

Burnett-Hurst, Alexander Robert. 1925. *Labour and Housing in Bombay: A Study in the Economic Conditions of the Wage-earning Classes in Bombay*. London: P.S. King.

Chandavarkar, Rajnarayan. 1994. *The Origins of Industrial Capitalism in India: Business Strategies and the Working Classes in Bombay, 1900–1940*. Cambridge: Cambridge University Press.

D'Monte, Darryl. 2002. *Ripping the Fabric: The Decline of Mumbai and Its Mills*. New Delhi: Oxford University Press.

Dangle, Arjun. 1992. *Poisoned Bread: Translations from Modern Marathi Dalit Literature*. Bombay: Orient Longman.

Gokhale, R. G. 1957. *The Bombay Cotton Mill Worker*. Bombay: Millowners' Association.

Government of Maharashtra. 2004 'Transforming Mumbai into a World-Class City: First Report of the Chief Minister's Task Force'. http://www.maharashtra.gov.in/english/reports/taskforce.pdf (accessed 3 April 2011).

Gupta, Dipankar. 1982. *Nativism in a Metropolis: The Shiv Sena in Bombay*. New Delhi: Manohar.

Heuze Brigant, Gerard. 1999. 'Populism and the Workers Movement: Shiv Sena and the Labor in Mumbai', *South Asia*, 22(2): 119–48.

Holmstrom, Mark. 1984. *Industry and Inequality: The Social Anthropology of Indian Labour*. Cambridge: Cambridge University Press.

Locating Caste in a Globalising Indian City ८ 131

James, Ralph C. 1962. 'Discrimination against Women in Bombay Textiles', *Industrial and Labor Relations Review*, 15(2): 209–20.

Jodhka, Surinder S. and Katherine S. Newman. 2010. 'In the Name of Globalization: Meritocracy, Productivity and the Hidden Language of Caste', in S. Thorat and K. S. Newman (eds), *Blocked by Caste: Economic Discrimination in Modern India*, pp. 52–87. New Delhi: Oxford University Press.

Joshi, Chitra. 2002. 'On De-industrialization and the Crisis of Male Identities', International Review of Social History, 47(S10): 159–175.

Katzenstein, Mary F. 1973. 'Origins of Nativism: The Emergence of Shiv Sena in Bombay', *Asian Survey*, 13(4): 386–99.

Krishnan, Shekhar. 2000. 'Murder of the Mills: A Case Study of Phoenix Mills'. Lokshahi Hakk Sanghatana and Girangaon Bachao Andolan Report.

Mhaskar, Sumeet. 2012. 'The Unmaking of the Worker-Self in Post-Industrial Mumbai: A Study of Ex-millworkers Responses to the Closure of Textile Mills in Girangaon'. DPhil Thesis, University of Oxford.

Morris, Morris David. 1965. *The Emergence of an Industrial Labor Force in India: A Study of the Bombay Cotton Mills, 1854–1947*. Berkeley: University of California Press.

Municipal Corporation of Greater Mumbai. 2005. Mumbai City Development Plan (2005 to 2025). http://www.mcgm.gov.in (accessed 21 March 2007).

Newman, Richard. 1981. *Workers and Unions in Bombay, 1918–1929: A Study of Organisation in the Cotton Mills*. Canberra: Australian National University.

Omvedt, Gail. 1994. *Dalits and the Democratic Revolution: Dr. Ambedkar and the Dalit Movement in Colonial India*. New Delhi: Sage.

Panini, M. N. 1996. 'The Political Economy of Caste', in M. N. Srinivas (ed.), *Caste — Its Twentieth Century Avatar*. New Delhi: Viking.

Patel, B. B. 1988. *Workers of Closed Textile Mills: Patterns and Problems of Their Absorption in a Metropolitan Labour Market*. New Delhi: Oxford and IBH.

Patel, Kunj M. 1963. Rural Labour in Industrial Bombay. Thesis, Bombay University, Popular Prakashan.

Pradhan, Gopinath Ramchandra. 1938. *Untouchable Workers of Bombay City*. Bombay: Karnatak Publishing House.

Solanki, Gopika. 2011. *Adjudication in Religious Family Laws: Cultural Accommodation, Legal Pluralism, and Gender Equality in India*. Cambridge: Cambridge University Press.

Thorat, Sukhadeo and Paul Attewell. 2010. 'The Legacy of Social Exclusion: A Correspondence Study of Job Discrimination in India's Urban Private

132 द Sumeet Mhaskar

Sector', in S. Thorat and K. S. Newman (eds), *Blocked by Caste: Economic Discrimination in Modern India*, pp. 35–51. New Delhi: Oxford University Press.

Thorat, Sukhadeo and Katherine S. Newman. 2010. 'Introduction: Economic Discrimination, Concept, Consequences, and Remedies', in Sukhadeo Thorat and Katherine S. Newman (eds), *Blocked by Caste: Economic Discrimination in Modern India*, pp. 1–34. New Delhi: Oxford University Press.

Weinstein, Liza. 2008. 'Mumbai's Development Mafias: Globalization, Organized Crime and Land Development', *International Journal of Urban and Regional Research*, 32(1): 22–39.

Wersch, Hubert Van. 1992. *Bombay Textile Strike, 1982-83*. Bombay: Oxford University Press.

Zelliot, Eleanor. 2013. *Ambedkar's World: The Making of Babasaheb and Dalit Movement*. New Delhi: Navayana Publishing.

IV

Legislating for Liberation? Dalit Electoral Politics and Social Change in Tamil Nadu

Hugo Gorringe*

In a newspaper interview in 2010, Dalit leader Ravikumar extolled the virtues of political participation, noting how the Government in Tamil Nadu had responded to his parliamentary demands for a hutless society with a programme to replace mud huts with *pucca* (brick or concrete) houses. Having spent three years raising the issue in the Legislative Assembly (State Parliament), he felt vindicated; 'more than an activist, a legislator can bring changes in the life of the people he represents' (Jayakumar 2010). Whilst this defence of parliamentary politics may be routine for Members of the Legislative Assembly (MLA), Ravikumar was no ordinary MLA. Not only is he an ex-Maoist, he was, until 2011, an elected representative of the *Viduthalai Ciruthaigal Katchi* (VCK [Liberation Panther Party]) — the largest Dalit[1] Party in

---

*I am indebted to Clarinda Still for extensive comments on the paper, and to David Mosse for a detailed discussion at the workshop. Fieldwork reported here was supported by the ESRC in 1998–99 and 2012 (Grant RES-062-23-3348), and Carnegie Trust for the Universities of Scotland in 2010.

[1] 'Dalit', meaning downtrodden, is the term adopted by radical ex-untouchables. 'Scheduled Caste' (SC) is the constitutional term for Dalits and refers to the castes entitled to positive discrimination (reservations) in politics, education and public sector employment. It excludes former 'untouchables' who have converted to Christianity or Islam. Several 'touchable' castes also receive reservations: Backward Classes (BCs) and Other Backward Classes (OBCs) are low castes, many of whom are impoverished. Several BC communities, however, are politically dominant in Tamil Nadu.

134 ௵ *Hugo Gorringe*

Tamil Nadu — which boycotted the polls until 1999 and called on Dalits to 'strike back' against oppressors.

The VCK decision to enter electoral competition engendered bitter debates within the movement as to the relative merits of autonomous grassroots mobilisation as opposed to political campaigning (Gorringe 2005; Wyatt 2009). The reluctance to commit to a political process seen as corrupt and ineffective was evident in the insistence that this was not 'a change of principle, but a change of tactics that could be reversed'.[2] The move to politics was presented as a necessary evil forced on the movement by police harassment and their depiction as militants. There was also the fact that rival caste groups had an electoral presence that they used to bolster their social dominance.[3] A decade on from their first foray into electoral politics the VCK is now an established and recognised political player. Before the May 2011 elections it had one MP (Member of the Lok Sabha in Delhi) and one MLA and having flirted with both major parties in Tamil Nadu, was in a settled alliance with the ruling party.[4]

Given this situation, and the positive assessment of his influence offered by Ravikumar, the VCK appears to offer an example of successful social mobilisation and political institutionalisation. Indeed, despite the success of Dalit parties in northern India one eminent commentator recently insisted that Dalit activists and scholars should pay more attention to developments in Tamil Nadu, which might offer 'some important lessons' for Dalit politics (Omvedt 2003: 14–24). Others, however, are less persuaded by the VCK, portraying the party as compromised and co-opted and their followers as increasingly marginalised. This paper draws on documentary sources and periods of ethnographic research in 1999 — when the VCK first entered political contestation — and more recently in 2010 and 2012, to examine the performance of the VCK and the extent to which their engagement in electoral institutions has addressed the concerns of their followers. This allows for a longitudinal analysis of activist perceptions and an

---

[2] Speech by Thirumavalavan, Madurai, July 1999.

[3] Interview with Thirumavalavan, Chennai, September 1999.

[4] MLA Ravikumar lost his seat in the State elections of April–May 2011, in which the VCK failed to win any seats.

Legislating for Liberation? 135

evaluation of the VCK's performance since its beginnings as a party. I begin by briefly outlining the contours of politics in Tamil Nadu and reviewing the literature on social movement institutionalisation before turning to the data.

Caste and Politics in Tamil Nadu

Tamil politics has a particular political logic. Whilst the Congress party dominated post-Independence institutional politics here as elsewhere, its vote was eroded in each election by the *Dravida Munnetra Kazhagam* (Dravidian Progressive Federation [DMK]). The DMK, a regional party, played on language nationalism (particularly the defence of Tamil from the imposition of Hindi as a national language) and espoused populist/ socialist policies that were mediated to the electorate through the means of cinema and an effective party organisation. It emerged out of the non-Brahmin mobilisation of the *Dravida Kazhagam* (Dravidian Federation) led by E. V. Ramasamy Naicker — better known as 'Periyar' (esteemed one) — an ideologue and propagandist who articulated a forceful critique of 'brahminism' and campaigned for social reform. Tamil Nadu, thus, was the first Indian state to elect a regional nationalist party to the government.

Under its founder, Annadurai, and his successor, Karunanidhi (the current leader), the DMK held office until 1976, but the party's linguistic and social radicalism were diluted in office. In 1972, when M.G. Ramachandran (MGR) (matinee idol of the Tamil silver screen) accused leaders of corruption and was expelled from the party, he formed the *Anna* (in reference to Annadurai) *DMK* (ADMK, now the All India Anna DMK, [AIADMK]). Building on MGR's popularity, portrayals as a pro-poor champion and populism (as typified by the free school meal for children) the AIADMK came to power in 1977 and controlled Tamil politics until MGR's death in 1987. Since then the two parties have alternated in power, and other parties have had to ally with them to succeed.

Although they are bitter rivals, the two parties are alike in many ways. Rather than envisaging inequality in class or caste terms both played on the Brahmin/Non-Brahmin divide to suggest a commitment to social change even as leaders and core constituents were drawn

136 ॐ *Hugo Gorringe*

from dominant, landowning Backward Castes. This, again, reflects a peculiarity of Tamil society in that the intermediate *varna* categories of Vaishya and Kshatriya have relatively little significance here meaning that political power is held by lower caste groups. By stressing language rather than class and playing non-Brahmins off against Brahmins, the DMK (and later the AIADMK) forged an imagined community of Tamils, that obscured their predominantly Backward Caste constituency. The emphasis on Tamil remains central to politics in the state today at the expense of stated commitments to land reforms, dowry and caste.[5] Indeed, the elections in 2011 were fought on the basis of corruption and family rule rather than any difference in policy — both were offering freebies such as cheap rice, fans, grinders and food mixers (Satyanarayana 2011).

Whilst both coalitions in 2011 contained Dalit parties, the failure to address structural inequalities means that caste remains central to social organisation in Tamil society. The contradictory articulation of anti-caste rhetoric by parties dominated by (and protective of) Backward Caste interests, therefore, combined to breed caste-based resentment amongst excluded groups (Gorringe 2006; Vaasanthi 2006). These sentiments, as Wyatt (2009) notes, have been used by political entrepreneurs seeking to mobilise followers. The emotive language of caste has an intuitive appeal (Chandra 2004) that is widely recognised and often seen as legitimate. Indeed, Tamil politics has arguably established 'an institutional learning process' (Offe 1990: 250) or 'repertoire of contention' (Tilly 1986) which has rendered caste-based mobilisation the definitive mode of political organisation for challenging groups in the state.

In the 1980s, for instance, the *Paatali Makkal Katchi* (PMK [the Toiling People's Party]) mobilised Vanniyars — a 'Most Backward Class' (MBC) concentrated in northern districts of Tamil Nadu — on the grounds that they lacked political recognition proportionate to their size and importance. PMK mobilisation was significant on three counts. First, its use of aggressive, sometimes violent, agitation has subsequently

---

[5] This account of Tamil politics draws mainly on the works of Washbrook (1989), Kohli (1990), and Subramanian (1999).

Legislating for Liberation? ਰ 137

been emulated by successive political challengers. Second, the PMK exploded the myth of non-Brahmin unity and brought the issue of relative caste deprivation to the fore. Finally, the political rise of this MBC group highlighted the continuing exclusion of Dalits, both by comparison and because the politically mobile Vanniyars increasingly countered Dalit assertion with violence (Arun 2007).

The VCK grew in direct opposition to the PMK after early attempts to forge a 'coalition of the oppressed' foundered on the caste-centric logic of the PMK. Autonomous Dalit mobilisation, thus, was both fuelled by, and generated, a forceful (often violent) casteist backlash (Gorringe 2006; Arun 2007). It is only in the past decade, following aggressive mobilisation of their own, that Dalit parties have entered political institutions. Since 1998, these new parties have shifted Tamil politics 'from a two and a half party system to bi-polar multipartism' (Wyatt 2009: 1). Smaller caste-based parties advanced this change by seeking to strip caste or Dalit voters away from the DMK and AIADMK (Roberts 2010: 18). Whilst these parties cannot win many (if any) seats on their own, their willingness to switch sides and ally alternately with each Dravidian party has meant that they have been able to field candidates in ever more constituencies as part of a coalition. Indeed, in the 2006 state elections no party gained an overall majority forcing the DMK to form a minority government shored up by electoral allies (Ananth 2006; Wyatt 2009). The 2011 elections saw the AIADMK return to power with a large majority, but the trend towards multipartism was seen in the fact that the DMK was beaten into third place by the DMDK (National Progressive Dravidian Federation) led by film-star Vijayakant (Subramanian 2011).

Despite the increasingly competitive nature of elections, the socio-political context precludes Dalit parties from emulating the electoral success of the *Bahujan Samaj Party* (BSP [Majority People's Party]) in Uttar Pradesh (Omvedt 2003). Bi-polarised electoral competition and the dispersed nature of Dalit castes, means that the number of votes required to win in any constituency exceeds the Dalit population. Even in reserved constituencies (from which only SCs may stand), therefore, Dalit Parties cannot win unaided. This situation is exacerbated by the fact that Dalits are themselves divided along caste lines. It is difficult enough to get members of the same caste to act in concert, and attempts

138 ₫ *Hugo Gorringe*

to consolidate the Dalit vote have been even more elusive. The two main Dalit parties — *Puthiya Tamizhagam* (PT [New Tamil Nadu]) and the VCK — map onto the two better organised and numerous castes: Pallars and Paraiyars respectively.

The most numerous and politically significant Tamil SCs are the Pallars, Paraiyars and Chakkiliyars. In the traditional caste order Pallars are the least impure of the three whilst Chakkiliyars perform the most menial and despised social tasks.[6] All three groups are represented across the state, but Paraiyars are preponderant in the northern districts (where the VCK are strongest), Pallars are most numerous in the south and west. Arundhadiars or Chakkiliyars are more dispersed across the west of the state. Although Pallar, Paraiyar and Chakkiliyar are caste categories — encompassing numerous sub-castes which are split along multiple lines including language, occupation and right or left-hand factions — the terms have political relevance and emphasise the creation of pan-Tamil caste links and movements. As such, they shape actions and perceptions on the ground.

The VCK first contested in the 1999 Lok Sabha elections with several other Dalit parties as part of a Third Front headed by the Tamil State Congress. That Front failed to win a single seat but it polled more than the margin of defeat in several constituencies and Thirumavalavan (leader of the VCK) beat the AIADMK into third place (Gorringe 2005). This performance gave it political recognition and helped it to supplant PT as the most successful and popular Dalit party, in large part because it was seen as a possible counter-weight to the politically volatile PMK. Both Dravidian parties have subsequently allied with the VCK and standing with the major parties, the VCK have gained three victories in the smaller constituencies of the State Assembly. Since it has always contested in alliance with others, it is difficult to gauge support for the party. However, rallies of over 100,000 people in the state capital and widespread recognition by lay-people clearly indicate that the party is now a recognised political player. Wyatt (2009: 120–21) suggests it can swing the vote in movement strongholds, but it failed to win a single seat in 2011 despite being allied to both the DMK and PMK. Its standing can be seen in that it contested eight seats as part of

---

[6] See Gorringe (2005: 58–59) for more details on caste categories.

Legislating for Liberation? 139

an (admittedly weak) DMK-led front in the 2001 state elections and party leader Thirumavalavan was elected as the MP for Chidambaram in 2009 (again in alliance with the DMK). In the past few years the VCK have reinforced their alliance with the DMK despite disagreements over the Sri Lankan crisis and other issues. Activists, therefore, expected to field more than the 10 candidates eventually agreed on in the 2011 state polls.[7]

Institutionalisation and Dalit Movements

Although many social movement scholars, such as Tarrow (1998) and Jenkins and Klandermans (1995), regard electoral participation as the end goal of mobilisation, many activists perceive politics as inherently corrupt and/or reformist. Offe's 'stage model of institutionalisation' (1990), thus, notes how increasing professionalisation and engagement in institutional politics can engender splits between radicals and reformists. Despite this, Offe (ibid.) presents institutionalisation as an inevitable response to movement stagnation as initial enthusiasm evaporates and further resources are required to sustain mobilisation. 'Institutionalisation' refers to the process whereby movements 'develop internal organisation, become more moderate, adopt a more institutional repertoire of action and integrate into the system of interest representation' (Della Porta and Diani 1999: 148). Coy and Hedeen (2005: 417) highlight the benefits that can accrue from this process in noting that 'most efforts at social change that enjoy even partial success must include collaboration between the challenging movement and the state and vested interests'. 'The Dravidian parties', as one respondent put it in 2012, 'are the *deciding* factor' in whether policy is realised or not. Equally significant are the less tangible gains of wider legitimacy

---

[7] A multi-sited ethnography focussed on Dalit activists, motivations, modes of operation, and ideological aspirations across Tamil Nadu, was conducted in 1998–99 (see Gorringe 2005). A Carnegie Trust funded project enabled me to update my research and capture attitudes towards the political Panthers with interviews and ethnography in 2010. Subsequently, fieldwork in 2012 brought me up to date (based on an interview with Chezhian, Madurai, 2010).

140 ☡ *Hugo Gorringe*

and the concurrent reduction in repression by state authorities and access to influential allies.

The process of institutionalisation also carries costs; movements may become 'bureaucratized and technique centred, losing [their] adaptive vitality' and there may be a dilution of movement critiques and tactics (Coy and Hedeen 2005: 407). It can, as Piven and Cloward (1979) show, result in demobilisation or co-optation. Melucci (1996: 231–32) further notes how institutionalised actors may lose the relative autonomy to criticise existing politics and articulate alternatives. In fact, Hasan (2006: 65) argues that the institutionalisation of identity-based groups can prevent 'fundamental change, such as land reform, because the new elite now have a stake in the existing system'. Support for this comes in Coy and Hedeen's (2005: 417) finding that newly-institutionalised actors seldom return to the politics of protest. They refer to this propensity for challenging groups to prioritise continued political participation as the 'paradox of collaboration'.

Understanding how movements make the transition from radical actors to political contestants, therefore, casts light on processes of democratisation and institutional efforts to address social exclusion (Kohli 2001). Charsley and Karanth (2001: 13) raise these issues in the context of caste inequalities and wonder 'whether the political leaders amongst them will be able to meet the rising expectations, without letting themselves be co-opted by the ruling classes based on the traditional upper castes'. Research in Uttar Pradesh echoes these concerns. In contrast to accounts which identify a 'Dalit revolution' in northern India (Kohli 2001; Jaffrelot 2003), Jeffery et al.'s ethnographic focus (2008: 1366) on 'people's consciousness of political change' highlights a 'marked disjuncture between formal political change and ground-level political realities' (ibid.: 1392). They conclude that many of the claims made about Dalit priorities and political views have 'not been adequately field-tested in contemporary India' (ibid.: 1391).

Pai's work (2002) on the BSP similarly argues that its political success has come at the expense of its social agenda. She distinguishes between empowerment from 'above' and 'below' and contends that the party primarily pursues the former, viewing empowerment in purely political terms. This emphasis on political power has led the BSP to ally with parties opposed to Dalit assertion, thus weakening their attempts to

Legislating for Liberation? 141

eradicate caste inequalities. Dalit parties in Maharashtra, which were at the forefront of post-colonial Dalit mobilisation, have suffered a similar fate (Omvedt 2003), indicating an enduring tension between grassroots movements seeking to transform social relations and political parties seeking electoral success. Dalit parties can entrench identities by emphasising the caste of parliamentary candidates rather than their policies and, once parties are in positions of power, those who mobilised to demand recognition anticipate beneficial outcomes on this basis (Chandra 2004). Caught between the compulsions and compromises of electoral politics Dalit parties have been unable to significantly erode caste discrimination (Mehrotra 2006). The inability of Dalit parties to determine public policy jars with the increased expectations of followers, resulting in a pervasive argument that Dalit politics has 'reached an impasse' (Shah 2004: 131).

Responding to this 'failure' of pioneering Dalit parties in UP and Maharashtra, Omvedt urged scholars and activists to 'look south' (2003: 17–18). Although Tamil Dalit parties have neither the longevity nor political success of their northern counterparts, their social context and more recent emergence makes them both important and interesting. Evaluations of their performance to date have been mixed. Roberts (2010) argues that the VCK has taken Dalit voters away from the Dravidian parties through its electoral engagement and espousal of Tamil nationalist rhetoric. Wyatt (2009: 132) concludes that it has 'helped to change the dynamics of the party system'. The 2011 results suggest that these processes are imperfect and incomplete at best and I would, thus, pose the same question to the VCK that Pai (2002: 1) puts to the BSP: 'Is it a movement with an agenda for radical social change, or a political party driven solely by the compulsion of achieving power?' In what follows this paper 'looks south' and draws on empirical data to offer an analysis of VCK politics.

From Cheri to Centre?

During its decade-long poll boycott the Liberation Panthers urged supporters to spoil their ballot papers with a different slogan in each election including: 'none of you are honest so none shall have our votes'; 'until there are separate electorates, our votes are for no one';

142 & *Hugo Gorringe*

and 'we lack the right to live, why get the right to vote?'.[8] The transformation to political participation, thus, was bitterly resented by many activists. Wyatt (2009) points to the significance of leadership and to Thirumavalavan's popularity throughout the controversial transition. It is inconceivable now that the VCK will turn its back on party politics, but institutionalisation is a long drawn out process (Coy and Hedeen 2005) and the risk of demobilisation and desertion of followers is real. During fieldwork conducted in 2010 and 2012 I found that several former activists had taken up full time employment and others were disillusioned with the party. Subramanian (2011) similarly suggests that Dalits deserted the DMK-front in 2011. The VCK, thus, needs to persuade followers that they remain a viable and attractive alternative to more established parties even as they seek to widen their support-base and deliver benefits to supporters.

One of the main dilemmas facing Dalit movements as they seek to grow out of the *cheris* (Dalit settlements on the outskirts of villages), is how to expand their appeal without alienating their core support. This fine balancing act is unavoidable given the inability of Dalit parties to win seats alone. Furthermore, whilst it serves as a powerful mobilising mechanism, 'caste appeal based on the interests of specific castes, [has] mattered in the state only in exceptional circumstances', because the Dravidian parties have successfully attracted voters belonging to different castes (Pandian 2006). A further impetus to broadening their appeal comes from the antipathy of other caste groups to Dalit mobility. One of the most pressing issues facing the VCK as a party was how to reduce the tensions raised by caste-based mobilisation that led to wide-scale electoral violence in Thirumavalavan's constituency in 1999 (Gorringe 2005). Entering parliament compelled the VCK to abandon its rhetoric of violent retaliation and self-defence. It subsequently had to persuade Dalits that it could still offer a bulwark against casteist violence. It is in this context that the party has turned to Tamil nationalism.

Roberts (2010) argues that the VCK's strategic and controversial adoption of Tamil nationalism needs to be understood both on its own terms and within the wider context. On its own terms, as his careful

---

[8] Speech by Thirumavalavan, Madurai, July 1999.

Legislating for Liberation? ॐ 143

reading of two volumes of Thirumavalavan's (2003, 2004) speeches demonstrates, the party constantly qualifies its nationalist Tamil rhetoric by insisting that it must be anti-caste and that it cannot be insular. As Roberts (2010: 19) puts it:

> In the historical context of modern Tamil Nadu, 'Tamil' refers not merely to a particular linguistic identity, but equally to the *universal* progressive values — anti-caste, feminist, pro-poor, democratic, and humanist — that Dravidian leaders, following the lead of early Dalit leader Iyothee Thass, sought to characterize as inherent to Tamil Nadu's authentic (pre-Aryan) culture. This appropriation of Tamil identity enables the VCK to claim the moral high ground vis-à-vis the Dravidian parties by calling upon them to live up to their own progressive rhetoric, while simultaneously depriving them of their most credible charge against the VCK (i.e. that it is a narrowly caste-based organization).

Crucially, he argues, that the turn to Tamil has succeeded in prising Dalit voters away from Dravidian parties. The evidence on which this argument is based is unclear. Contesting the elections has certainly allowed Dalits to vote for non-Dravidian parties, but there is no evidence that the Dalit parties' adoption of Tamil nationalism has had a similar effect. Indeed, insofar as it has led them into DMK and ADMK alliances it has made it more, not less, likely that Dalits will vote for Dravidian groups.[9] The key advantage to this approach, rather, is that it offers common ground on which to co-operate with other groups.

There have been four main alliances in the short political life of the VCK: the first, and most obviously principled of the four, was the Third Front of Dalit and non-Dravidian parties in 1999. That alliance was electorally unsuccessful and the diverse alliance of disparate groups came together in exceptional circumstances (Gorringe 2005). It proved to be unsustainable. The VCK subsequently allied with the AIADMK in a number of by-elections, which alienated numerous supporters who saw the party as anti-Dalit (Nambath 2000). It then formed a coalition with the DMK, but the third significant coalition brought the VCK together with the PMK — its bitter rival — under the banner of the

---

[9] Interview with Armstrong, Madurai, May 2012.

144 ᶻ *Hugo Gorringe*

Tamil Protection Movement. This pact, which had the potential to reduce caste violence in northern districts by uniting opposing caste parties, sought to 'protect' Tamil by lobbying against Tamil films using non-Tamil (primarily English) titles and dialogue, and calling for shop signs to be written in Tamil. The 'defence' of a threatened language led the TPM to perceive themselves as moral guardians of Tamil culture, best seen in the furious reactions to a film actress' comments about pre-marital sex (Anandhi 2005). Contrary to the claims for Tamil identity made above, it proved an unstable basis for an alliance that crumbled in the face of caste and political considerations. The TPM collapsed when the VCK opted to remain with the DMK — its fourth and most stable ally to date — when the PMK departed the front (only to return again in 2011).

Pandian (2006) argues that caste-based parties are 'aware of their relevance to the power dynamics of major political parties in the state. This is precisely why the opportunism of switching sides from one major party to the other becomes a survival opportunity for them'. As Nambath (2000) shows, however, this opportunism can only be taken so far before it alienates supporters. Chezhian, a long-time party activist, and Munniamma, an informed but non-aligned Dalit, bemoaned the constant shifting of alliances and called on the party to take a stand.[10] From this perspective the relatively stable alliance with the DMK was both welcomed and seen to be bearing fruit as seen in MLA Ravikumar's comments at the head of the paper. Similarly, an academic researcher insisted that the VCK offered a different, Dalit, way of doing politics rather than mimicking the established parties and pointed to welfare concessions that they had secured since allying with the DMK.[11]

The benefits of institutionalisation are apparent in other regards too: for one thing, the views of Dalit leaders are increasingly aired in the media. The broader appeal of the VCK also means that books of speeches (Thirumavalavan 2003, 2004) and analysis (Ravikumar 2009) have been translated into English. On the back of such exposure, in the

---

[10] Interviews with Chezhian, Allanganallur, 2010 and Munniamma, Madurai, 2010.

[11] Personal communication with Anandhi, Chennai, January 2010.

Legislating for Liberation? 145

opinion of one analyst, Thirumavalavan has become 'more than just a caste leader'.[12] A newspaper article (*The Hindu* 2010a) about the death of a VCK activist in an accident notes that Thirumavalavan 'provided relief money to the family of the deceased'. Another piece (*The Hindu* 2010b) reports Thirumavalavan distributing colour TV sets (Plate 4.1) — one of the election pledges of the DMK government.

Plate 4.1
Government Issue TV

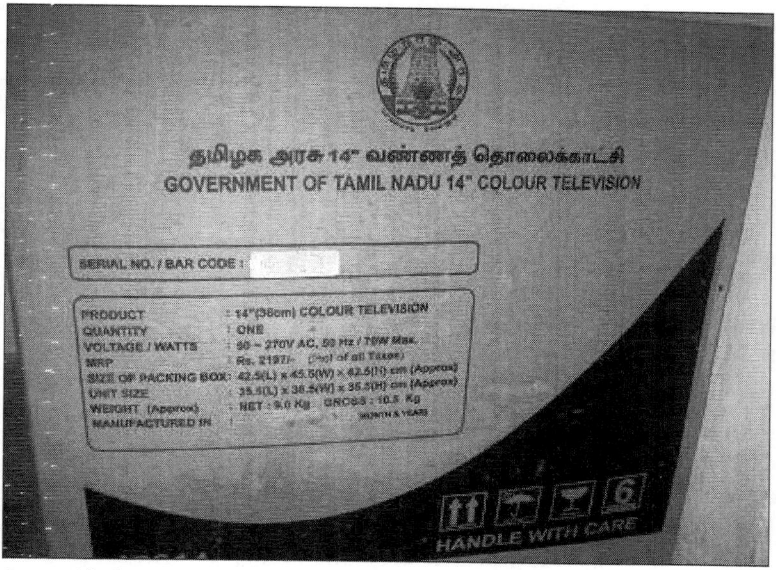

Source: All photographs by the author.

Given Mines' finding that 'a leader attracts a following by the benefits that he provides' (Mines 1994: 57), these gestures are important. Political participation by the VCK has opened channels to government resources and provisions that Dalits lacked before. Thirumavalavan's office is routinely mobbed by people seeking his intervention to secure a Government job, transfer or certificate.[13] The government is a major

---

[12] Personal communication with V. Alex, Madurai, 2010.
[13] Interview with Sankar, Delhi, 2012.

146 ᶻ *Hugo Gorringe*

employer and Dravidian parties have routinely distributed posts through patronage networks. Whilst the VCK was part of the ruling coalition it had access to such largesse and in most villages I visited in 2012 there were one or two people who benefited in this manner, even if they did need to oil the party wheels with money to do so.[14] Being a coalition partner also means that Dalit leaders — who are more accessible to the grassroots Dalits — have direct access to leading politicians and officials. Whilst the numbers entailed are small, the impact of one job extends beyond the individual in terms of families and wider aspirations.

The majority of Dalits now at least aspire to educate their children and the middle classes aim to put their children through English medium education. There is a wide consensus that the caste atrocities that characterised the 1990s have subsided. Successful prosecution of caste-Hindus under the Prevention of Atrocities Act, and the readiness of party activists to file cases and stage protests have resulted in a decline of extreme caste violence, thus facilitating education and stable employment. In some areas the gap between Dalits and non-Dalits in terms of access to resources is narrowing.[15] Of course, these developments cannot all be laid at the door of Dalit politics, but Dalit mobilisation has clearly put pressure on other parties to respond — if only to retain Dalit votes — and it has also increased legal and political awareness at the grassroots.[16]

Politically speaking, Dalits argue that Thirumavalavan has given them a voice in Parliament. The VCK are no longer excluded as they were in 1999 when cow dung was smeared over party posters (Gorringe 2005). Instead they are seen as small, but important, coalition partners. A corollary to this political acceptance is the cash flows that boost party coffers each election. The VCK thus is better off now, and this is reflected in the volume of billboards and walls bearing VCK symbols and messages. In addition to painted slogans, there were huge printed banners on show in both Chennai and the city of Madurai.[17] Whilst

---

[14] Author's fieldnotes, Tamil Nadu, 2012.

[15] See http://www.livemint.com/2012/06/21005650/Census-rewriting-SC-ST-narrat.html (accessed 20 April 2014).

[16] Interview with Lajapathi Roy, Madurai, 2012.

[17] Author's fieldnotes, Tamil Nadu, 2010 and 2012.

Legislating for Liberation? द 147

we should be wary of inferring *support* for a party on the basis of such symbols, they are clear indications of expenditure.[18]

The benefits of institutionalisation, however, have come at a price and the VCK is increasingly facing the disillusionment and distrust with which cadre viewed political institutions. A prevalent attitude during my fieldwork in 1998–99 was that movement activists were principled and committed to the cause rather than seeking to profit from their actions, unlike NGO staff and politicians who were portrayed as corrupt and venal. In 2010 and 2012, by contrast, the same respondents repeated widespread allegations of VCK corruption and profiteering, including numerous stories of VCK activists acting as brokers in caste disputes for monetary gain. Multiple respondents sympathetic to the VCK insisted that they were 'running *katta panchayats* (kangaroo courts)' in which they arbitrated in disputes for their own gain. As Jayakumar concluded: 'They have become a "proper political party" and do all the rowdyism, money-making and things that other parties do'.[19] The fact that rumours of this nature circulated openly in Dalit activist and VCK circles, intimates a degree of disillusionment and cynicism about their motives and achievements. The alliance with the DMK did not help here given the widespread anger about corruption, money and muscle power that culminated in the AIADMK's clean sweep in 2011.[20]

The allegations that middle rung officials were heavily involved in real estate businesses were corroborated by newspaper reports (e.g., *The Hindu* 2010c) on violence surrounding property deals. Profiteering from power, however, was not the main concern of Dalit observers. More pressing for them, was a sense that party members were losing sight of their values. One respondent spoke of a case in which she was a witness: a Dalit woman accused a co-worker of sexual harassment and the VCK got involved. Rather than seeking the truth of the matter, though, she says that they were primarily 'involved for the money' that could be

---

[18] Personal communication with Karthik, Madurai, 2010.

[19] Interview with Jayakumar, Bangalore, 2010.

[20] Personal communication with Nandan and Lakshmanan, Chennai, 2011.

148 द Hugo Gorringe

made by appropriating a significant cut of any compensation package.[21] Other accounts spoke of the Dalit victims of abuse being defrauded of compensation in this process. Whilst accepting that the VCK should be recompensed for their time and effort Muniamma deplored the lack 'of limits'. Additionally, three deeply disappointed activists spoke of an incident in which Vanniyar thugs brutally murdered a cross-caste couple but the VCK remained silent at the behest of, then ally, the PMK. Significantly, although this incident could have been rationalised as an attempt to preserve greater communal harmony at a time of caste tension, it was presented as a betrayal. The oscillation between marginality and mobilisation is nowhere better captured than in an interview[22] with a party post-holder near Madurai. He had achieved the 'impossible' in 2011, winning a panchayat president election in a *general* constituency. The appeal to other castes, the emphasis on Tamil and the focus on common issues can be seen to have brought Dalit politics into the mainstream here, but for the fact that a key plank in his campaign was the promise to resolve caste issues without resort to the Prevention of Atrocities Act. Victory, thus, comes at the cost of one of the most significant safeguards for Dalits.

At a state-level, Thirumavalavan and other VCK leaders' deference towards Karunanidhi and the DMK was seen as a loss of autonomy and the abandonment of long-held principles. Chezhian pointed to the rosette commemorating the VCK's land rights conference in June 2007 (Plate 4.2).[23] Rather than celebrating that event, however, he asked: 'Why is Karunanidhi on the badge and why is his image bigger than Thirumavalavan? He doesn't put Thirumavalavan on his notices!'

Indeed, in presenting Karunanidhi and the DMK as linked to 'Ambedkarism' and land reform the VCK could renew Dalit voters' support for Dravidian parties rather than weaning them away. A recurrent refrain from activists was that the VCK could no longer critique the government. Given that the fiery speeches of Thirumvalavan and others underpinned movement mobilisation, the changing tenor of party rhetoric could result in demobilisation. In this regard, political

---

[21] Personal communication with Muniamma, Madurai, 2010.

[22] Personal communication with anonymous individual, Madurai, 2012.

[23] Interview with Chezhian, Allanganallur, 2010.

Plate 4.2
Land Rights Conference Rosette

contestation can engender new demands and expectations. As Chezhian commented: 'I'm disappointed in him to be honest — he should be doing something for those of us who voted for him', and he pointed to declining numbers of village meetings as a problem for grassroots activists.[24]

---

[24] Interview with Chezhian, Allanganallur, 2010.

150 ꝯ *Hugo Gorringe*

Several respondents also felt that the compulsions of political engagement meant that there was 'no consistency' and they bemoaned the changing issues taken up by the party. As Inbaraj put it: 'Suddenly we are a "Tamil party"; how can we understand that?'.[25] Whilst a caste-free Tamil nationalism has always featured in VCK demands, the actions of the Tamil Protection Movement and interventions on Sri Lanka have downplayed the party's anti-caste demands. This may be a successful political strategy in a state where survey data suggests 58 per cent of people perceived the treatment of Tamils in Sri Lanka as a pressing issue even before the escalation of the conflict in 2009 (*Lokniti* 2006). The danger, however, is that the pursuit of a broader agenda can leave the core constituents behind:

> Now if you ask a member of the party what their demands are they should be able to tell you shouldn't they? But it is unclear whether it is Sri Lanka, Tamil nationalism or Dalit stuff ... Sri Lanka? What is it to us? We are suffering and struggling daily and need our own champion.[26]

Whilst the championing of non-Dalit causes moves the party beyond caste identity, unless this is 'sold' to core followers they can feel abandoned. As Mines and Gourishankar (1990) argue, unaccountable or aloof leaders are subject to accusations of self-aggrandisement. The debates surrounding Special Economic Zones[27] are a case in point. Vijayabaskar (2010: 36) documents the surprising absence of resistance to land acquisition and development in Tamil Nadu unlike other Indian states. One reason, he notes, is that 'the long history of anti-caste politics of the state' has portrayed 'the rural as a site of oppression'. From that perspective, Ravikumar MLA's assertion that 'if agriculture needs to be saved, agricultural labour has to be saved from agriculture' (ibid.: 42), is both consistent and principled. The argument is that investment in 'agriculture' tends to benefit landholders rather than the labouring poor.

---

[25] Personal communication with Inbaraj, Bangalore, 2010.

[26] Interview with Chezhian, Allanganallur, 2010.

[27] SEZs are demarcated areas within a country that have more liberal trading regulations than the host country.

Dalit movements, therefore, have long celebrated the potential of modernisation processes to break down structures of caste. The growing dissonance between leaders and followers in the VCK, however, means that their stance on SEZ's has raised allegations of corruption and profiteering. There is also a failure to connect disparate policies or reflect on how the compulsory purchase of agricultural land for poorly regulated industries might impact on Dalit's working conditions or aspirations to own land themselves. Furthermore, the SEZs advance a liberal agenda in which 'increasing privatisation means that reservations are increasingly useless'.[28] In an echo of Pai's work on the BSP, this respondent concluded that 'Dalit parties are doing well, but Dalit liberation is not'. Jevahar, a seasoned Dalit campaigner and academic, felt that caste discrimination remained a pressing issue: 'The structure remains intact. Capitalism has meshed with Brahminism to keep the downtrodden in poverty'. Worse still, the leaders who once spoke out against this, now often keep mum.

A Space within the Institution?

Given the pessimism and disillusionment characterising the performance of the VCK amongst Dalit respondents it is tempting to concur with Lakshmanan that the 'VCK is finished as a Dalit movement. It is just a party now'.[29] Far from constituting an advance for Dalit rights, thus, the institutionalisation of the movement is depicted as having vitiated the efficacy of the VCK as a champion for Dalit assertion. It is, however, worth recalling that institutionalisation invariably upsets some activists, and that their analyses of party performance are necessarily filtered through earlier expectations. As Gundimeda (2009: 58) notes of political developments in Andhra Pradesh, we should not see emergent Dalit parties as mythical saviours like 'Robin Hood'. Rather, we should analyse them in context and ask what spaces for negotiation are carved out in the process of institutionalisation. To focus overly on the *political* realm is to neglect the social conditions that gave rise to, and continue to generate support for the movement. It is significant in

---

[28] Interview with Jevahar, Madurai, 2010.

[29] Personal communication with Lakshmanan, Chennai, 2010.

152 ଟ *Hugo Gorringe*

this regard, that some of the most trenchant critics of the VCK quoted above remain dedicated to the party.

When I asked Chezhian why he did not turn his back on the VCK, he pointed to arenas in which they continued to articulate an anti-caste perspective. At a Dalit book launch in Madurai, for instance, Thirumavalavan delivered an impassioned speech on Dalit history and struggle. Whilst regretting that such speeches were increasingly confined to Dalit specific audiences, the engagement with these issues in such contexts was welcome. The profile of the party means that such perorations occasionally reach a wider audience; as when Thirumavalavan's speech to cadre at the 13th anniversary of the Melavalavu massacre was extensively covered in the media (*The Hindu* 2010d). The party have also developed their own media, publishing a magazine called *Tamizh Mann* (Tamil Earth) and websites that include video footage of Thirumavalavan speeches (http://www.Thiruma.net; https://www.facebook.com/evck.net.2012), whilst speeches and articles have tended to focus on Sri Lanka, they provide some space for the articulation of Dalit perspectives.

Fieldwork in 2010 and 2012 confirmed Chezhian's portrayal of the VCK's dual approach. Alongside the politics on public platforms and in coalitions, there is a residual commitment to the grassroots mobilisation that fuelled the party's rise. This was evident in mid-January when the streets of Madurai were suddenly decked in red and blue flags adorned with a white star. The emblems of the VCK led to a backstreet in a residential area where the flags were joined by posters, murals and large billboards. The symbols marked a party activist's house-warming at which Thirumavalavan presided. On one hand, a giant hoarding depicted Thirumavalavan alongside Ambedkar and Periyar but also Karunandhi and his son and heir apparent Stalin and Sonia Gandhi (part of the DMK coalition) (see Plate 4.3). Whilst this suggests his perfect integration into normal politics, other posters declared that 'a free society must be a casteless one'. If Thirumavalavan has been co-opted into hegemonic politics, thus, the VCK can harness other leaders to their cause.

The party leader, though a busy MP, clearly still makes time to attend such events. The fact that the imagery of the party was concentrated in the neighbourhood, and that several people I asked did not know

**Plate 4.3
Ambedkar, Periyar, Sonia Gandhi,
Karunanidhi, Thirumavalavan, and Stalin**

whose flag it was,[30] suggests that the VCK remains on the fringes of public consciousness.[31] In carving out such autonomous spaces for the articulation of an anti-caste agenda, however, it retains a connection to the movement on which it is based. Elsewhere, MLA Ravikumar — who routinely writes for *Junior Viketan* (a fortnightly Tamil language magazine) and contributes essays to other outlets — also 'creates a space for a Dalit perspective',[32] as do engaged intellectuals like Paari Chellian, whose documentary films on Dalit leaders and continuing atrocities have helped to raise awareness about important issues. The VCK has also followed other political parties in expanding into Trade Unionism (Plate 4.4). Whilst one Dalit worker at the central bus depot in Madurai

---

[30] Author's fieldnotes, Madurai, 2010.

[31] There was much more public recognition of 'Thirumavalavan's Party' in 2012.

[32] Personal communication with Anandhi, Chennai, 2010.

**Plate 4.4
VCK Trade Union Board, Madurai**

felt that the VCK as a union did very little to advance workers' rights, it certainly flagged up the issue of caste in the workplace.[33]

There are also the concessions wrung from the DMK as noted by Ravikumar. Whilst the fact that these are mostly 'welfare-related' has been a source of frustration for Dalit activists desiring more deep-rooted measures[34] non-activists take a different view. When asked about Thirumavalavan's performance, for instance, M. Dhanraj, a Backward Caste DMK supporter said: 'Oh he speaks up for them and has done pretty well for his crowd'.[35] Other BC respondents go further in seeing the Dalits as receiving preferential treatment. It is worth recalling that activists already view politics as tainted. To judge a party by their standards, therefore, may set the bar too high.

---

[33] Personal communication with Rajkumar, Madurai, 2010.
[34] Personal communication with Anandhi, Chennai, 2010.
[35] Personal communication with M. Dhanraj, Chennai, 2010.

Conclusion

The VCK's transition to political participation was bitterly contested. It is hardly surprising, therefore, that responses to the political Panthers are divided and often disappointed. This reflects Chandhoke's wider finding that people have 'lost faith in the ability of political parties to represent their interests' (2005: 326). The performance of the VCK must also be read through Lakha and Taneja's argument (2009) that India's democratic system has struggled to accommodate oppositional movements. Despite this, they view the recent upsurge of lower caste (Dalit and 'Other Backward Caste') groups as reshaping political institutions (ibid.: 316). Indeed, they describe the political accommodation and electoral successes of such movements as signifying 'a seismic shift in patterns of political participation and structures of power' (ibid.: 317). Given the work of Pai (2000) and Jeffery et al. (2008), we should be cautious of such assertions. The reality probably lies somewhere in-between the activist's tales of betrayal and the political scientists' over-reading of electoral results.

The VCK's electoral victories have come in alliance with Dravidian parties after all. Furthermore, the data presented here suggests that co-optation can take multiple forms and extends along a spectrum from adherence to the established rules of game, through deference to coalition partners, to abandoning afflicted Dalits for money or political advantage. Institutionalisation, by definition, requires different ways of operating. In Gamson's terms (1990: 28–29), caste-based mobilisation has proved more successful in securing political recognition (gaining acceptance as a legitimate party, electoral alliances and media attention) than in procuring 'new advantages' (policy changes, policy implementation or alterations to the structures of caste). Recognition, in other words, occurs on unequal terms since the Dravidian parties hitherto have been far less dependent on allies than the reverse. There are signs that this may be changing (Wyatt 2009) but until it does, smaller parties must seek to grow beyond their core vote.

The key for the VCK, as with other Dalit parties across India, is to expand without losing their core members or abandoning key demands. R. Manohar, a leading Tamil Dalit activist and NGO Director in Bangalore, argued that Dalit parties inevitably get 'sucked into

156 � Hugo Gorringe

administrative roles and the petty politics of bureaucracy'.[36] The result can be to cede the vital forefront of the struggle against caste discrimination to others such as the Communist Party of India (Marxist) linked Tamil Nadu Untouchability Eradication Front (TNUEF). In the past few years this Front has occupied the ground formerly dominated by Dalit movements like the VCK and *Puthiya Tamizhagam*. The TNUEF has not only published reports detailing continuing and evolving practices of untouchability (such as prohibitions on using mobile phones) it has also been at the forefront of struggles to demolish caste walls, that were built to separate Dalits from others in some Tamil villages[37] (see Dorairaj 2010a). Again the picture is more complex than this; that the CPI(M) are addressing caste head-on like this is in itself an outcome of VCK mobilisation.[38]

The politics of opposition is easier than that of government. Whilst the TNUEF publicly challenges the DMK to act against untouchability, the VCK must work with them to carve out space for a Dalit perspective. In March 2010, thus, when the National Commission for Scheduled Castes 'expressed anguish over the lack of initiative on the part of authorities to retrieve lands that were assigned to the SCs but were still in possession of non-Dalits' (Dorairaj 2010b), the VCK were conspicuously silent. On Ambedkar's birthday in April, however, the DMK leader attended a VCK event and 'made it categorical that lands allotted to the Dalits [that had been encroached] would be retrieved'. Thirumavalavan insisted on this occasion that he had 'only joined hands with the DMK for [Dalit] liberation' (*Express Buzz* 2010). Dalit politics, from this perspective, opens up opportunities for change. Simultaneously, however, it creates new modes of marginalisation. Speaking at a meeting of Muslims and Dalits in July 2011, thus, Abdul Rahman MP alleged that 'several MPs from TN ... were reluctant to go out for lunch or sit along with Lok Sabha member from Chidambaram (reserved) constituency Thirumavalavan in the Parliament, as he was a Dalit' (*Express News Service* 2011).

---

[36] Personal communication with R. Manohar, Bangalore, 2010.

[37] Personal communication with Nandan, Edinburgh, 2011.

[38] Interview with Rajangam, Madurai, 2012.

Institutionalisation always carries costs for political movements and, as illustrated here, these are accentuated in situations where the movement's constituents face daily discrimination. The Panthers are currently treading a tightrope between the compulsions of electoral politics and alliance formation on the one hand and the expectations of Dalit cadre on the other. They face the difficult task of translating the politics of recognition into that of redistribution; campaigns on land-reform, central government SC funds and reservations in the private sector begin to address this issue. For each campaign however, there are counter-stories of VCK leaders selling out in terms of land allotted to large companies or compromising in the face of disputes. Noting that caste structures remain intact and atrocities both continue and assume contemporary guises, Manohar asserted that 'Dalit parties are not standing on our behalf, but in our name'.[39] The success of the party, thus, is seen to have distanced it from its most vulnerable supporters and the demands around which it emerged. On the basis of this analysis it is clear that Dalit politics only offers limited mobility to the majority of Dalits and can lead to further marginalisation. If the political Panthers wish to retain their Dalit credentials and avoid the 'impasse' seen elsewhere, then more attention needs to be paid to bridging the gap between the party and the grassroots and on holding electoral partners to account. A focus on electoral results alone will further alienate the core supporters on whom the party depends.

$\mathcal{Y}$

References

Anandhi, S. 2005. 'Sex and Sensibility in Tamil Politics', *Economic and Political Weekly*, 40(47): 4876.

Ananth, V. 2006. 'Assembly Elections: Changing Dynamics in Tamilnadu', , *Economic and Political Weekly*, 41(13): 1232–33.

Arun, J. 2007. *Constructing Dalit Identity*. Jaipur: Rawat Publications.

---

[39] Personal communication with Manohar, Bangalore, 2010.

158 द Hugo Gorringe

Chandhoke, N. 2005. 'Revisiting the Crisis of Representation Thesis: The Indian Context', *Democratization*, 12(3): 308–30.

Chandra, K. 2004. *Why Ethnic Parties Succeed*. Cambridge: Cambridge University Press.

Charsley, S. and G. Karanth. 2001. 'Series Editors' Note', in G. Shah (ed.), *Dalit Identity and Politics*, pp. 11–13. New Delhi: Sage Publications.

Coy, P. and T. Hedeen. 2005. 'A Stage Model of SM Co-optation', *The Sociological Quarterly*, 46(4): 405–35.

Della Porta, Donatella and Mario Diani. 1999. *Social Movements*. Oxford: Blackwell.

Dorairaj, S. 2010a. 'Rally for Justice', *Frontline*, 27(13). http://www.frontline.in/fl2713/stories/20100702271310500.htm (accessed 4 July 2010).

———. 2010b. 'Facing Flak', *Frontline* 27(6). http://www.frontline.in/fl2706/stories/20100326270603800.htm (accessed 4 July 2010).

Express Buzz. 2010. 'Duty Bound to Reclaim Dalit Lands: Karunanidhi', *Express News Service*, 15 April. http://expressbuzz.com/cities/chennai/duty-bound-to-reclaim-dalit-lands- karunanidhi/165459.html (accessed 4 July 2010).

Express News Service. 2011. 'Tirumavalavan Faces Caste Bias from MPs', *IBNLive.com*, 31 July. http://ibnlive.in.com/news/tirumavalavan-faces-caste-bias-from-mps/171707-60-118.html (accessed 22 August 2011).

Gamson, W. 1990. *The Strategy of Social Protest*. Belmont: Wadsworth Publishing.

Gorringe, Hugo. 2005. *Untouchable Citizens*. New Delhi: Sage Publications.

———. 2006. '"Banal Violence?" The Everyday Underpinnings of Collective Violence', *Identities*, 13(2): 237–60.

Gundimeda, S. 2009. 'Dalits, Praja Rajyam Party and Caste Politics in Andhra Pradesh', *Economic and Political Weekly*, 44(21): 50–58.

Hasan, Z. 2006. 'Constitutional Equality and the Politics of Representation in India', *Diogenes*, 53(4): 54–68.

Jaffrelot, C. 2003. *India's Silent Revolution: The Rise of the Low Castes in North Indian Politics*. New Delhi: Permanent Black.

Jayakumar, G. 2010. 'Eklavya Bows to Arjun No More', *Express Buzz*, 28 February. http://www.expressbuzz.com/edition/print.aspx?artid=1ZYR7hRqmnY= (accessed 1 March 2010).

Jeffery, R., C. Jeffrey and P. Jeffery. 2008. 'Dalit Revolution? New Politicians in Uttar Pradesh, India', *Journal of Asian Studies*, 67(4): 1365–96.

Legislating for Liberation? 159

Jenkins, J. and B. Klandermans (eds). 1995. *The Politics of Social Protest*. Berkeley: University of California Press.

Kohli, A. 1990. *Democracy & Discontent*. Cambridge: Cambridge University Press.

———. (ed.). 2001. *The Success of India's Democracy*. Cambridge: Cambridge University Press.

Lakha, S. and P. Taneja. 2009. 'Introduction: Democracy, Governance and Civil Society: Rethinking the Study of Contemporary India', *South Asia*, 32(3): 315–25.

Lokniti. 2006. 'Tamil Nadu Pre Poll 2006 Report'. http://www.lokniti. org/pdfs_dataunit/Questionairs/tamil%20nadu,%20pre%20poll,%20 2006-report.pdf (accessed 4 July 2010).

Mehrotra, S. 2006. 'Well-being and Caste in Uttar Pradesh', *Economic and Political Weekly*, 41(40): 4261–71.

Melucci, A. 1996. *Challenging Codes*. Cambridge: Cambridge University Press.

Mines, M. 1994. *Public Faces, Private Voices*. Berkeley: University of California Press.

Mines, M. and V. Gourishankar. 1990. 'Leadership and Individuality in South Asia: The Case of the South Indian Big-man', *Journal of Asian Studies*, 49(4): 761–86.

Nambath, S. 2000. 'DMK Gained from Dalits' Apathy to AIADMK', *Hindu Online*. http://www.hindu.com/2000/02/29/stories/04292231.htm (accessed 2 July 2010).

Offe, C. 1990. 'Reflections on the Institutional Self-transformation of Movement Politics', in R. Dalton and M. Kuechler (eds), *Challenging the Political Order*, pp. 232–50. Cambridge: Polity.

Omvedt, Gail. 2003. 'Introduction: Thunder out of the *Cheri*', in R. Thirumavalavan, *Talisman*, pp. 14–24. Kolkata: Samya.

Pai, Sudha. 2002. *Dalit Assertion and the Unfinished Democratic Revolution*. New Delhi: Sage Publications.

Pandian, M. 2000. 'Dalit Assertion in Tamil Nadu: An Explanatory Note', *Journal of Indian School of Political Economy*, 12(3, 4): 501–17.

———. 2006. 'Does Caste Have a Future in Tamil Nadu, India?' *Tamil Brisbane*, http://www.tamilbrisbane.com/index2.php?option=com_content&do_pdf=1&id=158 (accessed 2 July 2010).

Piven, F. and R. Cloward. 1979. *Poor People's Movements: Why They Succeed and How They Fail*. New York: Vintage Books.

160 ੮ *Hugo Gorringe*

Ravikumar. 2009. *Venomous Touch: Notes on Caste, Culture & Politics*, trans. R. Azhagarasan. Kolkata: Samya.

Roberts, N. 2010. 'Language, Violence, and the State: Writing Tamil Dalits', *South Asia Multidisciplinary Academic Journal*, 3. http://samaj.revues.org/index2952.html (accessed 20 March 2011).

Satyanarayana, R. 2011. 'With a Longer List of Freebies, Jayalalitha Joins War of Populism', *The Times of India,* 24 March. http://timesofindia.indiatimes.com/home/specials/assembly-elections-2011/tamil-nadu/With-a-longer-list-of-freebies-Jayalalitha-joins-war-of-populism/articleshow/7779405.cms (accessed 24 May 2011).

Shah, G. 2004. *Social Movements in India.* New Delhi: Sage Publications.

Subramanian, Narendra. 1999. *Ethnicity and Populist Mobilization.* Delhi: Oxford University Press.

Subramanian, T. 2011. 'Clean Sweep', *Frontline*, 28(11). http://www.frontlineonnet.com/stories/20110603281101000.htm (accessed 24 May 2011).

Tarrow, S. 1998[1994]. *Power in Movement (2nd Edition).* Cambridge: Cambridge University Press.

The Hindu. 2010a. 'VCK Cadre Dies in Accident', *Hindu Online.* http://www.hindu.com/2010/07/02/stories/2010070261940800.htm (accessed 2 July 2010).

———. 2010b. 'Thirumavalavan Distributes Free Colour TV Sets', *Hindu Online.* http://www.hindu.com/2010/06/17/stories/2010061759420300.htm (accessed 2 July 2010).

———. 2010c. 'Murder Suspect's Father Found Dead', 28 January (Chennai Edition).

———. 2010d. '13th Anniversary of "Melavalavu Massacre" Observed', *Hindu Online.* http://www.hindu.com/2010/07/01/stories/2010070162140400.htm (accessed 2 July 2010).

Thirumavalavan, R. 2003. *Talisman: Extreme Emotions of Dalit Liberation*, compiled and trans. M. Kandasamy. Kolkata: Samya.

———. 2004. *Uproot Hindutva: The Fiery Voice of the Liberation Panthers*, compiled and trans. M. Kandasamy. Kolkata: Samya.

Tilly, C. 1986. *The Contentious French.* Cambridge: Harvard University Press.

Vaasanthi. 2006. *Cut-outs, Caste and Cine Stars: The World of Tamil Politics.* New Delhi: Penguin Books.

Vijayabaskar, M. 2010. 'Saving Agricultural Labour from Agriculture: SEZs and Politics of Silence in Tamil Nadu', *Economic and Political Weekly*, 45(6): 36–43.

Legislating for Liberation? द 161

Washbrook, D. 1989. 'Caste, Class and Dominance in Modern Tamil Nadu', in F. Frankel and M. S. A. Rao (eds), *Dominance and State Power in India (Vol. I)*, pp. 204–64. Delhi: Oxford University Press.

Wyatt, A. 2009. *Party System Change in South India: Political Entrepreneurs, Patterns and Processes*. London: Routledge.

V

A Book Also Travels

Circulating Small Booklets in Dalit Poorva

Badri Narayan*

'Talks have legs and books too have legs. In this world all the trees, bushes and animals walk and talk…'

(A.R. Akela, Paharipur resident and author of many popular Dalit booklets)

This chapter explores how the Dalit popular booklets travel from the writers of the booklets to the various agencies that disseminate the message of these booklets, to the educated, aware Dalits from whom they reach the grassroots comprising majorly illiterate Dalits. It also deals with the role and dissemination of Dalit popular literature in the development of political consciousness among the Dalits in the villages of Uttar Pradesh in north India, which enables them to fight for their social, political and cultural empowerment. The chapter throws light on the relationship between democracy, development and politics of knowledge in the context of Dalit mobilisation.

The chapter is based on the fieldwork conducted in a village called Shahabpur, which is a tiny village in central Uttar Pradesh approximately 20 kilometres from Allahabad. It is located 5 kilometres to the north of Hathiganh Chauraha on the Allahabad–Lucknow highway. It is nearly 2,500 metres in length and has almost the same breadth. The village is divided into 13 hamlets and sub-hamlets (known as *patti*s, *poorva*s and *tola*s), namely Shahabpur Bazar, Shahabpurtali, Godampatti (Chamrava), Shahabpur Kohrana, Shahabpur Purai ka Purva, Shahabpur Murain Tola, Shahabpur Pasiapur, Turkan, Inara, Shahabpur Judapur Chauraha, Shahabpur Chitanpur, Chitanpur Thakuran. People of various castes inhabit this village, most of them in the lower strata of

A Book Also Travels द 163

the Indian caste hierarchy. People belonging to castes like Patels, Pasis, Mauryas, Kumhars, Chamars, Turks (Muslims) and Dhobis, are mostly settled in their own *patti*s while other castes like Yadav, Darzi, Lohar, Nai, Bhuja, Dafali, Churihaar, which are less in number, live mostly in the Shahabpur Bazaar or are scattered in other *patti*s. The average distance between the hamlets range between 2 and 3 kilometres and they are linked by narrow pitch roads, un-metaled *kutcha* roads, or furrows (*chauri aris*) within agricultural fields. All the *patti*s are surrounded by lush green fields growing crops like rice, wheat, mustard, pulses, and vegetables.

If one were to visit a tea stall in a hamlet with a high Dalit population in the village in the mornings or evenings, one would find several semi-literate Dalit men sipping tea and reading small booklets printed on coarse and cheap newsprint. One such tea stall is in the Godampatti of Shahabpur that has a high population of Chamars (an untouchable Dalit caste), owned and run by Ram Kishor. In the evenings all the people congregate in the open space around the tea stall where the literate Dalits discuss whatever they have read, while the uneducated and illiterate Dalits sit by and listen with rapt attention. These discussions are an important medium for disseminating information and knowledge among the community since even the illiterate Dalits become aware of the contents of the booklets merely by listening to the conversation of their educated brethren. This in turn helps to create a socio-political and socio-economic awakening and awareness amongst them. Thus, the knowledge contained in these booklets is transmitted to the bulk of illiterate Dalits through the oral medium. The literate Dalits act as an agency for transmitting knowledge to the uneducated Dalits thus connect them with changing social values, as well as rupture some previously held values, thereby creating new social values.

These booklets, which we can call Dalit Popular Booklets, are cheaply priced between ₹1 and ₹25. They have neither attractive appearance, nor are they printed on superior quality or glossy paper like the books published by established Hindi publishing houses. Since these booklets are targeted at the poorer sections of the Dalit population, they are sold at Dalit political meetings, fairs and *Chetna Mandap*s (shops run by Dalits found in various cities and towns of UP where Dalit literature, which helps to raise Dalit awareness or *chetna*, is stored).

164 द *Badri Narayan*

The distinctive features of the literature contained in the Dalit Popular Booklets are simplicity, accessibility and acceptability. The writers and the publishers of these booklets come from lower-caste political activist groups and intellectuals and these booklets are written with a specific objective that is revealed by the authors in the introduction of the booklets. Most of these booklets are rooted in the lives and teachings of Buddha, Ambedkar, Ravidas, Kabir, Phule, and Periyar. Many of them also deal with caste histories, social criticism, Dalit politics and political struggles of Kanshiram[1] and Mayawati[2]. Dalit politicians engaged in mobilising Dalits for electoral politics use the narratives of these popular booklets in their electoral speeches and in their everyday mobilisational discourses (Narayan 2001: 3923).

The popular booklets played an important role in shaping the Dalit consciousness of two frontline Dalit leaders, namely Kanshiram and Mayawati, who went on to play major roles in the Dalit politics of Uttar Pradesh. When Kanshiram had lost his job and his political consciousness was being formed, D. K. Karpade, an activist of Dalit movement in Maharashtra, gave him several of these booklets to read, which helped to shape his political ideology (Yad 2005: 11). Mayawati was also an avid reader of these popular booklets in her early days. This literature is the fountainhead of her intellectual prowess that is expressed in her speeches and debates and in her political addresses during election campaigns (ibid.: 4). Once, during her tenure as the chief minister of UP, she came under flak by the media and the elite society after she made some controversial comments on Mahatma Gandhi. This led to a

---

[1] Kanshiram was an Indian politician of Dalit Raidasia/Ramdassia Sikh background. He founded the Bahujan Samaj Party (BSP), a political party with the stated goal of serving the traditionally lower castes of Indian society (which historically also included untouchables).

[2] Mayawati was the Chief Minister of Uttar Pradesh, India's most populous state. Her supporters refer to her as *Behen Ji*, which means sister. At age 39, she became the youngest politician to be elected chief minister in Uttar Pradesh and the first Dalit-woman chief minister of any Indian state. She is regarded as a symbol of dignity and political inspiration for millions of India's Dalits who were oppressed by the Hindu upper castes for centuries.

A Book Also Travels ᴅ 165

pandemonium in the State Assembly and she was asked to reply to the Assembly. To equip herself better with her reply, she asked one of her secretaries to buy these popular booklets. He bought booklets worth ₹5,000 from the Bahujan Kalyan Prakashan, belonging to Avinashji, a publisher of the popular booklets.[3]

The reconstructed myths that are printed in Dalit popular booklets help in the creation of a new political orality that provide political leaders the language of discourse. Several BSP leaders have used these stories in their speeches and discussions with common people and activists of the Dalit movement. BSP also formed a cultural squad of the folk singers, political poets and singers, who compose songs, ballads, poems, plays, and paint pictures about Dalit consciousness and transmit these messages to the villagers through songs, dances, dramas, other cultural forms of that region (Singh 1994: 122).

Writings, Writers and the Struggle for Freedom

The writers of these booklets are mostly the emerging Dalit middle class, educated, who want to spread the notion of 'Dalit empowerment' among the grassroots of this class. They occupy middle or a higher–middle status in society. Some of these authors like A. R. Akela, Sunderlal Sagar and Babulal Bhanwra are activists of the BSP, while others, who are not actively involved in BSP politics, are its sympathisers and supporters. Most of them are professionals, for instance Suresh Chandra Kushwaha, the author of popular booklet *Arakshan Ke Hatyare* (Killers of Reservation), is an advocate in the Allahabad High Court. Buddha Sharan Hans, author of *Kash Hum Hindu na Hote* (If We were Not Hindus), is a Provincial Civil Services (PCS) officer. G. P. Prashant, the author of *Bhim Pachasa* [Fifty Hymns on Bheem (as Ambedkar is endearingly called)], is a teacher by profession. Mata Prasad, who has written *Achhut Virangana* (Untouchable Valiant Woman Hero), is an Ayurvedic doctor and a dramatist (Narayan 2001: 3924). We talked to a few writers of Dalit popular booklets to investigate their backgrounds and to understand why they write these booklets.

---

[3] Interview with Avinash by Badri Narayan, Shahadatganj, Lucknow, 5 October 2009.

166 ॰ *Badri Narayan*

A. R. Akela is the writer of popular Dalit booklets. He publishes these booklets and sells them in meetings and rallies. Though he makes a small profit publishing and selling these booklets, it is also a mission for him.[4] In fact, Akela's association with this mission is both interesting and inspiring. He was born in a Dalit family of Paharipur village in Aligarh district, on 30 September 1960. His grandfather was a well-to-do farmer, and his father Talwar Bohrey, owned 40 acres of land. However he lost all his land to the moneylenders as he was caught in a debt trap. Akela's elementary education was in his village. He passed his junior high school examination from a nearby village called Datawali. Around this time, he also lost his father and in order to eke out a living he set up a general merchant shop in his village. At the same time, he started writing booklets based on Dalit issues as he was highly concerned about the plight of the Dalits. In 1980, his first book *Shambuk Rishi ki Barahmasi* (Evergreens of Sage Sambhuk) depicted the bare truth of the common Dalits. Annoyed with its popularity, the Brahmin village chief got him arrested for *Nashabandi* (Prohibition) under Section 7. When Akela was released on bail he started composing songs attacking the Brahminical system. He used to sing these self-composed *Barahmasi* (evergreen) lyrics in nearby villages during Ambedkar Jayanti celebrations. He also published his own songs and compositions and sold these in the form of small booklets for 60 paisa each. His growing popularity among the Dalits for singing against Untouchability and for celebrating Ambedkar Jayanti, angered the upper castes who forced him to flee his village in 1985. From the village Akela went to the Aligarh Cantonment where he established *Anand Sahitya Sadan* and started publishing his works. He has published several chapbooks both written by him and by other Dalit authors.

Another writer of these booklets is Ratnakar Bandhu Trisharan. He is involved in promoting political awareness amongst the Dalits. Trisharan, a native of Basti district, joined as a clerk in the State Public Works Department of Sisai, Gonda. To spend his spare time usefully, he purchased some social and religious books from *Bahujan Kalyan Prakashan* (Bahujan Welfare Publication), Lucknow. After reading these

---

[4] Interview with A. R. Akela by Brijendra Gautam, Aligarh, 9 July 2008.

A Book Also Travels ॐ 167

books, the sacrifices of Buddha and Ambedkar captured his imagination and conscience. They inspired him to evaluate the purpose of his own life and he decided to disseminate the thoughts of these personalities among the downtrodden in simple language in the form of folk songs, poems, etc., through small and easily comprehensible booklets.

His book *Bheem Sandesh* (Messages of Bheem) annoyed and upset the people of the upper castes, who allegedly implicated him in a false case. They conspired and framed him falsely, as a result of which Defense of India Rule (DIR) — that prohibited anti-national activities during the Emergency — was slapped against him and he was suspended from his job. During the period of his suspension, Trisharan lived in Basti. Since Haraiya, his birthplace, was close by, he established the Akhil Bhartiya Baba Saheb Dr Ambedkar Samaj Sudhar Samiti (All-India Baba Saheb Dr Ambedkar Social Welfare Committee) there to support his mission. The Samaj Sudhar Prakashan (Social Reform Publication) Haraiya was established under this Samiti.[5] A large number of people joined the organisation and used to visit various villages to disseminate the booklets and thereby awaken the masses. The modes used for this purpose were *katha* (parables), *pravachan* (sermons) and *geet-mandali* (choirs). The booklets of Haraiya (name of a place) Prakashan (publication) are printed in Samaj Seva Press (Social Service Press), Lucknow, which also handles its marketing.

Buddha Sharan Hans, another Dalit activist, has been writing and publishing small booklets written by him and other Dalit writers. He actively promotes these amongst the masses and has been doing so for over 40 years. Born on 8 April 1942 in village Tilori, district Gaya, of Bihar, Hans, who was a member of the Bihar Administrative Services, is endearingly called 'Dalit Paswan' (this name is given in affection to Hans for his contribution for the upliftment of marginalised people) for his long association with the Dalit cause. His involvement with this mission deepened with the publication of journals *Ambedkar Vichar Manch* (Ambedkar Ideological Forum) (1980) and *Ambedkar Mission Patrika* (Ambedkar Mission Publication) (1989). In addition, he has also authored small booklets like *Teen Mahaprani* (Three Great Men) (1996),

---

[5] Interview with R. B. Trisharan by Archana Singh, Basti, 2 August 2008.

168 द *Badri Narayan*

Soshiton ki Samasya aur Samadhan (The Problems and Solutions of the Exploited) (1970), *Daliton ki Durdasha* (Sorry Plight of Dalits) (1982), *Brahmanvaad se Bacho* (Save Yourselves from Brahminism) (1991), etc. After his retirement, he plunged into more missionary work promoting the Dalit cause.

Such writers are found all over UP. They strive hard to spread the message of Dalit consciousness through their books.

Reading, Writing and the Emergence of a Critical Dalit Public

The making of these popular writers and an educated Dalit public is linked with the history of the process of disseminating education among Dalits in modern India. Due to the intervention of various socio-cultural and political forces in pre- and post-colonial times, there has been a remarkable increase in the spread of education among Dalits. This happened due to the intervention of various socio-cultural and political forces. The Arya Samaj played an important role in educating the Dalits in Uttar Pradesh (Kshirsagar 1994: 128), as it opened the doors of its schools to the downtrodden. The Arya Samaj also gave the lower castes the right to read the Vedas. However, both the Samaj and the Dalits had to face a strong backlash from the Sanatan Dharma Hindus, who perpetrated great violence on them for flouting the orthodox Hindu notions. Although the Arya Samaj had its own politics for educating the Dalits, by linking them with the Brahminical knowledge system it gave them a new life through a revised version of Brahminism. While this revised version of Brahminism also helped to expand the territory of influence of Brahminical values, a major by-product of this phenomenon was that poor Dalits were enlightened through knowledge and education.

When a section of Dalits developed a critical consciousness they started distancing themselves from the Arya Samaj and began searching for new paths for Dalit liberation. Swami Achyutanand,[6] who had

---

[6] Swami Achyutanand, the pioneer of the anti-Brahminical Movement in North India, especially Uttar Pradesh. In his yearning for inner peace he got attracted to the Arya Samaj. Under the guidance of Swami Sachitanand he

A Book Also Travels ᴅ 169

made an immense contribution to the welfare and education of Dalits, himself attained consciousness through the Arya Samaj, but left it when he understood the inner conflicts of the organisation.[7] While a section of Dalits were obtaining education and knowledge from the Arya Samaj, a few Muslim organisations in UP also opened up their schools to Dalit students. These schools enabled many Dalits to acquire education and wisdom.[8] Around 1818, the British government for the first time made education a state responsibility by imposing the Common Code. This helped to increase the entry of Dalits in the education system. Christian missionaries also allowed the Dalits to study in schools run by them, due to which a section of the Dalits became educated (Bechain 1997: 177).

Around the same time, a section of Dalits who were influenced by Ambedkarite notions — a mixture of Western liberal ideas and the gradually emerging Indian Dalit consciousness — started converting education and knowledge into an instrument for Dalit liberation. Dr Ambedkar played an extremely important role in developing modern ideas among Dalits through a critical and subversive consciousness in the context of India's caste system. For him, the solution to all Dalit problems lay in education. By positioning education as an important agenda in social reform, he proposed knowledge as a tool to be used for Dalit liberation. In a situation where Dalits had been deprived of education under the Indian caste system, Ambedkar emerged as a powerful symbol in the campaign to link Dalits with education. Even during the colonial period, many Dalit communities started moving ahead by acquiring education through the numerous Ambedkar libraries

---

learned the Vedas but when he found it meaningless for social change he gave it up. He then started a social movement against Brahminical social authoritarianism. He started publication of two papers namely Achhut and Adi Hindu. He also established two important organisations in north India namely Achhut Mahasabha and Adi Hindu Mahasabha. His leadership and efforts for Dalit liberation were deeply acknowledged by Ambedkar.

[7] Interview with G. P. Madan by Brijendra Gautam, Allahabad, 16 February 2002.

[8] Interview with S. Sanjeevan Nath by Nivedita Singh, Allahabad, 12 August 2005.

170 *द Badri Narayan*

and Ambedkar trusts set up in Dalit colonies across India. In 1935–36, a registered Ambedkar Library had been established in Allahabad.[9]

A study of the oral history of the process of acquiring education and becoming intellectuals by a section of Dalits in Allahabad, Kanpur and Lucknow shows that migration to cities and settling in cantonment areas were important factors in this process. This can be seen as a 'cantonment phenomenon' since the cantonments and the British army officers played a crucial role in educating the Dalits who worked in their houses as domestic help. One such Dalit intellectual, the popular Dalit writer S. Rao Sanjeevan Nath, while reminiscing about his days in the cantonment says:

> We lived in the cantonment area. My father worked in the house of a British army officer. The officer himself got us admitted in a school. I must tell you that the British don't have any casteist feelings, which the so-called upper castes have that even the shadow of an Untouchable will pollute them. Since childhood, we saw one family member cleaning the boots of the British officers, while someone else would feed their children. In other words, we lived with them as a part of their family. The language spoken by all of us was a Pidgin English, which was called Garauti English stemming from the word *gora* that was used for the whites. In fact all the Dalits who spoke Garauti English were highly respected by the other Dalits in the Dalit colony. We learnt Garauti English just as children learn their mother tongues whether they could read and write or not. All of us who knew Garauti English later learnt English as a part of our education, which we all acquired till whatever level possible. Because of the British the urge for education increased among the Dalits. After leaving the cantonment some of the educated, intellectual Dalits started working for our community's liberation. All of them believed that spreading education among the grassroots Dalits was one of the ways to achieve this goal. In our colony lived an intellectual named Rai Sahib Kakarni who ran an Ambedkar library in his house. There were other intellectuals, too, like Bihari Lal and Dr Nand Lal Jaiswar, who were extremely knowledgeable. They used to write small booklets for the Dalits to read.[10]

---

[9] Interview with R. B. Trisharan by Archana Singh, Basti, 2 August 2008.

[10] Interview with S. Sanjeevan Nath by Nivedita Singh, Allahabad, 12 August 2005.

A Book Also Travels द 171

Among the intellectuals to emerge in the Allahabad region during the colonial period were a number of Dalits belonging to the Khatik, Bhangi, Pasi, Chamar, Dhobi, and other such lower castes. All of them were educated, intellectually strong and highly concerned about bringing about reforms in the Dalit communities. Often these Dalit intellectuals were influenced by two or more conflicting ideologies.

Democracy, Development and the Politics of Knowledge

The Dalit intellectuals who had been active during the colonial period remained so even after Independence. Alongside, a number of other intellectuals from the Dalit communities also emerged. Freedom produced a number of opportunities for the Dalit and backward classes for their development, education and for attaining equality. Despite the slow pace at which they could access these opportunities, there were some positive changes in the educational condition of the Dalits. However, oppression, exploitation and cultural dominance by the upper castes continued to plague them. This was the reason why education did not imply simply getting jobs like the other castes; for the Dalit intellectuals, education became closely connected with the development of their identity and self-respect. Since the 1950s and 1960s, while on one hand, new strategies of Dalit liberation were being planned, on the other hand, there was a strong urge within them to take advantage of the benefits and rights offered by the constitution to move ahead. In addition, their demand for equal participation and a share in the newly-formed government also increased.

However, the nation that was being formed was still under the leadership of the upper castes, with a strong Brahminical mindset. As a result, disillusionment with the existing system started setting in among the Dalit intellectuals and leaders. The uniform narrative for all communities that the government tried to propagate at the time of Independence was challenged by Dalit intellectuals by the 1960s, using the medium of their popular booklets, through which they attempted to highlight the glorious past of the Dalits, their contribution to India's liberation, and how they were being marginalised by the upper castes.

172 ङ Badri Narayan

In order to highlight the glorious past of the Dalits, the intellectuals started seeking out Dalit heroes, both mythical and historical, who had remained unsung and overlooked. They also increased their demand for a greater share in the Government by asserting their role in the 1857 movement and in the nationalist struggle. The writing and circulation of the small Dalit popular booklets became extremely powerful weapons (Narayan 2006: 53).

Dalit intellectuals used their popular booklets to assert even more vehemently the role of the lower castes in the nation–building process, both before and after Independence. It gained momentum during and after the Mandal Commission (in the 1990s). Once again a section of Dalit intellectuals tried to make the common Dalits aware of these burning issues through the small, inexpensive booklets that were accessible for all. It would be interesting to know that the intellectual section that emerged after 1990 included mainly the Chamars followed by the Pasis, Bhangis, Koris, Dhobis, Nais, Kurmis, and other such lower castes.

The analyses of the social biography of writers and intellectuals, who emerged after the 1960s and became even more active after the 1990s, reveal interesting facts. After studying the social background of 20 such popular Dalit writers it was found that 10 belonged to the Chamar and Jatav castes. Three belonged to the Bhangi caste, four belonged to the Pasi caste, one was a Dhanuk, one was a Dhobi and one belonged to the Kori caste. A comparison of their ideologies shows that 15 of them followed the ideologies of Buddha and Ambedkar. One was a follower of Kabir, while the rest were only involved in the fight to raise the dignity and self-esteem of their own castes. Most were indigenous doctors, school teachers and clerks. A few were government officers. Their writings were mostly concerned with the social, religious, philosophical, and political issues of the Dalits, and also with issues dealing with their own caste identities.[11]

Given the democratisation of education and knowledge because of the democratic movement, Mandal Commission, reservation, the

---

[11] Same as note 1.

A Book Also Travels द 173

emergence of BSP,[12] etc., great possibilities had opened up for the Dalits. When education spread among the Dalit communities, the number of readers also increased. Consequently, there was the awareness of a need for the formation of *their* literature. Gradually, these booklets began to be seen as a means of forming and spreading a new kind of democracy to deepen democratic values among the Dalits. There was a rising conflict between various castes and communities to enjoy the benefits given by the Indian welfare state and to move forward using those benefits. Simultaneously, these castes realised the importance of education and knowledge in accessing these benefits. The circle between education, knowledge and writing, and political empowerment opened many new avenues. In addition, the implementation of the Indian constitution and its amendment, by the Government from time to time — like the Mandal Commission report for granting reservations to the SCs and STs — created a situation whereby the Dalits became a growing part of India's education scenario.

Booklets, Agencies and Processes of Dissemination

Amarnath of Godampatti in Shahabpur, an aware and conscious Dalit who is a voracious reader of these booklets, informed us that the small booklets are brought to the village by various people like Lalji Premi,

---

[12] Bahujan Samaj Party (BSP) or Majority People's Party is one of the only five prominent national political parties of India, which is the largest democracy of the world. The ideology of the Bahujan Samaj Party (BSP) is 'Social Transformation and Economic Emancipation' of the 'Bahujan Samaj', which comprises the SCs, the STs, the OBCs, and religious minorities such as Sikhs, Muslims, Christians, Parsis, and Buddhists and account for over 85 per cent of the country's total population. The people belonging to all these classes have been the victims of the 'Manuwadi' system in the country for thousands of years, under which they have been vanquished, trampled upon and forced to languish in all spheres of life. In other words, these people were deprived even of all those human rights, which had been secured for the upper caste Hindus under the age-old 'Manuwadi Social System'. Now she has transformed her motto to sarvajan.

174 द Badri Narayan

Kamalji and another man who is simply known as *cyclewala* (because he arrives, with the books, on his bicycle), for distribution to the villagers. In addition, many people of this *patti* also buy the booklets when they visit Allahabad and Lucknow to attend the BSP rallies where these booklets are sold in makeshift stalls.[13] Following the lead of this source, we reached Lalji Premi, who lives in Shahabpur Bazaar and runs a school for Dalit children in the village. On being asked where he procured these booklets from, he said that he bought them in bulk from Lucknow's *Bahujan Kalyan Prakashan, Bahujan Chetna Mandap*s, *Bahujan Pustak Bhandar* and other such Dalit book centres and publishers. He added that he did not have any bookstalls from where he sold the booklets, but travelled all over the rural regions of Allahabad to distribute the booklets on his mission to arouse the Dalits.[14]

For Sangam Lal Bidrohi of Varanasi, ensuring that these booklets reach villages, quasbas and cities is his mission.[15] For this purpose, Sangam Lal established the *Dr Ambedkar Sahitya Kala Kendra* (Dr Ambedkar Literature and Art Centre) at Gellet Bazar, Varanasi. He has been involved in the propagation of Dalit literature for the last 35 years and carries these small booklets in a bag on his bicycle. He first delivers the books to his Dalit readers at their homes. Later, he visits their homes again, and discusses these books in such a manner that they ask for these books again. According to him, people buy lots of small booklets in the smaller villages.[16]

After 1990 there was a rising trend of writing these books and so the Dalit readership base multiplied. Now, people search for and read these books. Sangam Lal sets up stalls in villages on *Ambedkar Jayanti* and other such occasions, so that people can get these books. He has also set up his own publishing house, for printing books on relevant subjects. He aims to focus on the history of the Dalits. He informed

---

[13] Interview with Amarnath by Archana Singh, Godampatti, Shahabpur, 12 April 2009.

[14] Interview with Lalji Premi by Badri Narayan, Godampatti, Shahabpur, 14 April 2009.

[15] Same as note 1.

[16] Interview with Sangam Lal by Nivedita Singh, Varanasi, 2 November 2008.

A Book Also Travels द 175

that at present not only Dalits but also *Savarnas* (people from higher castes) buy these books. According to him, the latter read these books to correct past mistakes, to understand themselves and to present their own case accordingly. They say that they can see a change being brought about in society through the spread of these books.[17]

Bhullar, a 60-year-old Dalit who lives in Godampatti and is another avid reader of the booklets, told us that he recently visited a fair in Kanpur on the occasion of Ambedkar's birth anniversary, where he bought 20 small booklets for ₹100.[18] Interestingly, Dalit readers who want to know about Ambedkar outnumber others, as a large number of Dalits are keen to be acquainted with the struggles of his life. Books on the history of the community and Dalit folk forms, too, are in great demand.[19] In addition to them, books on Jyotiba Phule[20] and Savitribai Phule[21] are also sold at these fairs. Books on Kanshiram and Mayawati

---

[17] Interview with Sangam Lal by Nivedita Singh, Varanasi, 2 November 2008.

[18] Interview with Bhullar by Badri Narayan, Godampatti, Shahabpur, 21 April 2009.

[19] Same as note 1.

[20] Jyotiba, who belonged to the state of Maharashtra, revolted against the traditional religious beliefs, rites and customs of the Brahaminical system and felt that education is an effective tool to obliterate the Brahaminical hegemony. He alerted the common man about the religious sanctimony and superstitious beliefs prevailing in Hindu society. His greatest revolutionary step was to open a school to educate women who had been neglected and deceived since years. He also authored a number of books which included eminent literary works like *Gulaamgiri* and *Sarvajanik Satyadharma*. He worked not only for the emancipation of women and poor workers but also tried to sort the problems of peasants and worked for their welfare and prosperity. He formed the *Satyashodhak Samaj* that believed in the equality of human beings.

[21] Savitribai Phule was a great revolutionary social reformer and the first Dalit woman leader who favoured equality and education for women to provide them emancipatory potential. She was greatly influenced by the teachings of Lord Buddha and opened many *Mahila Seva Mandals* for improving the condition of women. She raised her voice against the conservative norms and customs of the Hindu society and worked for the betterment of the underprivileged and downtrodden people.

176 द *Badri Narayan*

are presently in great demand. However, the autobiographies of Dalit writers are not so popular at these fairs. People usually prefer to buy books with the pictures of Ambedkar or other Dalit heroes.[22]

Booklets that are cheaply priced are in greater demand, as people do not want to buy books costing more than ₹10. Women from the villages also like to buy booklets but they usually seek *kirtan*s (religious choirs) on Baba Saheb. If the pages of these booklets are thick and glossy, the women do not even bother to check the price, perhaps imagining that these publications are beyond their means. Cheap folk literature printed on coarse paper like *Aalha, Kirtan, Tota-Maina, Sadabriksha-Saranga,* and *Nautanki* attract them. The attractive covers or glossy print of books from big Hindi publishing houses like *Vani Prakashan, Pravin Prakashan, Rajkamal Prakashan, Natraj Prakashan,* and so on, do not attract the crowd at these fairs, who prefer small booklets printed on coarse newsprint. Their sense of aesthetics, which have an element of austerity, is different from that of the middle classes, who prefer attractive layouts. The Dalit readers at these bookstalls identify with books that are simple and modest like them. These can be folded and stuffed in their pockets or stored away in a corner of their rooms. Popular Hindi litterateur and bookseller K. Nath, who also displays and sells booklets at fairs, told us that when he displayed books and autobiographies by eminent Dalit writers like Kanwal Bharti, Sheoraj Singh and Naimisharay on *Ambedkar Jayanti* 2008, only a few copies were sold. But when buyers saw that these books did not contain love stories, *kirtan*s or lyrics of Hindi film tunes, they returned these. Similar is the fate of several anthologies of poems by Dalit poets. There is also no demand for *Jhootan,* an autobiography by Hindi literature's prominent writer, Om Prakash Valmiki.[23]

To understand the world order of these small booklets, we talked to Buddha Sharan Hans, who informed us that he travels through various Dalit villages to popularise these booklets and also organises events and birth anniversaries of great leaders. He wishes people would read these booklets at marriages and social gatherings so that their lives

---

[22] Same as note 21.

[23] Interview with K. Nath by Brijendra Gautam, Kanpur, 11 August 2008.

and thoughts would change.[24] He said that when he is invited to any wedding ceremony in and around Patna region, he always goes along with books and sets up bookstalls at the marriage *pandals*. Many of the invitees to the weddings buy books from these stalls. In fact, people even purchase these books at cremation grounds when he sets up his stalls there.[25]

Popular booklets have a large sweep, effective reach and deep penetration amongst the Dalits, cutting across the demography and class of the target audience. This is the situation at the macro level, where the myth and memories of the community is similar. But, at the micro level there are differences both at the levels of reception and articulation. A case in point is that of booklets of Valiant Jhalkari Bai. For the Dalits in the villages, issues of identity, pride and social honour are linked with the day-to-day struggle in their lives. The rural Dalits are not as vocal about their aspirations; their canvas is much smaller compared to the urban Dalits, who have better education and job. For the latter group, Jhalkari Bai's valour is linked with bigger ideological projects, such as nationalism, freedom movement, emancipation, empowerment, the class–caste struggle and the wrongs inflicted on her (and other similar heroes), at an individual level, and the entire Dalit community at the level of class and caste. For the rural Dalits it is a matter of pride that they too have brave, valiant leaders, but for the urban Dalits, the issue is very big as it goes much beyond — for them the narratives of the past represent the foundational element of identity construction of that particular caste. The urban Dalits crave for better and bigger share, which has hitherto been denied to them. They aspire for bigger demands in the development project of the state and express their angst for having been left behind in the historical process. Thus, the urge for identity construction (of that particular caste) is different at different levels. The urban Dalits made significant contribution towards freeing and building up the nation but this was overlooked after Independence, by the upper castes, who deliberately kept them behind, tucked away

---

[24] Interview with Buddha Sharan Hans by Brijendra Gautam, Patna, 1 December 2008.

[25] Ibid.

178 द *Badri Narayan*

in oblivion (Kushwaha 1993: 3). Kumar said that life sketches, history of the community, BSP songs and Ambedkar songs are sure sellers. The books are in great demand during Baba Saheb Ambedkar's birth anniversary celebrations, when fairs and rallies are organised at various places all over UP. Sushil told us that booksellers come to him before the event and take the books to sell during the fair. He also approaches some booksellers to sell the books before the fairs, when he hears of them through the organisers. Dalit magazines also have a lot of details and information about these fairs and gatherings.[26]

Bahujan Pracharaks (propagators) like Lalji Premi, *Chotey Kitabwale* Kamalji and Sangam Lal *Cycle-wale* are instrumental in the reach of these small booklets into Dalit settlements in villages. Publishers and distributors like Sushil Kumar, Mohan Lal Gautam, Buddha Sharan Hans, and Trisharan are also involved in the dissemination of these booklets. Bahujan propagators take these books from them in bulk or in retail to sell to Dalit readers.

Small Booklets, Political Knowledge and Legal Bans

The journey of these booklets is not without obstructions, as most of them instigate the Dalits to rebel against the oppression of the upper castes, which results in many tensions and clashes. Some of these texts attempt to divest the categories embedded in classical Hindu law by contextualising the oppression of Untouchables. The texts show clearly that they are a kind of ideological weapon for those groups who have been identified as Untouchables. This kind of struggle is not only limited to social and political levels but as Csikszentmihalyi has argued, 'The battle for the value of life is fought in the arena of meaning' (Schwartz 1997: 190).

For the literate and illiterate Dalits, these booklets help to subvert the dominant logic vis-à-vis Hindu religion, Brahminism, Dalit politics, Brahminical socio–culture, Dalit interests in state and system, Dalit history, etc. While reading and listening to them, the Dalits residing in

---

[26] Interview with Sushil Kumar by Archana Singh, Kanpur, 11 December 2008.

A Book Also Travels द 179

remote villages get to know and understand their cause as embedded in society, culture, history and politics. Armed with subversive logic, the Dalits are no longer silent when confronted by the dominant logic. They speak with confidence and their voice, through these booklets, gives rise to the Dalit politics which deconstructs established values, thoughts and the politics. This political awareness does not only determine the voting pattern in Indian electoral democracy but also constructs a Dalit socio-cultural awareness. The booklets were instrumental in shaping the political awareness of important north Indian leaders of Dalit Bahujan politics, like Kanshiram and Mayawati. It provided them with the logic based on which they could deconstruct and destroy the ideologies of the dominant groups and parties. Mayawati, during her student days, used to consult these booklets whenever she wanted to participate in debates. Kanshiram accepted that his Dalit awareness was fuelled by such booklets (Akela 2008: 49).

This may be the reason why a case was registered by the Local Intelligence Unit (LIU) in Kotwali police station under Section 153 A in 1980, on a chapter of his second book, *Ramayan Evam Manusmriti ki Holi Kyon* ('Why a Bonfire of Ramayan and Manusmiriti'), titled *Ramayan mey Ram-Sita* ('Ram Sita in Ramayan'). In 2006, an activist of the Rashtriya Swayamsewak Sangh (RSS), registered a case against one of his books, in police station Baitul, district Baitul, Madhya Pradesh. This case is still on in the Chief Judicial Magistrate's (CJM) court.[27] In the year 2007, an activist of the Bajrang Dal, Manodia, registered a case on Sagar's book *Garva se Kaho Hum Hindu Nahi Hai* ('Say it with Pride: We are not Hindus') under Section 153 A, at the Megh Nagar police station, Jhubua district.[28]

On 8 December 1969, the Uttar Pradesh government confiscated Periyar Lalai Singh's book, *Sacchi Ramayan* (True Ramayan), on the basis of the notification No. 9733-B18-G-2, case No 412/1970, in the Allahabad High Court. On 19 January 1971, Justice A.K. Yog ordered the quashing of the confiscation order. Singh's second book, *Samman ke liye Dharm Parivartan Karein* ('Convert Religion for the Sake of Honour') was confiscated on 25 August 1970 by the UP government,

---

[27] Ibid.
[28] Ibid.

180 द *Badri Narayan*

vide notification No 4431/-1963/70.[29] Three books of the popular Dalit writer Buddha Sharan Hans, *Mai Brahaman Kyon* ('Why Am I a Brahmin'), *Ko Rakshiti Ved* ('Who Protects Veda') and *Brahamanvaad se Bacho* ('Beware of Brahminism') were confiscated by the Bihar government. These books were published by Ambedkar Mission Prakashan, Chitkora, district Patna.[30]

Bhim Sandesh ('Bhim's Messages'), authored by R.B. Trisharan of Basti, was confiscated by the police from the press itself. On 15 February 1976, this book's manuscript was submitted at Bharat Press, Balrampur, Gonda (a stronghold of the Jan Sangh) for printing. It was being published by Sant Ram, the then president of *Navayuvak Harijan Sangha* (Young Harijan Orginisation), Balrampur (Gonda). The Brahmin compositor, after composing this book, showed it to some Brahmins. They lodged a complaint with the police stating that the book was anti-Hindu. On the night of 6 April 1976, the police raided the press premises and confiscated all the printed forms of the said book, alongside the original manuscript.[31] Trisharan was arrested from a chemist's shop even as his wife was released from hospital after an operation. He was jailed and faced rigorous imprisonment. Since he was a government servant, he was also suspended. The case was taken up in the Balrampur court of the judicial magistrate and he was finally released on bail on 4 May 1976.[32]

Several well-known Dalit writers and activists supported Trisharan during the course of this court case. Periyar Lalai Singh (Kanpur), Dr Gaya Prasad Prashant (Lucknow), Bhagwan Das, Guru Prasad Madan and Jaipal Singh Kashyap (advocate, Allahabad) and other committed social workers came forward to help him. Due to the untiring efforts of Moti Ram, MLA Kanpur and Babu Ram Verma, MLA Basti, the UP government decided to withdraw the case against him. On the basis of the judgement of the case, the ban order imposed on the said book was lifted. After two-and-a-half years of constant efforts, his suspension

---

[29] Judgement about *Sacchi Ramayana, Ambedkar Today* (Hindi Magazine), February 2008.

[30] Based on interview of Buddha Sharan Hans, Patna, 1 December 2008.

[31] Based on interview of R. B. Trisharan, Basti, 2 August 2008.

[32] Ibid.

orders were quashed. The charges against the book: 'to hurt the sentiments of other religion, cause unrest, defile a place of worship or provoke defilement', covered under Sections 153 A/295 A of the IPC, were found to be baseless.[33]

Conclusion

This chapter tried to study the relationship between democracy, development and politics of knowledge in the context of Dalit mobilisation and the role of Dalit Popular Booklets in raising consciousness among the Dalits. The Dalit Popular Booklets have played a significant role in the struggles of social upheavals and change in the social system as the marginal communities engaged in the process disseminated their ideas and ideology through these booklets. Since these literatures have popular content, their reach and penetration extends to both cities and rural areas. The illiterate Dalits become aware of the contents of the booklets merely by listening to the conversation of their educated brethren, who read out these books to them. The literate Dalits thus act as an agency for transmitting knowledge to the uneducated Dalits, connecting them with the changing social values, at the same time rupturing some previously held values, thereby creating new social values. This process has led to the creation of a Dalit socio-political and socio-economic awakening and awareness.

These small booklets function as the chief source of awareness at multiple levels like the Dalits at the grassroots, the intelligentsia and think tanks among the Dalits, and the Dalit political leadership. Some of the writers of these booklets are also actively involved in the BSP politics of mobilisation of the Dalits. These booklets played an important role in shaping the Dalit consciousness of two frontline Dalit leaders, Kanshiram and Mayawati, who went on to play major role in the Dalit politics of Uttar Pradesh. They provided Kanshiram and Mayawati with the logic based on which they could deconstruct and destroy the ideologies of the dominant groups and parties, while constructing and creating the Dalit political ideology.

---

[33] Same as note 1.

182 द Badri Narayan

The writers of these booklets are mostly from amongst the emerging educated Dalit middle class and are charged with missionary zeal. The making of these popular writers and consequently with the making of an educated Dalit public is linked with the dissemination of education among Dalits in modern India, right from the pre- and post-colonial times. There were multiple locations of education amongst the Dalits. While some of them were educated in Arya Samaji schools, others were educated in missionary-run institutions or schools run by Muslim clergy.

The chapter also showed how Dalit popular writings function as a site of contesting domain which produces contestations in the dominant section of society as they subvert their hegemony. Since the literature contained in the booklets subverts the dominant common sense, in retaliation, the dominant sections of the society take recourse to legal means to contain these uprisings and subversive literature. There are several examples of how the state machinery that was dominated by the upper caste Hindutva forces governed by the Brahminical system contested against the popular Dalit literature by taking some of the authors to court. Sometimes contestations also occur within the Dalits themselves which was observed when the Valmiki community from amongst the Dalits was up in arms against some of these books. Thus even those in the shackles of exploitation often resist the radical dissenting ideas contained in the booklets as they identify with the dominant common sense. This makes it amply clear that even within one social group there are always active public spheres, contesting and conflicting with each other.

५

References

Akela, A. R. 2008. *Behen Kumari Mayawati Ke Saakshatkaar*. Aligarh: Anand Sahitya Sadan.

Bechain, S. S. 1997. *Hindi Ki Dalit Patrakarita par Patrakar Ambedkar Ka Prabhav*. Delhi: Samta Prakashan.

Kshirsagar, R. K. 1992. *Political Thought of Dr Babasaheb Ambedkar*. New Delhi: Intellectual Publishing House.

Kushwaha, S. C. 1993. *Arakshan Ke Hatyare*. Allahabad: Kushwaha Publications.

———. 1994, *Dalit Movement in India and Its Leaders*. Delhi: M.D. Publications.

Narayan, B. 2001. 'Heroes, Histories and Booklets'. *Economic and Political Weekly*, 36(41): 3923–33.

———. 2006. *Women Heroes and Dalit Assertion in North India: Culture, Identity and Politics*. New Delhi: Sage Publications.

Phule, Jyotiba. 1995. *Gulamgiri*. Delhi: Sangeeta Prakashan.

———. 2007. *Sarvajanik Satyadharma: Pustak Navya Prastavnesaha*. Pune: Dnyanvilas Chhapkhana.

Schwartz, M. B. 1997. 'Indian Untouchable Texts of Resistance: Symbolic Domination and Historical Knowledge', in H. L. Seneviratne (ed.), *Identity, Consciousness and the Past: Forging of Caste and Community in India and Sri Lanka*. New Delhi: Oxford University Press.

Singh, R. K. 1994. *Kanshiram aur BSP: Dalit Aandolan ka Vaicharik Aadhar Brahminvaad Virodh*. Allahabad: Kushwaha Book Distributors.

Yad, Y. K. 2005. *Samajik Parivartan ke Mahanayak Manya Kanshiram Sahab*. Lucknow: Bahujan Sahitya Sanstha Ltd.

VI

Low-caste Elites and Re-traditionalised Responses

Status and Security in an Economically Uncertain Time

Jordan C. R. Mullard

The title of this book encapsulates the varying debates on the future of Dalits in India today. Dalits are experiencing transformations in status and fast becoming an important group of political and social actors in India and beyond and yet they continue to suffer social exclusion. The tension between advancement and stagnation is often described in relation to so-called *mainstream* or high-caste Indian society, revealing the persistence of caste discrimination on the one hand and the success of the government's social mobility policies on the other. Whilst examples of both these influences can be seen throughout India, it still embodies a particular view of Dalits as being buffeted back and forth by policies of affirmative action or reservations on the one hand, but still being subject to discrimination by mainstream Indian society on the other, and with very little chance of breaking through the constraints of either social processes. In fact, situating Dalit experience within a dichotomy that simply sees them advance only to be knocked back by an institutionalised discrimination masks a different, and in certain circumstances, unsettling, set of Dalit experiences and actions. As such, this article continues in the tradition of studies that look at the agency of Dalits, even when social, economic and political constraints are at large (such as Gorringe 2005; Hardiman 2007; Omvedt 1994; Shah 2006 to name a few). This chapter asks what happens when there is a Dalit elite, and how do successful Dalits see their identity and strategies for

Low-caste Elites and Re-traditionalised Responses ד 185

social mobility? It also asks what happens to Dalit identity more generally when there is competition amongst them for limited economic resources?

The relations I describe see affluent Dalits pitted against other Dalits in the struggle to maintain their wealth, status and power. In this context, concerns over material gains and political power begin to breakdown or thwart any sense of a shared identity of 'Dalit-ness', where concerns for status reinvigorate the so-called 'pollution-line', when actors aim to situate other Dalit communities well below it and themselves above it. This chapter examines how different Dalit communities view their mobility and marginalisation and how the struggle for status, power and access to resources underpins their relationships with each other.

The data presented here is drawn from my doctoral research in the Thar Desert region of North West Rajasthan, which took place between January 2005 and April 2007. The medium-sized, mixed-caste village of Mudharamsar[1] was unusual on two fronts. First, the village itself consisted of a low caste elite dominated by a family of Meghval (traditionally leather workers) and a family of Kumbhars (traditionally potters). Second, during my fieldwork the main source of employment for villagers had been suspended, causing mass unemployment in the region. From 16 May 2004 to 15 February 2007, the Rajasthani government had shut down many of the mines in the state to encourage mine owners to address environmental pollution and take measures to reduce carbon emissions. A total of 24,000 mines were temporarily closed causing widespread unemployment in the state. Bikaner, the district in which I was living, is famous for its mineral wealth[2] and was badly hit. Some 18,000 people in the *tehsil* (sub-district) in which I conducted fieldwork were made redundant causing considerable economic uncertainty for many families.

---

[1] The names of people and places have been substituted with pseudonyms to protect anonymity.

[2] The mines surrounding the village specialised in china, ball clay and gypsum.

186 द *Jordan C. R. Mullard*

This insecurity permeated many aspects of social life in the village, which in turn affected social relationships and solidarity between neighbours, kin and wider village relations more generally. The successful mobility of the lineage of Meghvals[3] produced a multitude of responses from both high and low castes that were further highlighted by the mine closures. Whilst the Meghvals' position had been a source of great gossip and conjecture prior to the mine closures, it was evident that their status had been elevated during that turbulent period.

This particular genealogy of Meghvals had been the largest landowners in the village, since the 1950–60s when the late patriarch of the family became a Member of the Legislative Assembly (MLA) through the reservation process. His government position enabled him to acquire more lands, educate his children and build bigger, better houses for his family. Indeed, it was this Meghval that commissioned the first and only tube well[4] in the village, which continues to provide fresh water to wells in every neighbourhood of the village today.

In the wake of the mine closures, industrial labourers sought jobs elsewhere. The second largest industry in Mudharamsar was farming, and as such agricultural labour became the primary source of employment for the villagers. Being the largest landowners, many different Dalit communities in the village approached the Meghvals for work. Before the mine closures it was not uncommon for Meghvals to take on agricultural labourers from different low castes, for example during peaks in the agricultural season. However, since the closures they preferred to recruit other Meghvals and especially their kin. The Meghvals' favouritism for employing their relatives led to greater competition for agricultural jobs during this period, and many Dalits in the village were left with no work. Consequently, the activities of this landowning Meghval family came to dominate much of the conversation amongst other Dalit communities about strategies for coping with the

---

[3] I carried out detailed genealogies during my fieldwork and this powerful family were all from a Gotr known as Panwar said to be descended from heroic Rajputs that had fallen from grace.

[4] Tube wells are expensive to install in Bikaner as the water table can be over 250m below ground level. The wells are highly prized as they provide a constant flow of clean water.

Low-caste Elites and Re-traditionalised Responses   ॡ 187

economic insecurity of the time and how to develop opportunities for social mobility.

In response to the Meghvals' dominance over the economic realm of the village, other low and intermediate castes sought to construct alternative economic and social relations. These relations attempted to marginalise the Meghval by using normative discourses of the 'traditional' caste hierarchy aimed at placing the socially mobile Meghvals firmly at the bottom. What ensued were exchange practices led by the family of wealthy Prajapat Kumbhars. Similar to the Meghvals, the Kumbhar family own considerable lands in the village, however, their income is not dependent on this occupation. Instead, the Kumbhar hold government positions in the village *Panchayat*[5] and engage in private-sector work outside the village. Thus for the politically-active members of the Kumbhar family, ensuring Panchayat support from other Dalits in the village was central to the exchange practices they orchestrated. I call these 're-traditionalised' village exchange practices because they incorporated elements of Jajmani, for which a long heritage has been constructed both by commentators on South Asian rural society, and also by villagers themselves (Fuller 1989; Mayer 1993). As such, Dalits that participated in the exchange claimed higher caste status for themselves and overtly rejected the Meghval.

This chapter, then, has two aims. The first is to describe how both mobility and marginalisation can be experienced simultaneously in a context of economic uncertainty, and the second is to show how these social processes can be used to construct power relations between competing Dalit castes in the same locale. As such, my ethnography highlights how a group or community can experience both mobility and marginalisation on the one hand, but can also practice exclusion against another similarly situated group on the other. I argue that these conflicting experiences lead to a fragmentation of Dalit identity at the local level. The lack of a shared identity between the Meghval and Kumbhar is partly due to historical differences between the two main lineages in the village and the ways in which they have sought advancement, but it was the mine closures that helped to crystallise these differences in economic terms.

---

[5] The Panchayat is the village-level unit of political administration.

188 द *Jordan C. R. Mullard*

This chapter begins with an overview of the two elite families in the village, their background and current position. It then introduces the key actors in the village exchange and how the system operates. However, material from one village can only provide us with a partial view; by drawing on the work of other scholars it can signify wider themes. As such, the penultimate section contextualises the data within wider debates on the mobility and/or marginalisation of Dalits in contemporary India. Finally, the conclusion revisits the questions introduced at the start of the chapter and aims to draw all the themes described together.

The Meghval Landlords and the Kumbhar Jajmans

In this section I describe the Meghval and Kumbhar elite, how they reached their positions, current tensions and economic activity. In total, the Meghval population is almost double that of the Kumbhars (502 and 266 respectively). There are 141 Panwar Meghvals in the village of Mudharamsar, representing 28 per cent of the entire Meghval population. Of the 141, 95 individuals have traceable descent from the last known patriarchs, Mungla Ram Panwar and Kharna Ram Panwar. Both of these men were born in the mid-19th century and their descendents make up two of the original Meghval families in the village. This group can then be sub-divided between those who descended from Mungla Ram and those who descended from Kharna Ram. The descendants of Kharna Ram are poorer than those that descended from Mungla Ram. Moreover, there is a further division between those descended from Mungla Ram's first son, Moti Ram, and his second, more economically and politically mobile son, Rupa Ram.

The two brothers Mungla Ram and Kharna Ram Panwar were brought to the village in the late 19th century by the Paliwal rulers as Chamars to remove dead animals and tan leather and work as agricultural labourers. Mungla Ram was able to establish a strong relationship with the Paliwal rulers of the village, which brought him certain privileges such as a larger house and cultivable land. Fifty or so years later, in the late 1940s, Mungla Ram's second son, Rupa Ram, became involved in the great political upheavals and low-caste tenant demonstrations in Bikaner. These protests sought to challenge the

Low-caste Elites and Re-traditionalised Responses ꟼ 189

exploitative *Zamindar*–tenant relationship and establish greater equality for cultivators. Around the same time, local Chamars (leather workers) and other untouchable castes were beginning to establish a caste council to discuss matters affecting the caste and to develop remedies. To lose the connotations of removing dead animals, the prescribed basis of their untouchability, the council opted for all those present to be called Meghval, and henceforth the Meghval caste was born. As part of this movement, the council also ordained that no Meghval shall in future drag or skin dead animals. This decision coincided with the Zamindari and Biswadari Abolition Act (1959), which led to the redistribution of land and enabled a majority of the Meghvals in Mudharamsar to leave their traditional caste occupations to take up agriculture. The uptake of agriculture was so prolific amongst Meghvals that the sanctions imposed on those practicing their caste occupation were rarely employed. According to village records and a village survey carried out by the Government's Census of India team, the last known Meghval in the village to break this ban was a man named Udar Ram in 1959 who was charged ₹11 (Bhargava and Gupta 1965).

As agricultural labourers and cultivators for the Paliwal landlords, the Panwar Meghval family acquired their own land. According to my informants, in the early 1940s a majority of land was held by a high-caste Paliwal landlord in the village, Ramchandhan Paliwal. He owned a reputed 202 hectares of land, 6 hectares of which were cultivated by Rupa Ram's father, an ancestor of the current Meghval lineage.

The greatest victory of the tenant movement in Bikaner, according to one of Rupa Ram's sons, was the establishment of the Rajasthan Tenancy Act (1955), an Act designed to secure the rights of tenant farmers. According to the Panwar Meghvals, it was through this Act that their ancestors were issued with their first official tenancy agreement. The agreement stated they only had to give 33 per cent of the total crops harvested from this land as rent and that they were entitled to keep the remaining 67 per cent for themselves. This agreement, coupled with the passing of the Zamindari and Biswadari Abolition Act four years later, led to the transfer of 6 hectares of land from Ramchandhan Paliwal to Rupa Ram's father.

Similar to the Meghvals, the Kumbhars had been brought to the village to perform their traditional occupations and to work as agricultural labourers. Also in receipt of tenancy agreements and later official land titles, these early Kumbhars were able to secure a living for their families and educate their children.

They too received 6 hectares of land during the legislative changes. However, instead of the land being given to one family as it was amongst the Meghval, the Kumbhars had to divide their land between three brothers. The decision to give a full 6 hectares to one Meghval landlord and divide a further 6 between three Kumbhars caused tensions between these two groups. As such, the re-distribution of land amongst these two castes started a feud that has continued to the present day.

The newfound status of the Meghval and Kumbhar as large landowners and political elites in the early 1960s meant they were able to educate their children raise their income levels and gain economic stability. Rupa Ram Panwar's educational achievements and involvement in local politics, for example, enabled him to become the first Meghval MLA in Rajasthan. His legacy lives on, and four of his eight sons have reserved government jobs today. Through their landowning and employment advantages, this family of Meghvals was able to acquire more land, including fertile farms in the irrigated region of the Indira Gandhi Canal command area.

According to my informants' calculations, crops grown in the irrigated area yielded over three times that of similar crops grown on non-irrigated farms. The average revenue from crops grown is based on the total average annual yield of 1.92 quintal or 192 kgs per hectare on non-irrigated land and 6.3 quintal per hectare on irrigated land, as per my informants' calculations. Irrigated land thus produces approximately six times the yield of non-irrigated land. The general cost of crops vary each year depending on the type of crop, levels of seasonal rainfall, demand, and the best price that can be arranged at one of the three *maṇḍī* or corn exchanges in the region. Type of crop and corresponding price do vary slightly, but all hover approximately between ₹1800 to ₹2700 per quintal. The figures in Table 6.1 are based on an average of ₹2300 per quintal, irrespective of the type of crop grown. The overall net income of the Meghvals then is substantially higher than the income of other landowning families, and whilst their income is split between six households, it is still over double the amount which each Kumbhar household, for example, is likely to receive.

Low-caste Elites and Re-traditionalised Responses ਰ 191

Table 6.1
Ownership and Average Revenue Patterns for the Largest Landowning Castes and Families in the Village

Largest Landowners in the Village (Caste)	No. of Large Landowner Households	Total Land (in Hectares)	Average Annual Revenue Per Hectare Irrigated (in ₹)	Average Annual Revenue Per Hectare Non-irrigated (₹)	Total Annual Income (in ₹)
Meghval–Panwar	6	97.50	271,687.50	347,760.00	619,447.50
Kumbhar–Prajapat	3	27.61		121,925.76	121,925.76
Darzi	2	27.52		121,528.32	121,528.32
Rajput	1	27.50		121,440.00	121,440.00
Paliwal	4	19.51		86,156.16	86,156.16
Total	16	172.14	271,687.50	798,810.24	10,704,97.74

Source: Prepared by the author.

Having land in the irrigated region had greatly improved the family's income. For example, the Meghval family own a total of 97.5 hectares of land, 18.75 of which was in the irrigated region. This land, according to the family, yields on average ₹14,490 per hectare per year compared to ₹4,416 per year from non-irrigated land. Kumbhars held 27.61 hectares of land in the village which generated an income of ₹121,925 which compared to the ₹619,447 earned by the Meghval was considerably less. Both Darzi and Rajput castes also held a lot of land in the village.

The position of the two large Meghval and Kumbhar land-owning families in the village, however, are not just determined by how they relate to each other, but rather are shaped by how they relate to other villagers with whom they have contact, which in turn come to form the basis for competing status claims. The choice of workers to work the land varies amongst the landlords and this is where the key ruptures between workers and owners exist. The Meghvals tend to employ kin members to cultivate the land and only during the peak harvest time employ daily-wage workers from other castes. The landowning Kumbhars in the village, on the other hand, tend to employ kin labourers and individuals who have a close relationship with the Kumbhars, although not necessarily from the same caste. For example, the Dholi

192 ॡ *Jordan C. R. Mullard*

are employed as agricultural labourers by Kumbhar landowners, and although the Dholi do not see this work as their primary occupation, most of their regular income, since the mine closures, is actually derived from work in Kumbhar fields. Rarely do the Kumbhar landowners work in the fields themselves, unlike the Meghvals. Moreover, some Kumbhar workers prefer not to work on farms owned by the Meghval, preferring to work on Kumbhar or Darzi plots, citing concerns over respectability as their motivation. The Darzi and Rajput landowners employ a combination of daily-wage workers from in or outside the village and longstanding cultivators that have worked the land for several generations. As such, these workers occupy a different position to those that work in Meghval and Kumbhar fields and are therefore not included in the discussions of this chapter.

Ownership of high-yielding land as well as their political involvement marked out the Meghval family as being quite distinct from the Kumbhar landowners who descended from the three brothers given lands in the past. The Kumbhar family's wealth was instead derived more from private and more recently government sector employment than agriculture. Unfortunately, however, I was unable to obtain reliable income data for the private-sector workers. Anecdotally, one of the brothers owned a successful wedding planning and float hire business that seemed to cater to many of the surrounding villages.

Similar to the Meghvals, the Kumbhars were also involved in village politics; however, this was a fairly recent phenomenon. Even so, the Meghval and Kumbhar families have risen to become the dominant landowners and political elite of Mudharamsar today. Nevertheless, their approach to social mobility was quite different.

During the time of fieldwork, Kumbhars were categorised as OBC in Rajasthan's reservation system. Previously they were classified as SC and many believed it was their re-notification as OBC that had contributed to the increased level of economic and political competition between them and the Meghvals. Whilst I discuss the construction of OBC and SC status in detail elsewhere (Mullard [forthcoming]), the Kumbhars' identity as OBC has contributed to their claim that their caste is 'cleaner' than the Meghval. The competition between the village's two wealthiest families can be seen as part of well-documented

Low-caste Elites and Re-traditionalised Responses ॗ 193

SC–OBC conflict found across India, even though the causes of their antagonism in Mudharamsar has slightly different historical roots. Today both families compete for reserved government jobs and political positions in the village.

The Kumbhars occupy a rank marginally higher in the traditional order of castes to that of the Meghvals, and as such have been considered a 'clean caste' in other areas of Rajasthan (Chauhan 1967). However, the traditional occupation of the Kumbhars was previously considered polluting in some parts of India. But in today's tourist-conscious Rajasthan, Kumbhar pottery has been elevated to the position of a recognised traditional handicraft through government policy, and the Kumbhars in Mudharamsar have benefitted from this.

As such, the Kumbhars hold a unique position within the village. Previously they were regarded as low-status Dalits, yet today they act as patrons to those castes engaged in traditional occupations such as the Dholi (Dalit musician caste) and Sadh (an OBC sectarian caste of temple keepers). This is in marked contrast to the Meghval who although of a similarly lowly position in the caste hierarchy, do not engage in their caste occupation. The Kumbhars, therefore, have come to govern much of the village's service economy, whereas the Meghvals run the village's agricultural industry. Relations between the two lineages, Kumbhar and Meghval, are at times strained. At best they maintain a civil distance, at worst relations can be violent. For example, early on in my research, and shortly after the mines had closed, a couple of young Kumbhar men set out to steal the goats of a Meghval family. Upon being rumbled in the act, a ferocious fight broke out between the Kumbhars and Meghvals living in the neighbourhood. Many villagers speculated that the men had tried to steal the goat because they thought the Meghvals were becoming too powerful in the village. It did not seem to matter, however, that the man whose goat was stolen was actually quite a poor relative to the wealthy Meghvals. What became clear some time after the event was that the tension signified disquiet amongst the poorer relatives of the dominant Kumbhar family.

These poorer Kumbhars were industrial labourers when the mines were operational and only periodically got work in the fields during peaks in the agricultural cycle. When the mines closed, these workers had nowhere to go as their traditional occupations were already filled

194 ॺ *Jordan C. R. Mullard*

by Kumbhar families closer to the Kumbhar Jajmans and the Meghval landlords turned them down in favour of recruiting kin. Angry with the Meghval landlords, the Kumbhar Jajmans and the lack of work more generally, these Kumbhars turned to the industrial actions orchestrated by the Trade Union Congress and the Communist Party of India against the mining companies and the state. This action actually brought these poorer Kumbhars closer to other Dalit castes, including Meghvals not related to the Panwars, as a 'labour class'. This class shared the same experiences of unemployment and a lack of village connections.[6] Thus it was the Meghval and Kumbhar families' position as the primary recruiter of village labour during the mine closures that led to an accelerated re-evaluation of existing social relations in the village. Given the economic crisis in the village, this analysis focused, not only on material interests but also on ideological discourses of caste, duty, and obligation.

I call the responses of the Kumbhar Jajmani elite 're-traditionalised' because they involve a set of assumptions concerning who is entitled to participate in the exchange and who is not and these are drawn from understandings of the so-called pollution-line. The re-traditionalised responses show how certain castes and groups within the village re-evaluate status and identity in times of economic deprivation. Such responses show how the powerless revive or reconstruct conservative principles of caste and untouchability. In doing so, they actively marginalise those close in the traditional hierarchy whilst also seek to advance themselves through lowering their own status from the social relations that placed them there.

Mosse (1994), for example, shows how low castes adopt strategies that may lead to greater economic rewards while, compromising their status. In case of the exchange relations in Mudharamsar, Dalit castes are choosing to engage in degrading patronage relations that place them in a lower position to those who actually occupy a similar Dalit status. This is accompanied by a discourse that places a positive status value on that relationship by claiming it to be dutiful, honourable and

---

[6] I describe the 'labour class' in great detail in my thesis and intend to publish on this aspect of the data in the future.

Low-caste Elites and Re-traditionalised Responses ढ 195

embedded in the glory days of the past where these traits apparently mattered.[7] As such, even though they subordinate themselves within the exchange they do so by claiming it to be preferable in status to agricultural work, which in the context of the mine closures, they were excluded from.

Therefore, on the one hand, social mobility through the use of 'traditional' discourse can be regarded as empowering by Dalit actors and even more so in a context where other Dalit castes are themselves the patrons. Yet, it also has the effect, borrowing Peter Mayer's term of 're-enslaving', particularly the poorer Dalits, in such a way as to create a new form of labour relationship that rapidly comes to be seen as 'traditional' (Mayer 1993: 36) and therefore pre-determined. In this respect, wealthier Dalits are establishing new inequalities between previously equal actors that are informed by sentiments associated with their own historical subjugation, for which there was a ritual rationalisation. This was particularly observable in the relationship between the Kumbhar Jajmans and Dholi drummers.

Re-traditionalised Occupations: The Dholi and Kumbhar

In the following sections, I offer a more detailed description of the 're-traditionalised' relationships referred to earlier. What I aim to show is that the discourses used by the Dholi, Kumbhar and Sadh castes located the origins of their exchange relations in history and tradition presenting them as immutable, exclusive and 'traditional'. Furthermore, the Kumbhar Jajmans in particular used this discourse to marginalise their political rivals and create a new hierarchy of status between

---

[7] It is important to note that there is a long tradition of romanticising the past in Rajasthan and the descriptive works of James Tod (2002[1829]), a 19th-century British political agent, who first visited the state in 1818 have contributed a great to deal to this. These have come to form what Erdman (1985: 14) calls the 'Nostalgic-Romantic tradition' in Rajasthani culture. What is interesting is that usually this romanticising is predominantly heard amongst high castes; however, in Mudharamsar the evidence shows how Dalits have also adopted this discourse.

196 द *Jordan C. R. Mullard*

themselves and the Dholi. In some respects this mirrors the process of Sanskritisation first outlined by Srinivas (1971) where low castes adopt high caste practices or discourses for their practice. However, the form of 'Sanskritisation' in Rajasthan is quite distinct. Rather than mimicking high castes more generally, Dalits in Rajasthan focus on the characteristics and practices of the Rajputs. It is important to note that Rajput culture is not a homogenous set of practices; however, there are some distinct characteristics that are frequently replicated and envisioned as Rajput. For example, the perceived innate qualities of loyalty, duty and honour. There is a long tradition amongst Rajasthan's Dalits of actively 'Rajputising' their caste either in the form of heroic origin stories or in establishing client patron relations (Erdman 2001; Snodgrass 2006). I term such activities — the Rajputisation of the caste — which I argue in my doctoral thesis, is a distinctly Rajasthani pursuit.

Although actors located their exchanges in the past, many of them had only recently joined the exchange. Prior to the mine closures, services such as barbering, leading ritual events, pottery, and music were performed by individuals living in the nearby town or by roaming peddlers from other villages. For my informants, re-establishing and locating these 'traditional' relations in the village gave them status by extending their social network to include a broader range of individuals and a secure local income. The exchange was similar in kind to the Jajmani system described below (in an abbreviated form) by Kolenda (1967). I quote it here:

> Briefly, the Jajmani system is a system of distribution in Indian villages whereby high caste landowning families called Jajmans are provided services and products by various lower castes such as carpenters, potters, blacksmiths… Purely ritual services may be performed by Brahman priests and various sectarian castes, and almost all serving castes have ceremonial and ritual duties at their Jajman's births, marriages, funerals and at some of the religious festivals… the landowning Jajman pay the serving castes in kind… Payment may amount to a little of everything produced on the land, in the pastures and in the kitchen… In this system, the middle and lower castes either subscribe to each other's services in return for compensations and payments, or exchange services with one another (ibid.: 287).

Low-caste Elites and Re-traditionalised Responses ਰ 197

The exchange in Mudharamsar was organised in this way. The Nai as Barbers performed rituals for the Sadh, Kumbhar and Dholi (drummers). The Sadh had taken over the role of village priest and controlled the main temple and performed rituals during *Shivaratri* for the Kumbhar, Nai, and Dholi. The Dholi were asked to perform music for the Kumbhar, Nai, Sadh, and Paliwal during religious, ritual and life cycle occasions. These castes acted as the patrons and gave both monetary and symbolic remuneration. Symbolic remuneration was in the form of favours, loans, invitations to events, as well as the use of services by other family members in different villages. However, far from being highly systematised as some accounts of Jajmani would have us believe, the exchanges in Mudharamsar were in fact highly sporadic, extremely unsystematic and quite different to those described by Kolenda, if they ever were so systematised in the past (Fuller 1989).

For example, in practice many of those involved in the exchange would still seek the services of well-known suppliers outside the village and there was no system in place to contact local village suppliers other than by sending someone to the particular person's house. If they were not available, the patron would seek the services elsewhere. Moreover, although the Dholi cited their traditional occupation as their primary source of employment, in reality they were agricultural labourers working in the Kumbhar Jajmans' fields. However, what was important to my informants, particularly the Dholi and Kumbhar Jajmans, was not how successfully the system operated as a whole, but the significance they attributed to the exchange relationships.

Whilst several castes were involved in the exchange, the entire system was orchestrated and controlled by the wealthy Kumbhar family and it was the association with this powerful family that encouraged the involvement of certain groups. For example, being part of this system represented an advance for the Dholi, according to my informants. Unlike some of the other castes in the exchange, prior to the mine closures the Dholi had in fact been daily wage industrial labourers working alongside Meghvals and other Dalit castes. Employment in the mines offered very little job security. Dholi informants took great pride in their new relations with the Kumbhar Jajmans and looked to them for status. Moreover, the fact that they were actually being employed as agricultural labourers also provided an economic incentive to speak well

198 द *Jordan C. R. Mullard*

of the exchange relation. The maintenance of this relationship with the Kumbhar Jajmans, who were eager to marginalise the Meghval elite, was immediately one that set them apart from other Dalit groups, most of whom had been made unemployed during the mine closures and were still struggling to find work or build connections in the village.

For the Dholi, the exchange relations were not only a way to make advancements in ritual status vis-à-vis the discourse constructed by the Kumbhar, they also managed to secure themselves regular paid work in the fields. Although being clients in the exchange placed them in a subordinate position to the Kumbhar, they believed their ritual status was increased as they were engaging in a system that in the past they would have been excluded from. Moreover, when discussing their position in the exchange, the Dholi continuously referred back to their status vis-à-vis the Meghval who although had economic and political wealth, were also fairly politicised around their Dalit or ex-untouchable identity and did not seek advancements in status in the same way as the Kumbhar or Dholi. Instead, they sought to construct their own status through revaluating their religious identity as Bhakts of a fairly recently acculturated Hindu and fully Hinduised and Rajputised saint, Ramdev. Ramdev has a long tradition in Rajasthan, where he is seen as an Islamic Pir amongst Muslims, an incarnation of Krishna by Hindus and the first Dr Ambedkhar and saint of the Meghvals by Dalits.[8] In my thesis I argue this saint has become increasingly Rajputised over the years and thus adds significantly to the Rajput origin stories and interests in Sanskritisation of many Meghvals.

A male Dholi informant stated quite clearly, for example, that they did not play for Meghvals because they considered them to be of a lower status, even though they occupied a similar position within the traditional hierarchy. The Dholi's marginally higher position is verified by Chauhan (1967: 86) in his ethnography of the Rajasthani village of Ranawaton-Ki-Sadri, where, he tells us none of the castes, even the lowest in the village would accept food from the Dholi. Mayer (1966) in Ramkheri village had similar evidence of the Dholi's exclusion from high and even low castes. For example, he found that 'No *Harijan* would eat from the Dholi, none would smoke with them, nor

---

[8] See Dominique-Sila Khan (1994, 1996, 1998, 1999, 2003[1997]) for a detailed picture of this deity.

Low-caste Elites and Re-traditionalised Responses　ढ　199

craftsmen serve them. However, the Dholi were expected to serve all untouchables without distinction' (ibid.: 38–59). The fact that the Dholi now performed for higher castes and refused to serve Meghvals shows how the re-traditionalised exchanges have led the Dholi to orientate themselves more firmly toward castes they considered cleaner or of higher 'traditional' status than the Meghvals. They likened their services to the *adhikar* (privilege) of performing ritual functions for a patron and considered the work devotional as it brought them closer to god. In turn, they regarded it as a 'proper' form of employment as it was what they were 'meant' to do. Informants also mentioned that it brought them many advantages, such as providing closer relationships with more strategic actors in the village and support during difficult times. The Kumbhar were likewise interested in building relations with poorer villagers who they believed could help them galvanise political support in the village during election time. When asked about building good relations in the village, one Kumbhar informant stated: 'It is important to develop strong relationships with people in the village. These people need our support during this time and they will support us in the future when we need them'.

By engaging in these client/patron relationships my informants were, at least ideologically, expressing an attachment to the 'ritual' division of labour, even if it bore very little resemblance to it in practice. The Dholi on some level viewed the adoption of their traditional occupations as an historical imperative for their advancement. Conversely, the Meghvals of 30 or 40 years ago regarded the renunciation of their traditional occupations as necessary for social mobility, especially as those in Mudharamsar had already achieved some advancement. In this respect there was a conscious effort on behalf of the Dholi to 're-traditionalise' their practices as a way to gain social status and establish a new identity as a *kamin* (or specialist) that brought them closer to higher and more wealthy and powerful castes in the village.

Even though such a caste-based discourse fuelled discussion surrounding the exchange, the power dynamics involved were not as vivid as the discourse suggested. Rather than simply replicating hierarchical Jajmani relationships many of these individuals had previously worked alongside each other in the mines as equals. The system they had created, in fact bore little resemblance to any idealised system of exchange they intended to reproduce. For example, it was ill-managed and not

200 ☙ *Jordan C. R. Mullard*

systematically employed. Yet it was the power of the discourse, the economic security the new social relations afforded and political support the exchange proffered that were most significant.

In re-positioning themselves to fit an ideal model, however, the castes involved were on some level forced to reject their traditional ranking and adopt new and for some lower positions because they did not accurately fit the normative ideal. The Dholi in serving wealthy Kumbhar patrons had to accept a position lower than the Kumbhar in the 'traditional' ranking. In doing so, the previous class and caste equality found between the Kumbhar and Dholi in the mines had been broken down and reconstituted to place the Kumbhar landowners as 'Jajmans' in a position of clear authority over the Dholi (see Beidelman 1959). As such, the Kumbhars' higher class status was firmly embedded. Although caste and class status formed much of the discussion surrounding the exchange, the Dholi were also interested in the ideas of obligation, duty and honour that they believed those exchanges ideally encapsulated. These traits or *guna* are regarded as the innate qualities that characterise Rajputs.[9] Moreover, the fact that the exchange secured them an income during the time of the mine closures was also very significant and disputing their subordinate position could have led to their unemployment in the fields and exclusion as a client (see Breman 1993).

However, that is not to say that the hierarchical components were without value. The Dholi did see, for instance, their exchange relations as a form of social mobility that likened them to higher castes. For them, the restricted exchange of their traditional services was a form of advancement that enabled them to raise their status and alter their identity as they were now tied to the fate of more wealthy and symbolically elevated Kumbhars.

Replicating Caste Hierarchy or a Response to the Political and Economic Power of Dominant Castes?

The response of the Dholi in some ways conforms to the relations between untouchables that Moffatt (1979) describes. Moffatt (ibid.: 3) suggested that Untouchables or Dalits reproduce the dominant caste

---

[9] See Harlan (1992) for a detailed account of gunas amongst Rajputs.

Low-caste Elites and Re-traditionalised Responses ढ 201

hierarchy amongst themselves. In choosing the castes with whom to exchange their services, the Dholi made a clear statement about the value they placed on a particular arrangement of caste relations. However, instead of simply replicating their subordination in the caste hierarchy, the Dholi and others in the exchange sought to re-position themselves in the caste hierarchy in a way that redefined it altogether. Moreover, the success of the Dholi, Kumbhar, Nai, and Sadh in creating a semi-functioning set of exchanges depended on the others involved to also re-evaluate their caste position and follow the same rules of caste interaction that saw them subordinate themselves to the Kumbhar patrons. Similar to the cases highlighted by Mosse (1994) and Still (2009), the Dholi accept patronage and subordination in return for economic security during the mine closures. However, this bitter pill was somewhat sweetened by the status discourse that accompanies the exchange relations. As such, what they lost in status by subordinating themselves to other Dalits, they made up for in a reinvented symbolic hierarchy that placed them above some of the most affluent Dalits in the village, the Meghval.

This was a substantial break from the past, where a majority of the castes exchanging services during the research would have in fact provided services for the entire village and not just for a restricted few. Moreover, some such as the Dholi would have actually been excluded from any restricted exchanges that may have existed in the past.

The actions of the Dholi, however, were in fact closer to those observed by Deliege (1992). In reassessing Moffatt's argument (1979), Deliege showed that there need not be a link between replicating caste practices and conforming to the dominant caste hierarchy, as Moffatt proposed. Instead, Deliege suggested that those who replicate caste practices need not necessarily subscribe to the dominant caste hierarchy. For example, he emphasised that not only do Dalits not accept their position within the caste system, but cases of replication that do exist are more likely to be in response to the power of high castes rather than a consensus with the caste hierarchy. In fact, in Mudharamsar, Dalits were interested in constructing an entirely new hierarchy, that although drew on motifs of past caste relations, and certainly had Sanskritising and Rajputising elements served to assert an alternative arrangement in response to the growing power of the Meghvals.

202 ᵷ *Jordan C. R. Mullard*

The Dholi and Kumbhar were in fact responding to the dominant Meghval landlords rather than just responding to the power of high castes. As even though both the Meghval and Kumbhar had appropriated the power in the village, they did not view themselves as high caste and nor did they see themselves reproducing the caste hierarchy. In fact, the Meghval actively rejected the caste hierarchy and their previous position within it. The Kumbhar Jajmans used their patronage relationships with other castes as a way to assert their status in a changing context, where the Meghvals had risen to prominence. Thus by constructing a system of exchange that symbolically drew on caste principles; they could construct a ritual status for themselves that laid claim to a higher status than their largest political rivals the Meghval and the most obvious method for this was through appropriation of caste related status markers.

Beidelman (1959), in his early comparative study of Jajmani, showed that economic power in rural India is not only strongly related to political power, but it also correlates to the ritual status of local caste groups. As such, the Kumbhars re-creation of Jajmani necessarily involved some appraisal or re-appraisal of the caste hierarchy. However, this was achieved with very little reference to the existing high castes in the village that had diminished in number and did not have much involvement in village affairs. Instead, the Kumbhar had created an alternative caste hierarchy in which they positioned themselves paramount. That is not to say, however, that the Kumbhars had little to do with the remaining high castes. On the contrary, the wealthy Kumbhar family's houses were located near to the old area of the village where the higher castes lived and as a result had created strong links with the higher caste Paliwal families.

However, the few remaining high castes in Mudharamsar were relatively powerless in everyday life. Whilst castes like the Paliwal did still hold a symbolic power as the descendents of the former founders and rulers of the village, this was largely irrelevant in the governance of the village. For example, the Panchayat (village government) was dominated by the Meghval and Kumbhar between whom there were disputes over who occupied the position of *Sarpanch* or Panchayat leader. Similarly, a Sadh OBC family had taken over the main temple from the

Low-caste Elites and Re-traditionalised Responses द 203

Brahmins and consequently had become the ritual elite, even though members of the Meghval lineage took very little notice of them.

Somewhat dependent on the Kumbhars for political representation, the higher castes in the village gave their support to the Kumbhars. These castes benefitted from the symbolic capital the high castes continued to hold in the traditional caste hierarchy. Consequently, with such an alignment of interests the caste status and power of the Kumbhar were elevated in the eyes of the Dalit clients of the Kumbhars. The Kumbhar used this caste status as a form of opposition to the Meghval lineage and in doing so mobilised that capital to marginalise the Meghval elite and construct a position of power for themselves.

This newly constructed set of social relations was then a direct response both to the power of the Meghval lineage, and unemployment due to the mine closures, particularly for the Dholi. In the household survey I carried out, the Dholi preferred to state 'traditional services' as their main job, even though more of their working day was actually taken up with agriculture in the fields of the Kumbhar. This, along with the status discourse surrounding traditional work in the village revealed how they valued their traditional occupations above the cash in hand work in the fields.

Whilst the Meghvals recruited from a range of castes, they preferred to employ their kin. This resulted in the exclusion of the Dholi. Aware of this, the Kumbhar, employed by the Dholi to work on their land and in return for employment, assisted in generating political support for their patrons in village elections. Thus, the Dholi were more likely motivated by a desire for economic security than proving political superiority over the Meghval. Proving the political superiority of the Kumbhars was just an added bonus that helped to confirm their advancement. Significantly, the Kumbhars who had been employed alongside the Dholi in the mines had not been elevated in the same way as their wealthy non-miner caste mates. Instead, many of the working class Kumbhars had joined other ex-miners in the industrial action that followed the mine closures. Thanks to their organisation as a 'labour class', it was clear that these Kumbhars would never achieve the status of the powerful Kumbhars. As such, the ritual advance of the Kumbhar precipitated by the 're-traditionalised' Jajmani was largely due to their higher class status.

204 *द* *Jordan C. R. Mullard*

Consequently, Dalit mobility in Mudharamsar comes in three primary forms: the first is class mobility, characterised by landownership and political power. The second is heightened ritual status through the 're-traditionalised' Jajmani. The third is a combination of the two, which sees class merged with a discourse of ritual status to provide an immutable justification for an economic and political mobility that in turn marginalises their largest rivals, the Meghval.

Conclusion

What conclusions might we draw on the issue of mobility and marginalisation in Mudharamsar? What is clear is that Dalits in the village adopt a range of practices that see them unite as a group, redefine caste inequality and subordination, acquiesce to Dalit elites as a way to secure jobs, and choose to advance their own caste and family rather than unite with other Dalits. In a context where there is no formal caste hierarchy, Dalits are increasingly in competition with each other to secure economic advantages and status. At times, actors use their caste to their advantage, such as the Dholi who actively chose to subordinate themselves in a system of village exchange for economic rewards.

Contributing to questions of what happens to Dalit identity when Dalits own land, become affluent, economically secure and politically influential; through the lens of economic devastation my data highlights how competing interests of dominance and economic security see caste used as a way to fragment Dalit relations. As Ciotti (2006), Still (2009) and writers in this volume and beyond point out, caste is an identity that operates as a set of motifs that Dalits can use to refashion a space for themselves in the contemporary Indian society rather than a fixed category into which people are placed.

That is not, however, to ignore how powerful and pervasive the ideology is that sees untouchability as ascribed and immutable. Mosse (1994) argues, for example, that Dalit subordination or marginality is 'ideologically constitutive' of untouchable identity. In the large part this may explain why the Meghvals are so keen to advance their own caste and kin rather than form alliances with other Dalits that were perhaps historically slightly better off in the caste system. Forming alliances with such Dalits could see their improved status put to question. This was

Low-caste Elites and Re-traditionalised Responses र 205

perhaps a wise move in light of the relationships being forged between other Dalits in the village. The Kumbhar, for example, exploited the economic needs of poorer Dalits by offering economic stability in return for a caste-based subordination and political support. This shows how significant caste superiority was to the Kumbhar on the one hand and how persistent the practice of caste interdependency is today and particularly so in times of economic turmoil when ordinary jobs are lost.

In this instance, Meghval and Kumbhar elites experienced social mobility during the mine closures by maximising on the unemployment of the time. Amongst the Meghval this was experienced through their monopoly over agricultural labour and the Kumbhars' through their invention of a Jajmani system of exchange. However, the Meghvals' advancement was very much linked to economic development, whilst the Kumbhars gained their mobility through a symbolic status deemed 'traditional'. So what does this mean for a united Dalit identity? It is not surprising that there is little unity around what constitutes Dalitness in practice in the village. In fact, it was this internal fragmentation and fluidity that enabled actors to reposition themselves according to the perceptions they had of their own social context. In doing so, the very act of Dalit identity making in Mudharamsar becomes a political act as each actor involved attempts to have an effect on the established social order. As Meghval landlords often quoted:

'There is only one caste, Human Beings, it was Man that created caste not god'.

र

References

Beidelman, Thomas. 1959. 'A Comparative Analysis of the Jajmani System', *Monographs of the Association for Asian Studies*. Locust Valley, New York: Association for Asian Studies.

Bhargava, Raj. C. and Ganesh R. Gupta. 1965. *Madh (Kolayat Tehsil, Bikaner District)*, 14(6a). Census of India 1961.

Breman, Jan. 1993. *Beyond Patronage and Exploitation: Changing Agrarian Relations in South Gujarat*. New Delhi: Oxford University Press.

Chauhan, Brij R. 1967. *A Rajasthan Village*. Delhi: Vir Pub. House.

206   द *Jordan C. R. Mullard*

Ciotti, Manuela. 2006. 'In the Past We Were a Bit "Chamar": Education as a Self- and Community Engineering Process in Northern India', *Journal of the Royal Anthropological Institute*, 12(4): 899–916.

Deliege, Robert. 1992. 'Replication and Consensus: Untouchability, Caste and Ideology in India', *Man*, 27(1): 155–73.

Erdman, Joan L. 1985. *Patrons and Performers in Rajasthan: The Subtle Tradition*. Delhi: Chanakya Publications.

———. 2001. 'Becoming Rajasthani: Pluralism and the Production of Dhartī Dhorān Rī', in Karine Schomer, Joan L. Erdman, Deryck O. Lordrick, and Lloyd I. Rudolph (eds), *The Idea of Rajasthan: Explorations in Regional Identity*, pp. 45–79. Delhi: Manohar.

Fuller, Chris J. 1989. 'Misconceiving the Grain Heap: A Critique of the Concept of the Indian Jajmani System', in Jonathan P. Parry and Maurice Bloch (eds), *Money and the Morality of Exchange*, pp. 33–63. Cambridge: Cambridge University Press.

Gorringe, Hugo. 2005. *Untouchable Citizens: The Dalit Panthers and Democratisation in Tamilnadu*. New Delhi: Sage Publications.

Hardiman, David. 2007. *Histories for the Subordinated*. Oxford: Seagulls Books.

Harlan, Lindsey. 1992. *Religion & Rajput Women: The Ethic of Protection in Contem-porary Narratives*. Berkeley: University of California Press.

Khan, Dominique-Sila. 1994. 'Deux rites tantriques dans une communaute d'intouchables au Rajasthan'. *Revue de l'histoire des religions*, 211(4): 443–62.

———. 1996. 'The Kamad of Rajasthan — Priests of a Forgotten Tradition', *Journal of the Royal Asiatic Society*, 6(1), April.

———. 1998. 'Is God an Untouchable: A Case of Caste Conflict in Rajasthan. *Comparative Studies of South Asia, Africa and the Middle East*, 18(1): 21–29.

———. 1999. 'Sacrifice, Martyrdom & Samadhi in the Tradition of the Meghvals of Rajasthan'.

———. 2003[1997]. *Conversions and Shifting Identities, Ramev Pir and the Ismailis in Rajasthan*. New Delhi: Manohar.

Kolenda, Pauline M. 1967. 'Toward a Model of the Hindu Jajmani System', in George Dalton (ed.), *Tribal and Peasant Economies*. Garden City: New York: American Museum of Natural History.

Mayer, Adrien C. 1966. *Caste and Kinship in Central India: A Village and its Region*. Berkeley: University of California Press.

Mayer, Peter. 1993. 'Inventing Village Tradition: The Late 19th Century Origins of the North Indian "Jajmani System"', *Modern Asian Studies*, 27(2): 357–95.

Low-caste Elites and Re-traditionalised Responses ੫ 207

Moffatt, Michael. 1979. *An Untouchable Community in South India: Structure and Consensus.* Princeton: Princeton University Press.

Mosse, David. 1994. 'Idioms of Subordination and Styles of Protest among Christian and Hindu Harijan Castes in Tamil Nadu', *Contributions to Indian Sociology*, 28(1): 67–106.

Mullard, Jordan C. R. (2013). 'Reserving The Untouchable Line: Political Formations of Low Caste Identity in Rural Rajasthan, India', in Alpa Shah and Sara Shneiderman (eds), *Toward an Anthropology of Affirmative Action.* Nijmegen: Stichting Focaal.

Omvedt, Gail. 1994. *Dalits and the Democratic Revolution: Dr Ambedkar and the Dalit Movement in Colonial India.* New Delhi: Sage Publications.

Shah, Alpa. 2006. 'The Labour of Love: Seasonal Migration from Jharkhand to the Brick Kilns of Other States in India', *Contributions to Indian Sociology*, 40(1): 91–119.

Snodgrass, Jeffrey G. 2006. *Casting Kings: Bards and Indian Modernity.* Oxford: Oxford University Press.

Srinivas, Mysore N. 1971. *Social Change in Modern India.* Berkeley: University of California Press.

Still, Clarinda. 2009. 'From Militant Rejection to Pragmatic Consensus: Caste among Madigas in Andhra Pradesh', *Journal of South Asian Development*, 4(1): 7–23.

Tod, J. 2002[1829]. *Annals and Antiquities of Rajasthan: Or, the Central and Western Rajpoot States of India.* London: Routledge.

VII

Dalit Women Becoming 'Housewives'

Lessons from the Tiruppur Region, 1981–82 to 2008–09

Judith Heyer*

In much of South Asia, and elsewhere, women withdraw from work as incomes rise to increase the status of their households and the status of the communities of which they are a part. This withdrawal of women from the labour market as incomes rise is often associated with a deterioration in the position of women, involving an increase in the degree of their subordination within the household and a decrease in

---

*The research on which this paper is based has been funded by the UK Department of International Development (DFID, formerly ODA), the Oxford University Webb Medley Fund, the Leverhulme Trust and the Queen Elizabeth House Oppenheimer Fund, at various stages. The 2008–09 research has been funded as part of a project on the effects of the expansion of the garment industry in the Tiruppur region funded by a DFID-ESRC Research Award (RES-167-25-0296), a project in which Grace Carswell, Geert De Neve, and M. Vijayabaskar were also involved. The research could not have been done without the support of Dr V. Mohanasundaram, my interpreter and co-researcher for most of the fieldwork since 1981–82, and without the contributions of M. V. Srinivasan, Paul Pandian, Selva Murugan, Arul Maran, and Gowri Shankar who acted as research assistants at different stages in the field. The research has also benefited from discussions at seminars in Oxford and elsewhere, and from discussions particularly with S. Anandhi, P. Swaminathan, K. Nagaraj, M. Vijayabaskar, S. Jeyaranjan, Karin Kapadia, and Barbara Harriss-White. I owe a special debt of gratitude to Clarinda Still for comments on this particular paper which helped me to pursue some of the arguments further than I had done hitherto.

Dalit Women Becoming 'Housewives' ॄ 209

their autonomy. This may not always be the case, however. In the case discussed in this chapter women in poor households have been withdrawing from the labour market as incomes rise not because men have put pressure on them to do so, but because women themselves have chosen not to continue with work that is arduous, exploitative, and poorly paid — work that exposed them to double exploitation, outside the household as well as within.

A whole range of factors determine whether engagement in paid work is to women's advantage or not. In some contexts it is clear that it is. In others it is not. This chapter looks at a group of Dalit women who have withdrawn from paid work under conditions in which engagement in paid employment did not appear to be associated with more autonomy, more control, and higher status within the household.[1] It was clear that their withdrawal was positively beneficial in many respects. The chapter looks at the respects in which Dalit women benefited from withdrawing from paid work, and the circumstances in which this was so, bearing in mind the position taken in much of the feminist literature in which it is argued that withdrawing from paid work is generally detrimental as far as women are concerned.[2]

The focus of the chapter is decreased participation in paid work by Dalit women in an area in which the income-earning opportunities open to Dalit men have been increasing quite significantly.[3] Dalit women have been taking on less paid work as Dalit men have been earning more. Dalit men have been able to access better-quality employment as agricultural labourers as well as better employment opportunities outside agriculture. Dalit women have been able to access much less well-paid employment opportunities both as agricultural labourers and in non-agricultural work. It is in this context that the labour force

---

[1] The research on which this chapter is based did not focus directly on empowerment and autonomy. Kabeer (2001) cautions us on the evidence establishing changes in empowerment and autonomy which has to be treated with care.

[2] See Sen (1990) which still forms the basis of many such claims, and Kapadia (1995) making the case in a rural South Indian context in particular.

[3] Opportunities for Dalit men have not improved nearly as much as those for non-Dalit men though (Heyer 2013, 2014).

210 द *Judith Heyer*

participation of Dalit women has decreased and Dalit women have been taking on less paid work.

Taking on less paid work has not necessarily weakened the position of Dalit women within their households however. Earlier, the paid work they were doing was draining and associated with poor health and low energy levels. The fact that they had large numbers of children, and had difficulty provisioning their households, took its toll too. They were not in strong positions with respect to decision-making, and control over their own labour, within their households. Later, when they were doing less paid work, were in better health, had smaller numbers of children, and less difficulty provisioning their households, they appeared able to assert themselves within their households more than they could before, gaining more control over decision-making.[4]

Clearly it is often the case that a reduction in employment outside the household signifies a deterioration in the status of women, putting them back into a more patriarchal relationship within the household and reducing their autonomy.[5] The evidence presented in this chapter suggests that the link between reduced employment outside the household and a deterioration in the status of women relies on a whole range of conditions that do not always hold however.[6] The quality of work outside the household is a key factor. If the work that women do outside the household is arduous, involves long hours and low pay, and involves relationships with employers that are exploitative in other ways too, women can be more empowered, more autonomous without it than with it. If, on the other hand, the work that they undertake outside the household is not too arduous, and involves reasonable hours, and reasonable pay, then the opposite may be true. It is not only the quality of work outside the household that is relevant however.

---

[4] See Nitya Rao (forthcoming) for an example of research that pursues this issue in a locality nearby. Her paper explores the influence that women staying at home have over decision-making, comparing it with that of those doing paid work. Her data show some categories of women having more influence when not doing paid work, some less.

[5] There is a large body of research showing this both in India and elsewhere.

[6] This is well-trodden ground, see Geetha (2007); Kabeer (1996, 2001).

Dalit Women Becoming 'Housewives' ♂ 211

Other factors are important too. One such in the context discussed in this chapter is social policy. The availability of subsidised food; free school meals; maternity, accident and disability benefits; and pensions; have been important features in the context under discussion over the past decade or two. These factors have helped to limit the rise in the cost of living, and have reduced vulnerability, making it possible for women to manage without doing paid work. Another relevant factor is the change in social attitudes to the valuation of domestic work, particularly those associated with the increased importance attached to children, and children's education, which women's domestic work supports in important ways. Age-related social norms, caste norms, and gender ideologies, so different in south from those in north India, have played important roles in the context under discussion too.

The chapter focuses on a specific context in which changes in male and female employment opportunities and changes in social policy have been associated with changes in Dalit women's patterns of work using micro level data on labour force participation rates (LFPR) of Dalit women as well as other evidence as a basis for discussion.

The context is western Tamil Nadu in the 1980s, 1990s and 2000s. Over this period, in the region concerned, Dalit women's participation in the labour force has been declining. It should be noted that women's participation in the labour force has been declining more generally at the all-India level over this period too.[7] The decline may be particularly strong in Tamil Nadu whose combination of effective social policy and widespread urban and non-agricultural employment distinguishes it from other states in India. The chapter looks at the role played by a combination of factors specific to a particular region in Tamil Nadu over the last two decades of the 20th century and the first decade of the 21st century, in Dalit women's changing patterns of work.

The chapter focuses on the Tiruppur region in the 1980s, 1990s and early 2000s. Over much of this period the region was going through a process of industrialisation spreading into the rural as well as the urban areas. This was a region known earlier for its highly commercialised agriculture, based on an oppressive system of exploitation of Dalit labour (Heyer 2000). Industrialisation centred on knitwear manufacturing.

---

[7] See Mazumdar and Neetha (2011); Thomas (2012).

212 द *Judith Heyer*

Other textiles, engineering, plastics, metalworking and other light industries also played a part. The industrialisation was relatively decentralised and small-scale. The growth of industry was accompanied by a decline in agriculture. It was associated with a general rise in incomes, for labour as well as for capital.

A whole range of state welfare programmes gradually put in place over the 1980s, 1990s and early 2000s, also contributed to rising standards of living particularly among the poor. These programmes included increased state spending on education and health, the provision of subsidised food and other essential commodities, mid-day meals, maternity benefits, pensions and accident benefits, Dalit housing, and latterly the National Rural Employment Guarantee Scheme (NREGS). Tamil Nadu has had a particularly strong record with regard to state welfare provision, and has been increasing its spending on welfare throughout the period of neo-liberal economic reform (Vijayabaskar 2011; Heyer 2012).

The chapter uses 1981–82, 1996 and 2008–09 data to look at the changing patterns of work of Dalit women in villages in the region. In 1981–82, when the first survey was conducted, the villages were still predominantly agricultural and the agrarian structure was still strong. Virtually everyone in the villages was working in agriculture, or activities derivative of agriculture. By 1996, the year of the second survey, the villages had been drawn into the region's growing industrialisation. Significant numbers of men in the villages were working outside agriculture, many commuting to work elsewhere. By 2008–09, when the most recent survey was conducted, the numbers of men working outside agriculture had not changed, but more were working in manufacturing, less in trade and services. Significant numbers of women were working in manufacturing too.

One might have thought that Dalits would have benefited from changes that undermined the old agrarian structure and led to a movement into non-agricultural employment outside the villages. In practice the old agrarian structure loosened its grip, though not nearly as much as might have been expected (Heyer 2000, 2010). Members of Dalit communities moved much more slowly out of agriculture than members of non-Dalit communities. The old hierarchies had been weakened but were still very much in place in the midst of all the change.

Dalit Women Becoming 'Housewives' द 213

In 1981–82 Dalit women were putting in long hours of work for very low pay: they could not manage their households on the earnings of their husbands (and/or sons) alone. They suffered from exploitation both inside and outside the household, the two sources of exploitation reinforcing each other. The fact that they were drained by work outside the household meant that they were less able to stand up to their husbands at home; the fact that they were under pressure at home meant that they were less able to stand up to their employers too. Far from employment outside the household strengthening their position within the household, it got weakened. It was physically depleting and the income it brought in was very low. Their outside employment was too arduous and too poorly paid.

As Dalit households became better off, in the 1980s, 1990s and early 2000s, Dalit women no longer had to put in long hours for low pay at some of the most vulnerable stages of their lives, through pregnancy and childbirth, and when their children were very young, as well as in old age. In 1981–82 Dalit women bemoaned the fact that they had to send their children out to work because they were burnt out by the time their children were old enough earn. Their work all through pregnancy and childbirth and when their children were still very young had taken its toll. By 2008–09 Dalit women were withdrawing in connection with pregnancy and childbirth, and to look after their children when they were young. They were going back to paid work and/or doing more paid work when their children were older and in school. Many were stopping paid work earlier in old age too. It was significant that the kind of paid work in which they were involved, agricultural labour, meant that they could enter and leave the paid labour force and they could also choose how many days of paid labour they did per week.

The position taken in this chapter is that Dalit women's withdrawal from paid work at crucial stages in their lives is a positive step given the poor quality of paid work available to them. It was a distinct improvement over the situation in which they had to put in all the work they could to make ends meet until they had children old enough to go out to work as well. As the earnings of their husbands increased, and state support limited the rise in the cost of provisioning their households, they no longer had to do this. It is also important to recognise, however,

214　द　*Judith Heyer*

that women would have been much better off had they also had better quality sources of income themselves.

The chapter proceeds by first introducing the villages and the data. It then looks at the way in which Dalit women's patterns of work changed between 1981–82 and 1996, and between 1996 and 2008–09, and the changing socio-economic environment that made this possible. The chapter concludes with a discussion of the inter-relationship between the different factors involved.

The Villages and the Data

The data on which the chapter is based come from surveys conducted in 1981–82, 1996 and 2008–09, additional interviews done in conjunction with the surveys, and additional interviews in 2003, 2004, 2010, 2011, and 2012. The 1981–82 data come from interviews with members of a 20 per cent sample of households in seven hamlets in two revenue villages.[8] The villages were known in 1981–82 for the strength of their agriculture and for being relatively 'remote', not on a main road. The 1996 data were collected from the descendants of 1981–82 sample households still resident in the villages in 1996 (Heyer 2010). The 2008–09 data were collected from a newly-selected 20 per cent sample of households in the same hamlets and revenue villages, as part of a project on the effects of the expansion of the knitwear industry in the Tiruppur region.

The study villages are 20–30 km north-west of Tiruppur, and 50–60 km north of Coimbatore. Tiruppur is the centre of a knitwear industry that has been very dynamic since the mid-1980s. Coimbatore is the older industrial centre that used to be known for its large textile mills and is now dominated by engineering and other industries as well as hospitals, colleges, and software units.

In the early 1980s the elite in the study villages were small-scale Gounder, Naidu and Chettiar agriculturalists running profitable

---

[8] I did a large number of the 1981–82 interviews, with the help of Dr V. Mohanasundaram who acted as my interpreter most of the time. In subsequent surveys M. Srinivas, Paul Pandian, Selva Murugan, Arul Maran, and Gowri Shankar also interpreted for me on occasion. They did interviews on their own as well.

Dalit Women Becoming 'Housewives' ₫ 215

commercialised operations. Members of these three groups made up 56 per cent of the households in the study villages and owned 92 per cent of the land (Heyer 2000, 2010). The majority of agricultural labourers, most of them landless,[9] came from two main Dalit[10] communities — Arunthathiyar and Pannadi.[11] They made up 30 per cent of the households and owned 1 per cent of the land. Other caste groups were represented in small numbers. They included small and marginal farmers and households involved in services and trade. Dalits were subject to serious stigmatisation and discrimination in 1981–82. Untouchability practices were still very strong (ibid.).

Women were very differently positioned in different castes in these villages. The majority of Dalit women worked as agricultural labourers in 1981–82. The majority of non-Dalit women contributed to household production, including agriculture and a few services. A minority of non-Dalit women in poorer households worked as labourers as well.

In 1996 the proportion of Dalits in the village population had risen but they still owned only 1 per cent of the land (Heyer 2010). Dalits were more dominant in the agricultural labour force with fewer non-Dalits working as agricultural labourers. Non-Dalits, and a few Dalits, had been entering non-agricultural occupations associated with industrialisation. The agrarian elite were no longer as dominant as before. By 2008–09 Dalits made up 40 per cent of the household population as non-Dalits had moved out in greater numbers than Dalits (Heyer 2014). The majority of Dalits were still agricultural labourers, but more Dalits had been moving into manufacturing than before. Dalit women were now entering manufacturing in small numbers as well.

Significant numbers of Dalit women, and fewer non-Dalit women, still worked as agricultural labourers in 1996. The majority of non-Dalit

---

[9] Apart from house sites which they owned.

[10] The category 'Dalit' is used in much of this paper to refer to the two main labourer groups, Arunthathiyars and Pannadis, and excludes the small number of Dalits in trade and service households.

[11] Arunthathiyars, otherwise known as Madaris, Chakkiliyars, are generally regarded as the lowest status of the three largest Dalit groups in Tamil Nadu. Pannadis, otherwise known as Devendras, or Pallars, are generally regarded as the highest status of the three.

216 ଟ *Judith Heyer*

women worked in household enterprises of various kinds. By 2008–09, some Dalit as well as non-Dalit women were working in manufacturing. The majority of Dalit women in productive employment were still agricultural labourers and the majority of non-Dalit women were working in household enterprises still.

1981–82 to 1996

In 1981–82, when fieldwork was first undertaken in these villages, more than 80 per cent of the working population was engaged in agriculture (Heyer 2000, 2010). A relatively successful, confident community of Naidu, Gounder and Chettiar *thottam farmers*[12] employed large numbers of labourers working long hours on terms and conditions that were harsh. Virtually all of the members of the two main Dalit groups in the workforce were agricultural labourers. Arunthathiyars were heavily involved in the tied labour (*pannayal*) system, in close relationships with thottam farmers and subject to a strictly enforced system of discrimination and untouchability in the villages at large. Most Arunthathiyars lived in tight-knit households in which all members of the household were obliged to work for the employers of the household heads. Pannadis, the other main Dalit group, worked as migrant sugar cane crushers all over Coimbatore district, as well as casual labourers in the villages. This gave them more independence from the village elite and substantial connections to the outside world. It also meant that many Pannadi women were used to managing their households on a day to day basis in the absence of the men.

In 1981–82 the village agricultural elite still dominated economic, social and political relationships to a very significant degree. The state also supported the agrarian elite (ibid.). Dalits' access to the state was indirect, through the agrarian elite.

Nearly all Dalit men in the two main Dalit labourer groups in the study villages worked as agricultural labourers in 1981–82. The majority of Dalit women worked as agricultural labourers too, taking very little time off for pregnancy, childbirth, or to look after young children.

---

[12] Thottam farmers were farmers with enough well-irrigated land to employ permanent labourers at the time.

Dalit Women Becoming 'Housewives' ┩ 217

The majority of Dalit women also did domestic work — buying food, fetching water, and firewood, cooking, cleaning, as well as looking after children, and the old, and the sick. Some Dalit families were still very large — there were nine or 10 surviving children in several cases in the sample in 1981–82. Once their children were old enough to go out to work, Dalit women withdrew to some extent from paid work, doing fewer days per week. Only a few stopped paid work altogether though. Very few Dalit women described themselves as 'staying at home' in 1981–82, unless they were incapacitated in some way. The sheer drudgery of their lives was very striking at the time.

Child labour was the norm among Dalits in these villages in 1981–82: 50 per cent of Dalit boys between the ages of five and 14 years were either herding livestock for their own households (a minority)[13] or working for others as agricultural labourers, most as pannayals. Many Dalit girls worked as casual agricultural labourers as well as doing domestic work. Less than 5 per cent of 5–14 year old Dalit girls, and 10–15 per cent of 5–14 year old Dalit boys, were in school. Sending children out to work did not do much more than cover their costs when they were young. As they got older the contribution that children made to the household budget rose, raising the opportunity cost of sending them to school.

Dalits lived in colonies that were overcrowded in 1981–82, with poor facilities, and squalid public space. The majority of their houses were constructed of mud, wattle and thatch. A few, financed either by employers, or in a very few cases by the state, had brick walls and tiled rooves. Water was a major problem. Dalit women had to rely on non-Dalit women to fill their pots from the main village wells, some distance from their own homes. The caste discrimination from which Dalits suffered included restrictions on the use of other facilities and space in the main villages outside the colonies in 1981–82 too (ibid.).

In 1996 agriculture was no longer nearly as dominant as it had been in 1981–82. Industry had expanded, reaching out into the countryside and the development of transport and communications had made it possible to commute to industrial and other non-agricultural work.

---

[13] There were relatively few livestock in these Dalit communities.

218 ढ *Judith Heyer*

A substantial proportion of the male, but not female, labour force was employed outside agriculture, large numbers commuting to work outside the villages. The proportion of Dalits working outside the villages was much smaller than the proportion of non-Dalits though (Heyer 2010). The majority of male and female Dalits were still agricultural labourers, albeit employed on terms that were considerably better than before. There had been a general increase in incomes, including those of agricultural labourer households. There had also been a general increase in state services and programmes.

The occupational distributions for male and female Dalits and non-Dalits in 1996 and 2008–09 are shown in Table 7.1. There are a number of points to note about the table. Firstly, there are significantly more men than women. There may have been some under-enumeration of women, but there is undoubtedly a real difference here too.[14] A second point to note about the table is the fall in the numbers of non-Dalits living in the villages. There was a small amount of outmigration of Dalits too. There were significant numbers of missing observations where women's occupations were concerned in 1996.[15] There is no reason to think that the percentages reported are not valid though.

The workforce includes those involved in 'productive' activities, those involved in 'domestic' activities, and the small numbers of men describing themselves as unemployed. The labour force includes those involved in 'productive' activities and the unemployed. Labour force participation rates, the percentages of the total population in the labour force, were 53.5 per cent for all women, 56.2 per cent for Dalit women, and 52.4 per cent for non-Dalit women. (The corresponding figures for men were 69.6 per cent, 72.7 per cent and 68.1 per cent respectively.) The differences between Dalit and non-Dalit women's labour force participation rates are not as great as one might have expected. It has to be borne in mind however that what counted as labour force participation for non-Dalit women was primarily work in household production, whereas what counted as labour force participation for Dalit women was agricultural labour and/or other waged work.

---

[14] There was a clear adverse sex-ratio in these villages (Heyer 1992).

[15] This was 17 per cent in the case of Dalits, and 8 per cent in the case of non-Dalits.

Table 7.1
Male/Female and Dalit/Non-Dalit Occupational Distributions: 1996 and 2008–09

Col. %	All Males		All Females		Dalit Males		Dalit Females		Non-Dalit Males		Non-Dalit Females	
	1996	2008–09	1996	2008–09	1996	2008–09	1996	2008–09	1996	2008–09	1996	2008–09
Own Agriculture	19	23	31	13	1	1			29	37	44	22
Livestock Keeping	3	2	4	4	2	1	2	3	3	2	5	4
Agricultural Labourer	28	30	31	25	65	66	74	53	8	8	13	8
Garments	9	21	1	7	4	16		8	12	24	1	6
Powerloom	3	2	1	0	4	4	1	0	2	1		
Other Non-agricultural	31	17	7	5	18	7	2	1	37	23	9	8
All in Non-domestic Employment	92	94	73	54	94	95	78	65	91	94	71	47
Domestic Work Only			26	46			22	35			29	53
Unemployed	8	6			6	5			9	6		
All Workers	100	100	100	100	100	100	100	100	100	100	100	100
LFPR	436	380	372	368	150	146	110	143	286	234	262	225
Total No. of Workers in Sample	69.6	66.3	53.5	41	72.7	65.9	56.2	47.7	68.1	66.6	52.4	36.6

Source: Village surveys, 1996, 2008–09.

220 द *Judith Heyer*

In 1996, 65 per cent of Dalit men in the workforce were still working as agricultural labourers (Table 7.1), for wages that were two to three times as high in real terms than they had been in 1981–82.[16] This contrasts with over 90 per cent working as agricultural labourers in 1981–82. Significant numbers of Dalit men were also working outside agriculture in 1996, unlike in 1981–82. There was only one Dalit man in the sample engaged in own account agriculture in 1996.

In addition, 74 per cent of Dalit women in the workforce were still working as agricultural labourers in 1996, receiving on average 50 per cent of the wages received by men for casual labour.[17] A very small number of Dalit women in the sample were working outside agriculture in 1996 (in construction, in a power loom unit, and as an assistant in a workshop). The remaining 22 per cent described themselves as 'housewives', 'staying at home', or 'not working'.

Women were described as 'housewives' in 1996 if they were married women only doing 'domestic' work. Older married women who were similarly placed described themselves as 'not working'. Unmarried women described themselves as 'staying at home'. All of these women would normally be involved in domestic work. The 22 per cent of Dalit women describing themselves as 'housewives', 'staying at home' or 'not working' in 1996 compares with 29 per cent of non-Dalit women. It is significant that being 'housewives' was an option for Dalits in 1996, unlike in 1981–82. Women with young children spoke proudly of

---

[16] Daily agricultural wages for men were ₹5, ₹6 and ₹7 in 1981–82. In 1996 they were ₹40, ₹45, ₹50. This represents an up to 200 per cent increase using the Coimbatore rural rice price, and up to 175 per cent using the consumer price index for agricultural labourers (CPIAL). See the *India Labour Journal* for the source of both the rice price and for the CPIAL. This overstates the real rise though. There are a number of items of increased expenditure that are not included in the CPIAL, including things like health care, etc. Patterns of expenditure have changed much more dramatically in Tamil Nadu than in other parts of India, with many new items being regarded as necessities now.

[17] This might have been seen as an improvement on 1981–82 when Dalit women's wages were nearer to 40 per cent of men's, but men were also doing contract labour in 1996. This meant that their average wages were higher than the daily wage figures suggest.

Dalit Women Becoming 'Housewives'   ॐ   221

being able to look after the children properly until they went to school. Others spoke of not having the double burden of work. A number of Dalit men said that they liked their wives staying at home too, 'to cook proper meals' among other things. The domestic labour that was a major part of Dalit women's lives was in some ways easier, in some ways more demanding, than it had been earlier. Access to water was easier and there was less difficulty procuring food, but standards were higher — there were more clothes to be washed, and food was more elaborate, etc.

Also significant as far as women were concerned was the decline in fertility. By 1996, the numbers of surviving children per couple had declined substantially both among Dalits and among non-Dalits.[18] Having fewer pregnancies, and fewer children to bring up, also contributed to improvements in Dalit women's health and well-being over time.

There was much less child labour in 1996 than there had been in 1981–82. Only 25 per cent of boys aged 5 to 14 were still herding or going out to work, and only 5 per cent of girls. 50 per cent of 5–14-year-old Dalit boys and 65 per cent of 5–14-year-old Dalit girls were in school. There had been an expansion in state funding for education. Initiatives like free school meals, and free school uniforms and books, had helped as well (Kajisa and Palanichamy 2010). It was significant that households had been able to accommodate the loss of income associated with no longer sending their children out to work and still remain better off with respect to such things as consumer goods, clothing and utensils. What made this possible was the two- to three-fold increase in daily wages in agriculture, though the increase in earnings was less as days worked were fewer in 1996 than in 1981–82.

Dalit colonies also improved between 1981–82 and 1996 (Heyer 2010). New colonies being planned in 1981–82 were up and running in 1996. They were more spacious and the houses were constructed out of better quality materials. There was also provision for individual

---

[18] The majority of Dalit couples in the sample had three to six surviving children (with a mode of 4) in 1981–2, and one to five (with a mode of 3) in 1996. These numbers are for surviving children only and include children born some time ago as well as children born more recently.

222 ≺ Judith Heyer

electricity connections. There were improved public services including water and street lighting. The better-quality housing and improved services had a major impact on Dalit lives, particularly those of Dalit women and children who spent so much more time in the colonies than men.

A number of other state policies introduced in the 1980s had strengthened the position of women (and children) in the villages too. The Integrated Child Development Services (ICDS) provided support and supplementary feeding to pregnant women and children, together with crèche facilities for three- to five-year-olds. Maternity benefits helped too, as did the noon, later mid-day meals scheme in schools.[19] There were pensions for widows, and deserted wives, and although the coverage was only partial, these sent valuable signals too. The public distribution system (PDS) which was a flagship scheme in Tamil Nadu provided subsidised food and essential commodities. This was already in place in a limited form in 1981–82. It had expanded substantially by 1996 significantly reducing the difficulty Dalit women had provisioning their households (Government of India 2005; Heyer 2010).

To summarise: Significant numbers of Dalit women were 'staying at home', 'not working', and/or being 'housewives', at some of the most vulnerable stages of their lives in 1996, unlike in 1981–82. As important, in 1996, were higher incomes, better living conditions, and fewer children. It was also very significant that there was less child labour. The next generation of children were getting a much better start.

1996 to 2008–09

In 2008–09 similar numbers of Dalit men were still working as agricultural labourers, earning higher wages than before, and there were still only one or two engaged in own account agriculture. However more of those working outside agriculture were in manufacturing, less in trade and services. More Dalit women were working in manufacturing too.

---

[19] The 'Chief Minister's nutritious noon-meals scheme' for children in schools was introduced in the rural areas of Tamil Nadu in 1984. This was an early pre-cursor of the mid-day meals scheme that was introduced at the national level in the early 2000s.

Dalit Women Becoming 'Housewives' ₫ 223

There had been a further rise in incomes since 1996, but this was not as great as that between 1981–82 and 1996 when the village economy first became integrated into the regional economy. There had also been a further expansion of social policies benefiting Dalits. Dalits were getting a voice through the revitalised panchayati raj institutions (PRIs) as well.

Labour force participation rates had fallen very significantly, from 53.5 per cent to 41.0 per cent for all women; from 56.2 per cent to 47.7 per cent for Dalit women; and from 52.4 per cent to 36.6 per cent for non-Dalit women. Dalit women's labour force participation rates were now well below those recorded by non-Dalit women in 1996. (Male labour force participation rates had also fallen, but not as much: from 69.6 per cent to 66.3 per cent for all men; from 72.7 per cent to 65.9 per cent for Dalit men; and from 68.1 per cent to 66.6 per cent for non-Dalit men.) One of the reasons for the fall in labour force participation rates was that more were in education for longer.

The majority of Dalit men in the workforce were still agricultural labourers (Table 7.1), working fewer hours for higher wages than in 1996.[20] Many worked for part of the year outside the study villages, to supplement the work available within the villages. Work was less regular even so and sometimes combined with construction when there was not enough work in agriculture. The proportion of men engaged solely in non-agricultural occupations had barely changed between 1996 and 2008–09.

A smaller proportion of Dalit women in the workforce were working as agricultural labourers. The male/female wage gap in agriculture had increased between 1996 and 2008–09; 8 per cent of Dalit women in the workforce were now working in the knitwear sector. This was a recent departure in 2008–09. All of those involved were young unmarried women.[21] Whereas virtually all the Dalit women working outside agriculture were working in the knitwear sector in 2008–09,

---

[20] Daily agricultural wages increased by roughly 20 per cent in real terms between 1996 and 2008–09. The CPIAL is used as a deflator here. If one takes into account the fact that most men's work was on contract in 2008–09, the increase in their wages is nearer 35 per cent. The increase was much lower than the increase between 1981–82 and 1996 either way.

[21] Unlike women living in Tiruppur town that feature in De Neve (2012).

224 ठ *Judith Heyer*

Dalit men were also working in powerloom units, and in petty trade, construction, spinning mills, engineering, low-level government, etc.

More women described themselves as 'housewives', 'staying at home', or 'not working' in 2008–09 than in 1996. Whereas in 1996 only 22 per cent of Dalit women in the workforce had so described themselves, the proportion in 2008–09 was 35 per cent. Meanwhile, the proportion of non-Dalit women so describing themselves in 2008–09 had risen to 53 per cent. These represent very significant increases in withdrawals from 'productive' work since 1996. The 'domestic work' on which they were now engaged full-time had become easier in some respects — water was more plentiful and nearer by, there were better PDS supplies, some people were cooking with LPG, and some were using mixi-grinders to prepare food. Fertility rates had come down further too.[22] In other ways domestic work had become more demanding though, as standards continued to rise.

The age distributions of female occupations are shown in Table 7.2. It was difficult to get reliable data on ages so these should be treated as rough approximations. The general patterns shown in the table are revealing nevertheless and supported by more casual evidence too. The proportion of Dalit women only engaged in domestic work is relatively high in the 15<30 age group when many are getting married, pregnant and/or looking after young children. It falls in the 30<45 age group by which time children are going to school. It rises again in the 45<60 age group, and then peaks in the 60+ age group, 60 per cent of whom were only engaged in domestic work; 26 per cent of the 60+ age group were still working as agricultural labourers though, many with few other means of support. The pattern is very different among non-Dalits. The proportion of non-Dalit women only doing domestic work is relatively high in the 15<30 age group (though not as high as in the Dalit case as more non-Dalits in this age group were in college or school). It rises in the 30<45 age group which is when the proportion among Dalits falls. It then stays at the same level in the 45<60 age group, and goes on to peak at 81 per cent in the 60+ age group. Less than 20 per cent of non-Dalit women aged 60+ were engaged

---

[22] The majority of Dalits had one to three surviving children, with a mode of two in 2008–09.

Table 7.2
All Females 2008–09

Row %	Young	At School	Domestic	Knitwear	AL	Livestock	Agriculture	Other	All	Sample Nos*
0<5	100								100	22
5<15		97	1	1					100	66
15<30		26	35	15	21		1	1	100	117
30<45			30	5	37	4	20	5	100	128
45<60			38		21	8	21	11	100	71
60+			77		7	2	9	5	100	81
All	5	20	35	5	19	3	10	4	100	485

Source: Village Surveys, 2008–09.

Note: *Excluding those with missing data here.

Table 7.3
All Dalit Females 2008–09

Row %	Young	At School	Domestic	Knitwear	AL	Livestock	Agriculture	Other	All	Sample Nos*
0<5	100								100	12
5<15		94	3	3					100	34
15<30		12	39	15	32			2	100	65
30<45			12	2	83	2			100	48
45<60			29		64	7			100	14
60+			64		27	9			100	22
All	6	21	26	6	39	2		1	100	195

Source: Village Surveys, 2008–09.

Note: * Excluding those with missing data here.

Table 7.4
All Non-Dalit Females 2008–09

Row %	Young	At School	Domestic	Knitwear	AL	Livestock	Agriculture	Other	All	Sample Nos*
0<5	100								100	10
5<15		100							100	32
15<30		44	31	15	8		2		100	52
30<45			40	6	9	5	33	8	100	80
45<60			40		11	9	26	14	100	57
60+			81				12	7	100	59
All	3	19	41	4	6	3	17	6	100	290

Source: Village surveys, 2008–09.

Note: *Excluding those with missing data here.

228 ढ़ *Judith Heyer*

in 'productive' work. All of this was within the household too. All in all, considerably higher proportions of Dalit than non-Dalit women were engaged in 'productive' activities at all stages. The 'productive' work of Dalit women was also generally more demanding than that of non-Dalit women.

There was virtually no child labour in the study villages in 2008–09. Virtually all Dalit children aged 5–14 years were in school, the majority on track to complete secondary as well as primary schooling. Dalit households were focusing on children in 2008, seeing children, and children's education as an investment in the future. Women's domestic work is key here, supporting children's performance in school. The fact that many non-Dalit children were in private schools gave Dalits a stronger role in state schools, reducing the discrimination to which they were subjected there. Very few Dalits were in private schools. Untouchability was no longer explicitly practised in village schools in 2008–09. Its explicit practice had only been abolished relatively recently though.[23] There were still cases of discrimination in a neighbouring High School which some Dalit children from the villages attended however.

There were several Dalits from the villages in higher education in 2008–09. There were none who had got anywhere near this in 1981–82, and only one or two in 1996. There were more girls than boys among those in higher education in 2008–09 too. This raised real possibilities of upward mobility. Reservations that gave Dalits preferential access to government employment made post-SSLC qualifications attractive, enabling them to go on to apply for government employment in schools and elsewhere. Experience in surrounding areas had given them reason to expect success here, unlike in other parts of India,[24] or even in Chennai now too.[25]

---

[23] The Ambedkar People's Movement had successfully lobbied for the abolition of separate seating, and separate drinking vessels in schools in the study villages, in 1998. Other forms of discrimination and untouchability were abolished more slowly though.

[24] This was a real possibility in this context unlike in other contexts. See Jeffrey et al. (2008).

[25] I am grateful to Karin Kapadia for raising this point.

Dalit Women Becoming 'Housewives' द 229

There were more Dalit housing colonies in 2008–09 and still more were being planned. The colonies were cleaner, healthier and more spacious than they had been in 1996, and quite unrecognisable compared with what they had been in 1981–82.

Revived village panchayats had been in place for some time by 2008–09, with their systems of reservations for Dalit women, Dalit men and non-Dalit women. They had been established shortly after the 1996 fieldwork, following elections in October 1996. They made a substantial difference to the position of Dalits, raising their visibility, enabling them to make themselves heard and to be treated with somewhat more respect. Increased representation had not led to the abolition of untouchability practices however. Hotels and tea-shops still practised the two-tumbler system,[26] and there were strict rules about where Dalits sat and moved in the hotels and tea-shops as well as in the farm compounds in which many Dalits worked.

Women's self-help groups (SHGs) were actively promoted in the study villages in 2000–01 when a local NGO received state funding to start a number of groups, including several consisting only of Dalit women. The NGO funding was not sustained however and the situation soon lapsed into a pattern in which groups came and went, none continuing for long enough to build up to anything very substantial. SHGs which might have been expected to contribute to Dalit women's self-employment opportunities were not doing this in the study villages in 2008–09. A coir project introduced in the early 2000s was another initiative that was similar to the SHGs, and also short-lived. It ran for a year or two and then closed down.

The coverage of the ICDS, maternity benefits and pensions had increased by 2008–09. The first health centre had been established in one of the study villages too. The PDS had also expanded further, to include more commodities, and higher subsidies. In 2008–09 people

---

[26] The two-tumbler system in which separate drinking vessels are kept for Dalits has been the subject of protest in many parts of Tamil Nadu. The system had been abolished in one of the neighbouring villages to the study villages but Dalits in the study villages had not been successful in getting it abolished there.

230 ☡ *Judith Heyer*

commented on the impact it was having on the amount of paid work that both women and men needed to do.[27]

The NREGS is the most recent development holding out promise for Dalit women. There were earlier employment generation programmes but none as comprehensive or as accessible to Dalit women as this. The scheme was introduced in the study villages in 2008. In late 2009 and early 2010, after rather a slow start, it was attracting 50–60 people per day in one revenue village, and more than 70 in the other. By February 2011, a number of households had already exhausted the 100 days to which they were entitled for the year and by March 2012 nearly all had.[28] The uptake was almost exclusively female. The wages were not high enough to attract men. The majority of people involved were Dalits too. NREGS work was regarded as less arduous than agricultural labour. There was competition within households for NREGS work, older women complaining that younger women within the household got precedence when it looked as though the household would come up against the 100 day limit for the year. The NREGS was having a significant impact on female agricultural wages. These had been raised in January 2010 to match the ₹100 being paid by the NREGS. They had been raised again in 2011 and 2012. Women getting more work that was more appealing, and women getting better wages in agriculture, were both very significant benefits associated with the NREGS.

To summarise: The numbers of Dalit women 'staying at home', 'not working' and/or being 'housewives', both when they were going through pregnancy and childbirth, and/or had young children, and when they were very old, had increased since 1996. Dalit women were benefiting from somewhat higher incomes, better living conditions, and fewer children too. It was a major achievement that child labour had virtually disappeared. The next generation of girls were getting a much better start than their mothers had had. Women were not yet getting significantly better employment opportunities though.

---

[27] Male agricultural labourers, discussing the number of days of paid work they did per week, said that what was available in 2008–09 under the PDS meant that they only had to do one to two days per week to feed their families, as opposed to the five to six necessary earlier.

[28] This was confirmed on a brief re-visits in February 2011 and March 2012.

Conclusion

The main points that have been established so far are that:

1. Dalit women had decreased their participation in paid employment and were also benefiting from an improvement in the quality of paid employment in which they were engaged.
2. Dalit women had not benefited nearly as much as men from the general improvement in employment opportunities though. There was more in all this for women as dependents of men who were earning more than before.
3. Dalit women's decreased participation in paid employment had been made possible by a substantial rise in earnings of men and an increase in state welfare interventions.
4. Dalit women had benefited from higher standards of living while decreasing their participation in paid employment.
5. Dalit women were more dependent on others in their households for income than before, which meant that the basis of their autonomy was less secure.
6. Children and children's education were being given higher priority in Dalit households and Dalit women benefited from this not least because the domestic work that Dalit women did was seen to enhance the performance of children in school.
7. The possibilities of the current generation of Dalit women benefiting from improved employment opportunities themselves were limited, but the outlook seemed better for the generation to come.

Dalit women were better off in material terms in 2008–09 than they had been in 1981–82. Their status within their households appeared to have improved too.

This calls into question the link between women's status within the household on the one hand, and women's participation in paid work on the other. It is not just a question of whether women do paid work outside the household or not. There are a number of other factors that also come into play.

232 द *Judith Heyer*

First and foremost is the quality of paid work — its terms and conditions, and the employment relations involved. It was certainly a step forward in this case for Dalit women not to be doing so much work outside the household that was associated with drudgery and low pay. Their standards of living increased as they reduced their involvement in paid work outside the household too. Their status within the household had also increased in many respects. Their bargaining power within the household appeared to have increased as they were no longer so overworked and poorly paid — earning so little and working so hard for these earnings did not appear to have given them much bargaining power before. They were still burdened by patriarchal relations within the household however, which meant that they shouldered virtually all of the domestic work. This, together with norms about what it was appropriate for women to do, meant that they did not have access to many of the improved employment opportunities open to men. There had been a substantial increase for men, and very little increase for women, in the availability of better quality employment. The exception was young unmarried women who did not have domestic responsibilities who worked for a few years in the knitwear industry, but they were not well paid. The majority of Dalit women in paid employment were still agricultural labourers receiving less than half of the wages of men. It was because Dalit women had such limited alternative opportunities that their agricultural wages remained so low.

The fact that women were able to reduce their participation in poor quality paid work outside the household was made possible by the increase in men's earnings, and the substantial proportions of their increased earnings that men contributed to the household budget.[29] One of the things that was crucial here was that women could take agricultural labour up again at any stage if men were not contributing enough. Threats of going back to work were effective bargaining counters to put pressure on men. Men gained prestige from supporting their families, enabling their women to stay at home. Social pressures reinforced their playing positive roles.

---

[29] This did not mean that men contributed all of their earnings to the household budget or that women felt as able as men to spend household income on themselves. See Kapadia (1995) and Geetha (2007) on this.

Dalit Women Becoming 'Housewives' द 233

Had it not been for the fact that men made substantial contributions in this context it would not have been possible for women to reduce their paid work nearly as much. The position of widows and deserted or separated wives brings this point home. They suffered acutely from the lack of male contributions to the household budget, and the fact that they had to rely on their own poorly paid employment alone.

State social policy also played an important role in enabling women to reduce their participation in poor quality paid work outside the household. State social policy limited increases in the cost of living and also provided some cushion against adversity in this case. Had the social policy not been in place, women would not have been able to reduce their paid work nearly as much.

Relevant also here is the fact that the valuation of domestic work had undergone substantial changes over the period under consideration. One of the reasons for this was the changing position of children. In 1981–82 children were regarded as burdens, sent out to work as soon as they were old enough, going to school for limited periods if at all, and getting low priority within their households overall. By 2008–09, children were seen as investments that would bear fruit through education and good quality care. Women's roles in caring for children, supporting children's performance in school, were highly valued in this respect.[30] The valuation of domestic work had increased in other ways as standards of living had increased too. This had strengthened women's status within the household as their participation in paid work fell.

While there had been real improvements in the lives of women in these Dalit communities, what remained very unsatisfactory was the absence of better quality independent sources of income. One can point to the general improvement in material well-being, for Dalits as well as non-Dalits, women as well as men, and the fact that state welfare programmes had benefited women as much as men. What also needs to be stressed is that women were still paid so much less than men for agricultural labour, and that women had not had access to many of the other independent sources of income available to men. This point is particularly relevant in the context of the discourse of labour shortage in the area, the response to which had been to bring migrant labour

---

[30] Rao (forthcoming) notes this too.

from further and further away, and to raise the wages of men, rather than to develop work regimes that would allow increased contributions from women.

Thus, while the position of women had improved in many respects as they withdrew from paid employment, it remained the case that women were reliant on the goodwill of men. One only had to look at cases in which men were not delivering to see how vulnerable this left them[31] in a population in which the majority were doing quite well.

References

De Neve, G. 2012. 'Fordism, Flexible Specialisation and CSR: Indian Garment Workers Critique Neoliberal Labour Regimes', *Ethnography*, 22 November: 1–24.

Geetha, V. 2007. *Patriarchy*. Kolkata: Stree.

Government of India. 2005. *Tamil Nadu Development Report*. New Delhi: Planning Commission.

Heyer, J. 1992. 'The Role of Dowries and Daughters' Marriages in the Accumulation and Distribution of Capital in a South Indian Community', *Journal of International Development*, 4(4): 419–36.

———. 2000. 'The Changing Position of Agricultural Labourers in Villages in Rural Coimbatore, Tamil Nadu between 1981/2 and 1996', Queen Elizabeth House Oxford Working Paper Series no. 57: 27.

———. 2010. 'The Marginalisation of Dalits in a Modernising Economy', in B. Harriss-White and J. Heyer (eds), *The Comparative Political Economy of Development, Africa and South Asia*, pp. 225–47. London: Routledge.

———. 2012. 'Labour Standards and Social Policy: A South Indian Case Study', *Global Labour Journal*, 3(1): 91–117.

———. 2013. 'Integration into a Global Production Network: Impacts on Labour in Tiruppur's Rural Hinterlands', *Oxford Development Studies*, 41(3): 307–21.

Heyer, J. 2014. 'Dalits in Industrialising Villages near Coimbatore and Tiruppur: 1981/2, 1996, and 2008/9', in V. K. Ramachandran (ed.), *Dalit Households in Village Economies*, pp. 133–69. New Delhi: Tulika.

[31] See Rao (forthcoming) for examples.

Jeffrey, Craig, Patricia Jeffery and Roger Jeffery. 2008. *Degrees without Freedom: Education, Masculinities and Unemployment in North India?* Stanford: Stanford University Press.

Kabeer, N. 1996. 'Agency, Well-being and Inequality: Reflections on the Gender Dimensions of Poverty', *IDS Bulletin*, 27(1): 11–22.

Kabeer, N. 2001. 'Conflicts over Credit: Re-evaluating the Empowerment Potential of Loans to Women in Rural Bangladesh', *World Development*, 29(1): 63–84.

Kajisa, K. and N. V. Palanichamy. 2010. 'Schooling Investments over Three Decades in Rural Tamil Nadu, India: Changing Effects of Income, Gender, and Adult Family Members' Education', *World Development*, 38(3): 298–314.

Kapadia, K. 1995. *Siva and Her Sisters, Gender, Caste, and Class in Rural South India.* Boulder and Oxford: Westview Press.

Mazumdar, Indrani and N. Neetha. 2011. 'Gender Dimensions: Employment Trends in India, 1993–94 to 2010', *Economic and Political Weekly*, 46(43): 118–26.

Rao, Nitya. Forthcoming. 'Caste, Kinship and Life-course: Rethinking Women's Work and Agency in Rural Tamil Nadu, India', *Feminist Economics*.

Sen, A. 1990. 'Gender and Cooperative Conflicts', in I. Tinker (ed.), *Persistent Inequalities: Women and World Development.* New York: Oxford University Press.

Thomas, Jayan Jose. 2012. 'India's Labour Market during the 2000's', *Economic and Political Weekly*, 47(51): 39–51.

Vijayabaskar, M. 2011. 'Global Crises, Welfare Provision and Coping Strategies of Labour in Tiruppur', *Economic and Political Weekly*, 46(22): 38–45.

VIII

Finding One's Place among the Elite

How Dalits Experiencing Sharp Upward Social Mobility Adjust to Their New Social Status

Jules Naudet

The experience of shifting from one social class to another, from a dominated group to a dominant group, raises the question of how the upwardly mobile person relates to his group of origin. The process of acculturation to the new group implies a certain deculturation from the schemes of action and of perception and the dispositions inherited from the group of origin. The upwardly mobile person is in the situation of a 'stranger': he quits his group of origin, begins a laborious process of deculturation, and attempts to acculturate himself to a new group. But total amnesia and perfect acculturation remain mere ideal types. The memory of the group of origin is always present and can cause the upwardly mobile person to be torn between his attachment to his group of origin and his desire to recognise the social legitimacy of his new group. This tension and this double bind constitute the major challenges people experiencing upward social mobility have to deal with (Naudet 2011).

In this chapter I attempt to highlight the particular way in which upwardly mobile Dalits make sense of this tension and adjust to their new professional status.[1] Such trajectories of sharp upward mobility can be seen as a direct consequence of the 'silent revolution' (Jaffrelot 2003) that enabled the rise of low castes in India. Though this revolution is still 'unfinished' (Pai 2002), it left a particularly strong mark on

---

[1] Part of the analysis presented in this chapter has been developed in an earlier article (Naudet 2008).

Finding One's Place among the Elite द 237

the representations of the Dalit middle-class. My analysis thus intends to shed light on how individual success stories are connected to the broader historical process of social and political emancipation through which the 'untouchable' subject became Dalit (Rao 2009). If the 'Dalit identity' is generally associated with the rejection of the social domination inherited from the brahmanic order and with a quest for a new social order (Ilaiah 2005; Omvedt 1995; Shah 2001), such a radical agenda is not completely hegemonic. Some authors now start to argue that, capitalism being the most efficient means of Dalit emancipation, Dalit politics need to be more in phase with the free-market ideology and should rely more on the emergence of a 'Dalit bourgeoisie' (on these debates, see Nigam 2002; Omvedt 2005; Prasad 2011; Teltumbde 2011). The analysis I offer here will thus try to assess to what extent these politics are prevalent among upwardly mobile Dalits.

I will draw on 44 biographical interviews for this with Dalits originally from a poor economic background (people whose parents were landless labourers, small farmers, manual workers, service employees or occupying low clerical positions) who attained qualifications from prestigious institutions of higher education and achieved prominent positions in the private sector,[2] in public service (the Indian Administrative Service [IAS], the Indian Police Service [IPS] and the Indian Revenue Service [IRS]) and in academia (researchers and faculty members). All the interviews were face-to-face interviews carried out in nine different cities of north India. One interview with a non-resident Indian (NRI) was conducted over the phone and another via the internet. Among the 44 interviews, 16 were conducted with employed academic faculty, 11 with people from the private sector and 17 with people from public service. The semi-guided interviews lasted from 50 minutes to over three hours. The average length of an interview was one hour and thirty minutes. Three-fourths of the interview consisted of biographical questions and the last fourth of more reflexive questions about the way mobility was experienced. The sampling technique consisted of random

---

[2] The interviewees working in the private sector graduated from the Indian Institutes of Technology (IITs), Indian Institutes of Management (IIMs), Birla Institute of Technology and Science and Indian Institute of Foreign Trade (IIFT).

interviews with people who were contacted through various channels (e.g., networks of civil servants and scholars, running announcements on professional and alumni newsletters), as well as snowball sampling. This sampling technique necessarily introduced some bias and to some extent limited the representativeness of my sample. But this bias is largely reduced by the great diversity of the sources through which the interviewees were contacted. This study is part of comparative research that also involves France and the United States (Naudet 2012).

In the first part of this chapter, I shall analyse the impact of primary and secondary socialisation on the way in which mobility is experienced. Then I will describe the chief narrative repertoires drawn upon by my interviewees in order to justify the legitimacy of their place in the social sphere. The two poles of the narratives of my interviewees are, first, the moral imperative of 'paying back to society', which may be considered as the ideological platform from which most of the Dalit interviewees narrate their experience of social mobility; and, secondly, what I call 'legitimist' discourses, that is, discourses which show an acceptance of dominant social norms.

Primary and Secondary Socialisation

Primary Socialisation and Schooling

Somewhat astonishingly, every single one of the people I interviewed insisted on the fact that they had parents who had constantly stressed the importance of education. Even though in practically every case their parents were unable to help them with their homework (many of them being illiterate), all of them reported that their parents had very positive attitudes towards school (making financial sacrifices so that their children would be able to study, providing strong encouragement to work, etc.). This was all the more striking as some of these interviewees, due to the straitened financial circumstances of their family, were forced to work at a very young age.

As a result, none of these interviewees claimed to have felt that the adjustment to academic norms placed them in contradiction with their group of origin. Quite to the contrary, almost every single one of them saw their success as the accomplishment of their parents' wishes, rather than as some form of class betrayal. This observation is supported by

Finding One's Place among the Elite द 239

various studies on education in India, which never demonstrate the existence of an 'oppositional culture' (Ogbu 2008). On the other hand, Jeffrey et al. (2005) show that, in spite of poor school results people from the lower castes continue to put a high premium on education.[3] Sarangapani (2003) reveals that faith in the benefits of education is widespread, and particularly evident in the respect which is usually shown towards teachers and professors. Likewise, in her study on the education of Dalit girls, Paik (2009) has shown that their access to education is fraught with more difficulties than other students', that the teaching staff tend to display a more hostile attitude towards them, and that they adhere less spontaneously to school norms and codes, but that in spite of all these obstacles, Dalit girls persist in believing that education is the 'magic wand' which will help them improve their living conditions (Paik 2009: 195). For Manuela Ciotti, the access to education of Manupur Chamars is comparable to an 'ontological experience' which allows them to acquire a new 'substance', most often of a 'moral' nature (Ciotti 2006: 900, 2010). This strong valorisation of education is particularly clear in the interviews I carried out with Dalits.[4]

Thus, in spite of family dispositions which are quite distant from the school ethos, there does not seem to be an inherent incompatibility between the family thought structures and the dispositions demanded by school. Even though Dalit families do not have the means of transmitting a legitimate cultural capital to their children, they rarely express hostility or distrust towards school. In fact, in the narratives I collected, school always appears as a space removed from the social sphere, or a space which provides a hope of escaping, in the future, from the ruthlessness of social relationships. The same narratives, however, paradoxically reveal that it is also the space where caste discriminations are most violent, in the sense that they reach their highest intensity of cruelty and hypocrisy. My interviewees' narratives thus present a

---

[3] In 1961, the literacy rate for Dalits was 10.2 per cent. In 2001, it was 57 per cent (according to census data as quoted by Still [2008]). Unfortunately, gender inequalities in Dalits' access to education remain extremely high.

[4] Some studies, however, insist on the idea that education is not always unanimously perceived as a resource which guarantees access to upward social mobility (Balagopalan and Subrahmanian 2003; Subrahmanian 2003).

240 *ढ़ Jules Naudet*

paradoxical, almost carnivalesque vision of school, which constitutes both the motor of social reproduction, the place where social injustices are perpetrated, and the place which bears all their hopes of a reversal of roles and of a reversal of the social order.

Thus, all the people I interviewed had parents who, even though they were strangers to the school environment and ethos, believed in the benefits of education. The mere fact of paying school fees, even if they only amounted to ₹40 a year, can be seen as an indication of their faith in education. This is particularly noteworthy in a context where, as my interviewees were prompt to point out, many other families in the same financial situation deemed this an unnecessary luxury. So it is in keeping with the family ideology rather than in opposition to it that social success is forged in these situations.

Secondary Socialisation and Higher Education

It is possible to distinguish two types of trajectories in higher education, leading to different experiences of mobility: higher education in universities and higher education in elitist and competitive institutions. Those who studied in universities have a different experience from those who studied in institutions which are marked by forms of socialisation based on elitism and which prepare students for entry into IIMs, IITs, and elite colleges such as St Stephen's in Delhi, or St Xavier's in Bombay, for instance.

The chief difference between these two experiences of higher education for Dalit students lies in the way these students are confronted with social otherness. More precisely, it is in the way in which they cope with the caste stigma that the most significant distinctions can be observed.

In schools like the IIM or the IIT where students highly valorise and even fetishise achievement, competition and meritocracy, benefiting from reservations is harshly stigmatised. Displaying one's Dalit origins is thus a public admission of having benefited from reservations, which is, in turn, a kind of indirect recognition of one's inferiority. Though entering IIMs through reservations requires very high results in CAT (Common Admission Test), many students still consider these 'reservation students' as being less meritorious. In a context where intelligence

Finding One's Place among the Elite द 241

and aptitude are highly prized and 'accurately' measured in terms of percentages and scores, being a Dalit student casts a serious shadow on one's reputation among one's batchmates. Given the fact that there are no SC–ST student associations on these campuses, students have very few incentives to reveal their caste origins. This is further reinforced by a management ideology (Boltanski and Chiapello 1999)and the politics of the secular (Lukose 2010) that taboo any reference to one's social origins.

As a consequence, these students are caught in a no-win double-bind: on the one hand they are strongly attached to their group of origin and aware of caste discrimination, on the other hand they are subject to a strong social pressure towards the interiorisation of the dominant stance on reservations (that indirectly implies a negation of their caste identity). This leads to paradoxical discourses. For example, Deepak,[5] a 30-year old IIM Ahmedabad (IIMA) alumnus at once denounces 'upper-caste' caste discrimination against Dalits ('they don't want us to achieve better than them') and yet at the same time asserts that he is strongly against reservations (despite having entered IIMA through reservations). At first he says he never hides his caste, but later in the interview he explains that he does his best to make sure that nobody knows his caste at his workplace. He also did not reveal his caste background to his two roommates, even though one of them is also from a Dalit background. He seems convinced that in the corporate sector people only respect or notice you if you're from a family that is successful in business, if you have prestigious degrees, if you have achieved a good ranking at national level quiz contests, if you do not speak in vernacular languages, if you do not discuss vernacular literature but only read the latest American or British best sellers and so on. Thus he describes his years in IIMA as a time during which he 'completely reshaped [him] self' He spent hours every day correcting his English accent, reading American best sellers and he made it a point never to speak about Bankim Chandra Chatterjee, his favourite author. When I suggested that he might be exaggerating the possible reaction of his colleagues if he revealed his caste, he vigorously reacted and told me: 'No! You

---

[5] All names are pseudonyms. Based on an interview with Deepak, Mumbai, 26 October 2006.

242 ॾ *Jules Naudet*

have to understand them ... That's the way it works in business! And if you don't play this game, you'll never find your place in this world'. Here the expression 'you have to understand them', in which 'them' seems to refer both to his 'upper-caste' batchmates and to the business elite in general, acts like a veiled confession of his intimate desire to belong to this 'corporate world', even if the price to pay for it is the repudiation of his group of origin. Notably, he began this repudiation by defending an anti-reservation position even though he had himself benefited from these policies.

At the other end of the spectrum, people who studied in less competitive institutions (although not necessarily less prestigious) had quite different experiences. In the first place, the economic disparities between them and the other students were less glaring, as the context is not quite so favourable to ostentatious consumption practices which distinguish the well-to-do students from the less well off. According to one of my interviewees who studied in Jawaharlal Nehru University (JNU), the wealthier students tended to 'play down their wealth'. Nevertheless, for students who came from extremely poor backgrounds, living on campus still implied a confrontation with stark social difference. As Raj (another former JNU student I interviewed) puts it:

> Actually arriving in JNU was a cultural shock. People were all speaking English, nobody knew me. Being from a Scheduled Caste, with my own complex, coming from a reserved seat, not being able to speak properly ... So it was a lot of problems. It was difficult to read the English texts of Marx, Durkheim, etc.[6]

He, too, undertakes a process of correction of his dispositions, repeating the same word hundreds of times in front of the mirror, reading the newspaper aloud to improve his accent, and so on. However, unlike some IIM students, he does not remain isolated but instead soon meets and strikes up friendships with other students in similar situations. On this type of campus, which welcomes large numbers of students, it is far easier to regroup on the basis of one's native state, one's caste, one's level of income or political views. More importantly, Raj soon

---

[6] Based on an interview with Raj, Delhi, 18 January 2007.

Finding One's Place among the Elite ॿ 243

discovers an environment that fosters political involvement, he meets Dalit activists and discovers Ambedkar's writings. He claims this experience changed his life:

> My life was changed in 1992 when I was introduced to Ambedkar's writings in a class. It appealed all of a sudden. And there was a psychological transformation going on inside me. I left everything, you know. I was wearing a zodiac ring and I gave it up. I stopped remembering any God, any religion. All became useless for me. It was a radical transformation. I began fighting, I began speaking for Dalits. Dalits became the hub for me.[7]

Raj's example clearly shows that the greater number of students on campus and the stronger political activism result in a very different way of experiencing social alterity. My interviews consistently show clear evidence of this difference between elitist institutions and universities.

Secondary Socialisation and Professional Context

Almost all the people I interviewed in the private sector had completed their higher education in elite establishments such as the IIMs or IITs. As the environment in which they studied made a strong impression on them, they carried over the norms they interiorised during their degree into the corporate world.[8] Thus, only a minority of my interviewees working in the private sector lay a strong personal emphasis on their Dalit identity:[9] most of them, as a general rule, try to conceal their caste identity.

---

[7] Ibid.

[8] As noted by Jodhka and Newman in their comparative study of Indian and American hiring managers, recruitment practices in the Indian private sector are characterised by a very strong attention to the 'family background' of candidates: 'For Indian employers, there is no contradiction between an emphasis on individual merit and the notion of valuing "family background", which, virtually every hiring manager emphasised, was critical in evaluating a potential employee. Americans would view this notion as a contradiction in terms.' (Jodhka and Newman 2010: 58–59).

[9] The people concerned always come from families who are themselves influenced by the Dalit movement. Unlike academics and senior civil servants,

244 ट *Jules Naudet*

Interviewees working in senior administrative positions are far more prompt to state the fact that they belong to SCs. There are at least two reasons for this. First, most of them studied in universities where the Dalit cause was defended. Second, since their peers can easily find out whether or not they had benefited from reservation it is better to display an attitude that shows they accept and even embrace this aspect of their identity. Moreover, unlike the private sector, there are professional organisations for senior administrative officers from SCs (like the All India Backward and Minority Communities Employees' Federation [BAMCEF], for instance), and this allows a form of institutional officialisation of Dalit identity.

SC interviewees in academia are also more likely to accept and disclose their Dalit identity. Like senior administrative officers, university professors usually obtained degrees from universities in which the expression of caste identity was easier than in elite institutions. Similarly, professors from SCs or STs generally benefited from reservation policies and their colleagues are, most of the time, aware of this fact. This form of recruiting thus has a direct impact on the way in which students come to terms with their social origin: they have no reason for hiding their caste when most of their colleagues already know what it is.

Repertoires of Adjustment to the New Status

The 'Paying-back to Society' Moral Imperative

If we look at my interviewees' narratives as a whole, the single most striking aspect of these narratives is without a doubt the fact that all of their success stories hinge on the strength of the bonds they have maintained with their group of origin. Significantly, practically all of them reported that they helped their parents financially.

These efforts to keep in close touch with their original background despite their change of social status seems to be buttressed by references to the Dalit movement, although it can also be detected in the discourse of people who do not explicitly refer to it.

---

those private-sector interviewees who were not exposed to this movement at home are less likely to appropriate this type of discourse in university or in their workplace.

Finding One's Place among the Elite द 245

The interviews I collected are characterised by an insistence on the need to maintain strong bonds with the group of origin. This imperative is very often presented as a moral obligation, as something that is imposed from without rather than from within. This explains why many interviewees decide to build schools, to create micro credit organisations, to set up libraries, to endow scholarships, etc., in their family's village. These types of activities are extremely common among Dalit interviewees. More than half of my interviewees mention that they work as volunteers for organisations, leading campaigns and development programs in their social group of origin. This can be linked to an ideology, upheld by the Dalit political leader Kanshi Ram, of 'paying one's debt to society' (Ram 1982).

These people's successes are cases of an individual's success. It is a person, at most a family, who benefits from this mobility. And yet these individuals choose to speak of their mobility as if it were the community as a whole that was elevated by their success. Even though some of them acknowledge the individual character of their success, they still place their individual story within the wider frame of their group. Thus most of the interviewees resort to narrative strategies characterised by a much stronger negation of their individuality.[10] When the interviewees were questioned about the reasons behind their success, many answered, without hesitation, that it can be explained by the movement led by Ambedkar. Not only did the teachings of Ambedkar enable their parents to structure their education around an ethos of academic and social success, but furthermore Ambedkar was known to be the architect of the reservations system without which it would have been near impossible for these people to experience such mobility. The figure of Ambedkar in particular and the Dalit movement in general are therefore always implicitly present as the structuring force behind the personal narratives of the interviewees.

It is striking that nearly all the Dalit interviewees who work as senior administrative officers or university professors pay tribute to

---

[10] In her ethnography of Manupur, Manuela Ciotti points out that the Chamars she is observing tend to consider that the benefits of the education received by only a small number of them are actually 'collectively shared' and thus benefit the Chamar community as a whole (Ciotti 2006, 2010).

246 ∂ *Jules Naudet*

Ambedkar, insisting on the fact that his example played a decisive role in their own success. This clearly reflects the constant effort made by these interviewees to reintegrate their individuality into the Dalit collective identity, and militates against the idea that upward mobility necessarily involves a process of individualisation, or at least a blurring of group attachment.[11]

In her ethnography of a Chamar community in Uttar Pradesh, Manuela Ciotti shows that the term *Dalit* is little used by the Chamars themselves, and is often used to designate political leaders (Ciotti 2010). It is striking that the term is on the contrary widely used by my interviewees to refer to their own selves: they perceive themselves as Dalits, struggling against caste domination. When they claim to belong to a discriminated and exploited caste, they attempt to directly legitimate their ethical and political stance. The way they consistently interweave their definition of themselves with their attachment to the Dalit community can be illustrated by the following example: one of my informants who had not returned to his native village in 15 years gave an example of the discriminations which he had had to face there. He bitterly reported that the last time he went to his village he was not allowed to enter the temple. His words seemed sincere enough, however other information collected in the course of the discussion revealed that this was *not* something that he had personally experienced, or at least not recently. He was projecting himself in one of the emblematic experiences of discrimination to which his group is subjected, even though he had not experienced this himself. Yet it is this type of experience — at least in part — which provided him with a justification for his activism and his involvement in the Dalit movement.

This ready access to a repertoire of discourses enables upwardly mobile Dalits to give a meaning to past experiences and to work them into a coherent narrative. This repertoire undoubtedly enables them to use their origin as a resource to justify their new social status. This perception of themselves as Dalits allows them to build their self-esteem and to fully accept and come to terms with their social origin. Revealingly,

---

[11] For a critical review of the theoretical literature on social mobility, see Naudet (2011).

Finding One's Place among the Elite द 247

many of my interviewees admitted that they stopped hiding their caste only after being introduced into the Dalit networks of their campus. In fact, they often claim that the years devoted to higher education were a time of emancipation which was made possible by a renewal of their outlook on society and their place within it. For those who were acquainted with Dalit repertoires earlier on in their lives, the period of higher education became a time of reinforcement of these repertoires which were as yet only imperfectly mastered.

It is possible to argue that Dalit identity, despite being a subaltern identity, is structured around an ethos of mobility in the sense that it places a project of social mobility at the heart of the identity of a group which is socially dominated. The Ambedkarite ideology and the Dalit movement do not merely promote education: they also provide strict guidelines about the behaviour to adopt once one has succeeded, thereby establishing a moral imperative of 'paying back to society'. In other words, social mobility is *programmed* within Dalit identity.

This Dalit ethos directly echoes the Gramscian notion of the 'organic intellectual' who acts as a link between the subalterns and the institutions (Gramsci 2001: 652). One of the most telling examples of this Dalit version of the organic intellectual is to be found in the following excerpt from an interview I conducted with Pankaj, who teaches economics in Mumbai:

> I am no longer poor, I am teaching in university and I could say I don't want to get involved in any social activity, in the movement. I could do that. But if I do that, what would I think of myself? What would have been the purpose of getting so much education? If Babasaheb Ambedkar had said 'Ok, I got a good education, now I am gonna live a comfortable life' then all we people would not be here out of the village. So he had sacrificed everything and therefore we could come up to here. Now it is our duty to pay back to society. So we should not say: 'I am somebody different, this and that. I took distance with my people'. I am here because of him. I should not forget that. And therefore if I am here it is because of all these people who fought before me. They fought for me; I will also fight for them.[12]

---

[12] Interview with Pankaj, Mumbai, 25 October 2006.

248 ढ़ *Jules Naudet*

The bonds these academics and senior administrative officers feel they still share with their group of origin are so compelling that their narratives hardly ever betray any unease deriving from their change of status. The adjustment to their new social position is rarely presented as a source of tension: the narratives are more centered on the relations maintained with the group of origin than with the difficulties presented by integration to the new group.

In her study of class mobility in urban India, Sara Dickey argues that 'family serves as the source of an individual's class' (2010: 195). Such an assertion contradicts the position held by Kapadia (1995) and Thiruchendran (1997) who contend that individuals within families occupy different class positions. My ethnography brings a new element to this debate by suggesting that, even if people can occupy various class positions within a family, the 'paying-back to society' moral imperative acts as a counter-force to the fragmentation and individualisation of family members. It prompts upwardly mobile Dalits to make sure their own status does not differ radically from that of their family and community members. Such a moral imperative relies on the intimate belief that the uplifting of a Dalit necessarily calls for the uplifting of the whole community.

I have just developed an analysis of what could be called the ideological 'kernel' around which most of the Dalits I interviewed narrate their experience of mobility. Yet the explicit reference to the Dalit movement does not appear in the narratives of all of my interviewees. It is more rarely mentioned by people who work in the private sector.

Anil[13] is one of the rare interviewees in the private sector whose socialisation is strongly marked by the Dalit movement. Anil is from a weaver community in Gujarat. His father was a clerk for the village gram panchayat and a landless labourer; his mother was also an agricultural labourer. Anil's education was much influenced by a local Dalit non-governmental organisation (NGO), and throughout his schooling he worked with his parents in the fields. He started reading Ambedkar's works when he was in the seventh standard and from eighth standard onwards he benefited from an educational programme scheme. According to him the goal of the scheme was 'to promote students like

---

[13] Interview with Anil, Mumbai, 26 October 2006.

Finding One's Place among the Elite द 249

me, from my caste, and they wanted us to become IAS officers and to get into positions of power and from there to influence decision making'. After his matriculation he wished to conform to the NGO's expectations and he 'wanted to contribute towards social justice' by becoming an IAS officer. He left his hometown to undertake a Bachelor of Law diploma from a prestigious law university. The first years of university were very painful for him. He felt very different from other students during that period and he was afraid to disclose his caste or his economic background. He felt like a usurper whose place was not in such prestigious surroundings, and he said that he would often cry at night alone in his room. In spite of his strong inferiority complex, he managed to obtain his diploma and started thinking about his career. Since he had grown up influenced by the Ambedkarite movement, he still believed that one day he would have to pay back his debt to the community. After graduating from law school and doing a short professional stint in a finance company, he got an opportunity to study in an American Ivy League university and left to study. Once back from the United States he gave up his corporate job and thought about a career in academia, as this would make it easier for him to 'contribute towards social justice'. After a first experience as a research assistant, he abandoned the idea of doing a PhD as he could not imagine doing such work all his life. He also gave up the idea of becoming an IAS officer. He then found a job as a consultant for a large company in Mumbai, and at the time of the interview he earned more than ₹100,000 a month. However, he felt ill at ease with his new position. He became depressed and finally decided to consult a psychotherapist who 'made [him] aware' that he was feeling guilty for not doing anything to help his community. The psychotherapist helped him to overcome this guilt: 'He is the one who made me aware that there was nothing wrong if I don't tell my... if I was in the corporate world, earning money and not doing any social work'. In a way the therapist helped him accept his new position and understand that he could live his life for himself and that he did not have to carry the burden of all the misery of his community of origin. Anil then bought a house for his parents far from the village, in a big city, and bought a photocopy shop for his brother who was a landless labourer. Since then Anil has scarcely gone back to his village and no longer has any desire to return there.

For Anil, the moral imperative of paying back his debt to society weighed heavily on his shoulders, acted as a constraint on his personal desires, and exacerbated the tension he perceived between his group of origin and his new group. His narrative reveals the extent to which the moral imperative of 'paying back to society' heavily structures the experience of social mobility for Dalits. It also shows that drawing upon the discursive repertoires of this moral imperative is far more difficult in contexts where it is less well established, or where it carries a stigma. In addition to my interviewees, the Dalit activists in senior positions in the private sector whom I met in the course of my investigations were generally engineers who had obtained their degree in IITs. Engineers are not compelled to interiorise the neo-managerial discourse (Boltanski and Chiapello 2007) in the way that IIM graduates are; their work does not imply a stark contradiction between their support of the Dalit movement and the managerial ideology. Conversely, IIM graduates from SCs or people like Anil constantly face this very contradiction and the tension that results from it.

The absence of references to Ambedkar and to Dalit struggles seems to prevail in the interviews with Dalits people working in the private sector. These interviewees develop narratives which reveal the difficulties they experience when they try to situate themselves in the 'social space' (Bourdieu 1984): the fact they are ashamed both of their origin and of the fact they are ashamed of it, makes it difficult for them to put together a coherent discourse to justify the place they occupy in society today. Thus they tend to be caught in between two worlds, having the impression of being neither here nor there.

The Legitimist Discourse in the Indian Context

Evidently, the 'paying back to society' moral imperative or the impulse of remaining loyal to one's group of origin provide the framework for the narratives of most of my interviewees working in the public service and in academia. They all acknowledge that their mobility gives them the opportunity to enjoy a more comfortable lifestyle and that higher education was the means of opening the doors of emancipation. They enjoy being able to command 'respect' and having a prestigious social position. But although they claim that they are now able to 'choose' the

Finding One's Place among the Elite द 251

life they wanted to live, yet the firm conviction that they still intrinsically belong to their group of origin dominates their narratives in spite of all these changes and transformations in their lives.

It would be nevertheless simplistic to suggest that these interviewees are shining examples of constant altruism. Upward social mobility never goes without a certain acknowledgement of legitimate hierarchies and upwardly mobile Dalits are no exception to the rule. Here it is important to avoid painting an ideal picture of complete, disinterested devotion to the collective struggle. Personal interests are never entirely dissolved in the attachment to the group of origin. This ethos of social conscience and selflessness also disguises these upwardly mobile persons' position of dominance in the Dalit community. Given their position in a society which is still structured around caste relationships, it is extremely difficult, perhaps even impossible, for a person from a Dalit background to be entirely integrated into a society dominated by the higher castes. Severing ties with the group of origin in order to merge more perfectly with the approached group is a dangerous wager which could result in humiliating isolation. It is thus easier to be dominant among the dominated rather than dominated among the dominants.

Throughout my fieldwork, I was able to observe a great number of situations which showed that the social mobility of the interviewees was accompanied by an assimilation of 'schemes of action' (Bourdieu 1998) which did not have currency in their group of origin. The most obvious aspect of this assimilation is undoubtedly, for many of my interviewees, a tendency to emphasise the prestige and respectability which their new status confers on them. In their narratives, this is evidenced by their insistence on the influence and power which their new status gives them, as well as recurring remarks on the fact that they arouse fear, respect, flattery, envy, jealousy, or even hatred in others. All of my interviewees admit that they derive great satisfaction from the power that their new status gives them over other people. Significantly, my interviewees, especially the senior administrative officers, place a lot of emphasis on the power they have over people who occupy a lower rung in the socio-professional ladder. It is through this power that they hope to contribute to the struggle for 'social justice', that is to say, to help Dalits confront with situations of domination. Several IAS officers thus explained to me that they organised regular sessions where people

252 ट Jules Naudet

from SCs could come to see them directly to express their grievances and place claims, without passing through the different steps of the administrative system, which might have censured them at some point. If they deemed it necessary and legitimate, they would then use their influence to solve their problems.

Having power implies wielding it, of course, and I have several times in the course of my fieldwork witnessed situations where the interviewees used the privileges of their position for less noble causes. One IAS officer lent me his chauffeured car to bring me to the interview and take me back to my office afterwards. Another IRS officer, when I asked him for recommendations about accommodation in town, got the manager of one of the best hotels to rent us a room free of charge. He then explained such generosity by saying that this person 'owed him a few favors'. An eminent Dalit intellectual whom I interviewed early in the morning at his home had his shoelaces tied up for him by his servant while he went on answering my questions. Another senior administrative officer, known for his activism in the Dalit movement, called out for his servant for a whole minute, to ask him to fetch a notebook which was lying barely two steps away from the spot where he was sitting. When the servant made a mistake and brought him the wrong notebook, it was violently flung at his head, along with a biting insult. These anecdotes are certainly not the general rule, but they occur regularly enough to be worthy of being noted. They reveal that despite belonging to a group which has been and continues to be the victim of terrible discrimination, the interviewees themselves are willing to accept the privileges of power which their new status gives them, without showing signs of any critical distance.[14] However, this kind of behaviour does not go uncriticised. For example, Ashok, who refuses to employ domestic help for his family and cleans his toilet himself, is

---

[14] These observations remind us of the disjuncture that often exists between narratives and actual behaviours, and thus highlight the limits of the interview methodology. However, the mere fact that our interviewees' narratives are so consistent clearly shows how structuring and constraining is the 'paying-back to society' moral imperative. Such a repertoire clearly acts as a major force in the construction of the self of upwardly mobile Dalits.

Finding One's Place among the Elite ∂ 253

one of the rare interviewees who develop a discourse which is sharply critical of these widespread practices.

Yet acceptance of domination is often laid at the door of others rather than their own. For instance, when I ask interviewees if they feel they have moved away from their group of origin, their reaction is quite indignant and followed by an emphatic insistence on the bonds maintained with the people whom they left behind in their native village or in the slum where they grew up. Quite often the interviewee will quote examples of people who, after they succeeded professionally, severed every tie with the rest of their community to concentrate fully on their careers. At the end of these interviews I would always ask if it would be possible to be put in contact with these people. Most of the time, my request was not granted but two senior administrative officers agreed to introduce me with civil servants they had labelled as 'renegades'. The interviews I conducted with these so-called 'renegades' turned out to yield results quite similar to the others, and even if these persons had not set up any micro-credit or development organisations, they still used the same discourse marked by references to the Dalit struggles, they made the same claim of fighting for 'social justice' through their job, they shared the same conviction that they had remained close to their community, and they used the same kind of reference to Ambedkar.

A well-known public figure, Narendra Jadhav, was often called upon to represent the archetype of the 'renegade Dalit' by my interviewees. This former economist at the IMF and at the Reserve Bank of India is the author of an autobiography — translated in 17 languages —in which he recounts the story of his family. He is now a member of the prestigious Planning Commission, and he never hesitates to insist on his Dalit identity. Like my informants, he also claims to contribute to the struggles towards greater social justice. Yet, according to several of my interviewees, he merely uses the Dalit movement in order to further his career. Such a recurrent invocation of Narendra Jadhav, who is known for his public declarations in defense of the deprived, clearly shows that the idea of betrayal has a special significance for Dalits. It is not so much his work with the IMF or the Reserve Bank of India that is resented but rather the weakness of his bonds to the Dalit community and his alleged careerism. This, it is claimed, leads

254 ट Jules Naudet

him to refuse to use his power to help other actors in the 'movement'. The reaction that Jadhav provokes can be seen in the email an IIT engineer sent me as we were exchanging messages about his trajectory. As I deliberately suggested that the story of his family made me think of Narendra Jadhav's, he replied:

> The difference between Narendra Jadhav and us is that even though our people were treated as Untouchables (i.e., worse than slaves); Narendra has remained 'Hindu by heart' and 'lower by Caste'. In Maharashtra this is a hot issue nowadays because he participated in the 'Ganesh Pooja' (Worship of the Elephant Headed God) of 'Brahmin–Shudra Varna Hindus' along with his wife and family... Our family is a staunch Ambedkarite and Buddhist. From heart we believe in the '22 Vows' given by Bodhisattva Dr. Ambedkar. We are no more Hindu by religion and lower by Hindu caste. So it is a request: please don't compare our family with a 'lower caste Hindu like Mr. Narendra Jadhav' who is still Hindu even after tremendous atrocities done by his own Hindu people. It is insulting for proud people like us.[15]

The indignant response of this engineer, who lives abroad and is very active in the Dalit movement, shows that there is a Dalit 'activist capital' [*capital militant*] (Matonti and Poupeau 2004) and that it is used as a principle of distinction among the Dalit elite. In this perspective, the 'traitor' is someone who does not respect the codes of this activist commitment in relation to the group of origin. But the narratives of academics and senior civil servants suggest it is impossible to imagine such a 'traitor' not trying to claim that he is serving his community. This is the minimum expected from anyone from a Dalit and a destitute background.

Ravi, a Dalit essay writer who has published a number of books on the situation of Dalits in India, articulates a different and more original discourse through which he intends to denounce the tyranny of the 'paying back to society' moral imperative. Although he is personally very close to activist Dalit networks (he is considered as one of the 'voices' of the movement) and although he has remained in close contact with his peers from his native village, Ravi asserts that it is his duty as

---

[15] Email interview with Sanjay, 6 September 2006.

an intellectual to expose and criticise this imperative felt by upwardly mobile Dalits and to underline the positive effects of uprooting:

> Some of them manage to get out of this [the degrading living conditions of rural areas]. They are likely to be more scattered and less inserted in the day-to-day life. Less united. What is the ideal situation for a Dalit leader? To remain united? Or rather that everybody should get out of this? In sum it is better to be less united, less rooted to your past, but less discriminated. It is worse to remain more united, more together, more rooted to your past but condemned to humiliation. That is a bad situation, *na*? So what I am saying *ki* let us not all think for all times that this class [of Dalits] must keep on helping this class [of Dalits]. At least in terms of ideal, let us think of a situation in which everybody becomes like this. At least in the realm of ideal, if not real. Because only when you have something ideal can it happen in reality. You have seen yourself the kind of life that rural India has. It is worse than prison. So, even if one gets out of that and gets dissolved in society, gets lost in individualism, I think that is better than remaining united and having more people in this kind of situation.[16]

Ravi's stance is particularly idiosyncratic and his public declarations on this subject have provoked heated debates. He argues that capitalism offers Dalits the best opportunities for emancipation from the 'feudal caste system'. According to him, only through the creation of a class of capitalist Dalits will they be able to overcome the old prejudices for it will allow the idea of a successful Dalit to be more widely accepted. For Ravi, Dalit mobility strategies should become more individualistic, more selfish. To attain this aim, a form of uprooting is necessary. This 'organic intellectual' argues that the model of the 'organic intellectual' is not a viable model for upwardly mobile Dalits. But his position is still based on the optimistic paradox that uprooting always results in a form of return to the original group. He contends that the deracinated Dalit will always return to his original group, displacement being only a necessary transitional phase:

> They [upper caste people] will never allow a Dalit, even if he is trying to escape from his people, to escape... He will always be a Dalit. Suppose

---

[16] Interview with Ravi, Delhi, 17 December 2006.

256 द *Jules Naudet*

he gets into a good job, he thinks he has escaped his community, and nobody knows in his society, in his office that he is a Dalit. People talk about Dalits in his surroundings, even if they don't know he's a Dalit. It ultimately pushes him. Because if he's known as a Dalit... I mean people talk about Dalits in such a way that it links him to his people. If it comes to be known he's a Dalit, people's first reaction will be 'But he does not look like that!' Because they have a standard image of a Dalit. Then they start sympathising, at least in their action and all that and this pushes him back to his community because he feels he's not seen for who he is, but he's seen as a representative of the larger community back home. So the society ultimately pushes Dalits to keep connected to their roots. Like Oprah Winfrey in Paris. She entered in a shop in Paris and was insulted, or something like that. For those who have not seen her on TV, she remains a Black. So it pushes her back to her community. So it forces you to come back to your people.[17]

Conclusion

The ideological borrowings which characterise Ravi's discourse are unique among the interviews I have carried out for this study. But it still seemed necessary to present Ravi's point of view since this critique of the ethos of Dalit mobility by an influent Dalit intellectual who nonetheless obeys the 'paying back to society' imperative reveals the tensions faced by upwardly mobile Dalits. Ravi insists that this imperative is a handicap for upwardly mobile Dalits, as Anil's case shows. Mobility implies a choice between careerism and activism. The socialisation of young Dalits seems to point to a perpetuation of the 'paying back to society' ideology. However the examples of Anil and Ravi suggest that this conception of mobility is not completely hegemonic and that the attraction of capital may result in a partial rejection of the 'paying-back' moral imperative. Such a rejection seems more likely to happen among those who have opted for a career in the private sector. So in the end, the values of resistance and solidarity might well in the future be defeated by the diffusion and growing hegemony of market-oriented values.

ꜩ

---

[17] Interview with Ravi, Delhi, 17 December 2006.

References

Balagopalan S. and R. Subrahmanian. 2003. '*Dalit* and *Adivasi* Children in Schools: Some Preliminary Research Themes and Findings', *IDS Bulletin*, 34: 43–54.

Boltanski, Luc and Eve Chiapello. 1999. *Le nouvel esprit du capitalisme*. Paris: Gallimard.

———. 2007. *The New Spirit of Capitalism*. London: Verso.

Bourdieu, Pierre. 1984. *Distinction*. Cambridge: Cambridge University Press.

———. 1998. *Practical Reason: On the Theory of Action*. Stanford: Stanford University Press.

Ciotti, Manuela. 2006. '"In the Past We Were a Bit "Chamar"'': Education as a Self- and Community Engineering Process in Northern India', *Journal of the Royal Anthropological Institute*, 12: 899–916.

———. 2010. *Retro-modern India: Forging the Low-caste Self*. New Delhi: Routledge.

Dickey, Sara. 2010. 'Anjali's Alliance: Class Mobility in Urban India', in Diane P. Mines and Sarah Lamb (eds), *Everyday Life in South Asia (Second Edition)*, pp. 192–205. Bloomington: Indiana University Press.

Gramsci, Antonio. 2001. *Selections from the Prison Notebooks*. London: Electric Book Company.

Ilaiah, Kancha. 2005. *Why I Am Not a Hindu: A Sudra Critique of Hindutva, Philosophy, Culture, and Political Economy*. Calcutta: Samya.

Jaffrelot, Christophe. 2003. *India's Silent Revolution: The Rise of the Lower Castes in North India*. London: Hurst.

Jeffrey, Craig, Patricia Jeffery and Roger Jeffery. 2005. 'When Schooling Fails: Young Men, Education and Low-caste Politics in Rural North India', *Contributions to Indian Sociology*, 39:1–38.

Jodhka, Surinder S. and Katherine S. Newman. 2010. 'In the Name of Globalization: Meritocracy, Productivity, and the Hidden Language of Caste', in Sukhadeo Thorat and Katherine S. Newman (eds), *Economic Discrimination in Modern India*. New Delhi: Oxford University Press.

Kapadia, Karin. 1995. *Siva and Her Sisters: Gender, Caste and Class in Rural South India*. Boulder: Westview Press.

Lukose, Ritty. 2010. *Liberalization vs Children: Gender, Youth and Consumer Citizenship in Globalizing India*. Durham: Duke University Press.

Matonti, Frédérique and Franck Poupeau. 2004. 'Le capital militant. Essai de définition', *Actes de la recherche en sciences sociales*, 155: 4–11.

Naudet, Jules. 2008. '"Paying Back to Society": Upward Social Mobility among Dalits', *Contributions to Indian Sociology*, 42(3): 413–4.

258 द Jules Naudet

Naudet, Jules. 2011. 'L'expérience de la mobilité sociale: plaidoyer pour une approche par le discours', *Bulletin de Méthodologie Sociologique*, 111(1). http:// bms.sagepub.com/content/112/1/43.abstract (accessed 10 March 2014).

Naudet, Jules. 2012. *Entrer dans l'élite: Parcours de réussite en France, aux Etats-Unis et en Inde*. Paris: Presses Universitaires de France. http://www.puf.com/ Autres_Collections:Entrer_dans_l'%C3%A9lite (accessed 8 March 2014).

Nigam, Aditya. 2002. 'In Search of a Bourgeoisie: Dalit Politics Enters a New Phase', *Economic and Political Weekly*, 37(13): 1190–93.

Ogbu, John (ed.). 2008. *Minority Status, Oppositional Culture and Schooling*. New York: Routledge.

Omvedt, Gail. 1995. *Dalit Visions: the Anti-Caste Movement and the Construction of an Indian Identity*. New Delhi: Orient Longman.

———. 2005. 'Capitalism and Globalisation, Dalits and Adivasis', *Economic and Political Weekly*, 40(47): 4881–85.

Pai, Sudha. 2002. *Dalit Assertion and the Unfinished Democratic Revolution: The Bahujan Samaj Party in Uttar Pradesh*. New Delhi: Sage Publications.

Paik, Shailaja. 2009. 'Chhadi Lage Chham Chham, Vidya Yeyi Gham Gham (The Harder the Stick Beats, the Faster the Flow of Knowledge): Dalit Women's Struggle for Education', *Indian Journal of Gender Studies*, 16: 175–204.

Prasad, Chandrabhan. 2011. 'Rise of Dalit capitalism'. *Daily Pioneer*, 16 January, http://www.dailypioneer.com/310860/Rise-of-Dalit-capitalism.html (accessed 20 January 2011).

Ram, Kanshi. 1982. *The Chamcha Age: An Era of Stooges*. New Delhi, http:// www.ambedkarintellectuals.in/attachment/25.TheChamchaAge1_text[1]. pdf. (accessed 10 March 2014).

Rao Anupama. 2009. *The Caste Question: Dalits and the Politics of Modern India*. Berkeley: University of California Press.

Sarangapani, Padma M. 2003. *Constructing School Knowledge: An Ethnography of Learning in an Indian Village*. New Delhi: Sage Publications.

Shah, Ghanshyam (ed.). 2001. *Dalit Identity and Politics*. New Delhi: Sage Publications.

Still, Clarinda. 2008. 'Dalit Women in the Social Justice Revolution in India', *Public Policy Research*, 15: 93–96.

Subrahmanian, R. 2003. 'Introduction: Exploring Processes of Marginalisation and Inclusion in Education', *IDS Bulletin*, 34: 1–8.

Teltumbde, Anand. 2011. 'Dalit Capitalism and Pseudo Dalitism', *Economic and Political Weekly*, 46(10): 10–11.

Thiruchendran, Selvy. 1997. *Ideology, Caste, Class and Gender*. New Delhi: Vikas.

About the Editor

Clarinda Still is Lecturer of Modern Indian Studies in the Contemporary South Asian Studies Programme, University of Oxford; and Junior Research Fellow at Wolfson College. She trained as an anthropologist at Edinburgh, University College London (UCL) and London School of Economics and Political Science (LSE), and has conducted ethnographic fieldwork among Dalits in South India. Her research interests include inequality, discrimination, poverty, and upward mobility. Her monograph *Dalit Women: Honour and Patriarchy in South India* (forthcoming) explores Dalit politics and gender relations under conditions of rapid social change.

Notes on Contributors

Hugo Gorringe is Senior Lecturer of Sociology, University of Edinburgh. He has authored *Untouchable Citizens: The Dalit Panthers and Democratisation of Tamilnadu* (2005) and articles on protest policing, violence and identity politics. He has recently completed an ESRC (RES-062-23-3348) Grant looking at Dalit Politics in Tamil Nadu.

Judith Heyer is Emeritus Fellow at Somerville College, and Associate in the Contemporary South Asia Programme, Oxford University School of Interdisciplinary Areas Studies. She was formerly Lecturer in the Department of Economics, and Tutorial Fellow, Somerville College, Oxford University. She has written and edited a number of books on rural and agricultural development in Kenya and Africa. She has also co-edited books on issues relating to development in other parts of the world, including India. Her more recent work based on long-term research in villages in western Tamil Nadu has focused on different aspects of rural development, including Dalits and rural labour.

Sumeet Mhaskar is Visiting Scholar at the Center for South Asia, Stanford University. Prior to Stanford, he was based at the Max Planck Institute for the Study of Religious and Ethnic Diversity, Göttingen, Germany. He has obtained his doctorate from the Department of Sociology, St. Antony's College, University of Oxford. His doctoral thesis explored Mumbai's ex-millworkers' responses to their job loss as a result of textile mill closures during the last decade and a half. His research interests include labour studies, political economy, economic sociology, discrimination and exclusion at workplaces, Indian politics, urban transformation and social movements.

Jordan C. R. Mullard's works on the comparative study of inequality, discrimination and social transformation in Europe and India. She received her Anthropology doctorate from the London School of

Economics and Political Science in 2010. Her ethnographic research looks at the interplay between caste, class and religion in processes of social change amongst Dalits in North India. She is currently working on a book exploring poverty, inequality and social mobility amongst Dalits in rural Rajasthan.

Badri Narayan is Professor, G. B. Pant Social Science Institute, Allahabad. His interest lies in Dalit history, power, politics and culture, social memory and popular articulation of democracy, subaltern and most marginal issues in Indian society. His latest publication is *Kanshiram: Leader of the Dalits* (2014). His other critically acclaimed books are *The Making of the Dalit Public in North India* (2011), *Fascinating Hindutva- Saffron Politics and Dalit Mobilisation* (2009), and *Women Heroes and Dalit Assertion in North India* (2006). He has also been a recipient of the Fulbright Senior Fellowship (2004–05) and the Smuts Fellowship, University of Cambridge (2005–06).

Jules Naudet is Researcher at the Centre de Sciences Humaines, New Delhi. He holds a doctorate degree in Sociology from Sciences Po Paris. His book *Entrer dans l'élite* (2012) is dedicated to a comparative analysis of the experience of upward social mobility in France, in India and in the United States. His most recent research is concerned with the study of elites. He is currently working on the representations of poverty by residents of upper-class neighborhoods in Delhi, Paris and São Paulo.

Sudha Pai is Professor at the Centre for Political Studies, Jawaharlal Nehru University, New Delhi. Her areas of interest are state politics, Dalit politics and public policy. She was Senior Fellow, Nehru Memorial Museum and Library, Teen Murti, New Delhi for a period of three years. Her recent books are *Democratic Governance in India: Poverty, Development and Politics of Identity* (2001, edited with Niraja Gopal Jayal), *Dalit Assertion and the Unfinished Democratic Revolution: The BSP in Uttar Pradesh* (2002), *Developmental State and the Dalit Question in Madhya Pradesh: Congress Response* (2010), and *Interrogating Reorganization of States: Culture, Identity and Politics in Independent India* (2011, edited with Asha Sarangi).

262 द *Notes on Contributors*

Kaushal K. Vidyarthee is a postgraduate student pursuing DPhil in Social Policy at the University of Oxford and DPhil Scholar at Green Templeton College, Oxford. His current research is focused on Dalit's incorporation into India's business economy and its implications for social and economic policies. He has immense interest in caste inequality, informal economy and spatial analysis. He is also working on a co-authored book titled *Dalits and Adivasis in India's Business Economy*. Apart from being a qualified urban planner, he has previously worked on agricultural markets and done fieldwork among grain traders in Tanzania.

Index

Avarnas 4
Achhut Mahasabha 169
Achhutananda, Swami 168
activism 25–26, 246, 256
activists 1, 3, 15, 25, 45, 68, 133, 139, 141–42, 148, 151, 154, 164–65, 179–80; Dalit 17, 31, 134, 167, 243; global networks of 25
Adi Hindu Mahasabha 169
Adi-Dharms 4
Adi-Dravidas 4
Adi-Hindus 4
adivasis/tribal people 8, 14, 50–52, 54, 66–67, 74, 77, 100; as entrepreneurs 54, 57–58, 64, 66
affirmative action 1, 10, 12–13, 45–47, 49, 65, 184; policies of 11–12, 184
agrarian elite 215–16
agricultural labourers 13, 22, 62, 150, 186, 188–89, 192, 197, 205, 209, 213, 215–18, 220, 222–24, 230, 232–33; wages of 220, 220n16, 223, 230, 232
Akela, A. R. as BSP activist 165–66
Akerlof model 72
Akhil Bhartiya Baba Saheb Dr Ambedkar Samaj Sudhar Samiti 167
All India Anna DMK (AIADMK) 135, 137–38, 143, 147
Ambedkar Mission Patrika 167
Ambedkar People's Movement 228, 228n23

Ambedkar Vichar Manch 167
Ambedkar, B. R. 5, 47, 111, 152–53, 164–65, 167, 169, 172, 176, 198, 243, 245–46, 250, 253–54: as architect of reservations system 245; critical of Communists 115
Ambedkarism 148
Anandhi, S. 19
Annadurai. See All India Anna DMK (AIADMK)
annihilation of caste 5
Antyajas 4
Arunthathiyars/Chakkiliyars 29, 138, 215–16; as tied labour (pannayal) system, 216
Arya Samaj in educating Dalits 168
atrocities 20, 26, 153, 157, 254
Atrocities Act 20, 26
Atyalkar, Dattatray 120

Babu, Shyam 2, 48
Backward Classes (BCs) 12, 115, 133, 171, 173, see also Other Backward Classes (OBC)
Bahujan Kalyan Prakashan 165–66
Bahujan Pracharaks (propagators) 178
Bahujan Samaj Party (BSP) 24, 28, 45, 137, 140–41, 151, 164–65, 173
Bajrang Dal, case on Sagar's Garva se Kaho Hum Hindu Nahi Hai 179
Balmiki 29
Beidelman, Thomas 202

264 द Index

Below Poverty Line 8
Béteille, André. 7, 20, 23
Bhan, Chandra 73
Bhangi caste 172
Bhanwra, Babulal 165
Bharti, Kanwal 176
Bhim Sandesh (Bhim's Messages) 180
Bhopal District Trade Centre (DTIC) 46, 51–52, 54, 56–58, 66
Bhopal Document (BD) 45–49, 51, 65
Bhowmik, Sharit K. 127
Bhuja caste 163
Bidrohi, Sangam Lal 174
Bombay Mill Owners Association (BMOA) 114–16; to recruit Dalits 115
booklets 26, 162–67, 79, 181–82; agencies and dissemination 173–78; political knowledge and legal bans 178–81
Bourdieu, Pierre 7, 15–16
Brahmanvaad se Bacho (Save Yourselves from Brahminism) 168
Brahmins 6, 28, 124, 136, 180, 203
Breman, Jan 30, 125
Buddha 164, 167, 172
Buddha Sharan Hans 165, 167, 176, 178, 180
business economy, Dalit participation in 71
business opportunities 44, 50, 65
business/industrial class 46

Calandrino, Michele 9
Carswell, Grace 26
caste Hindus 125; clashes with 27
caste: atrocities 48, 146; bias of 62–63, 65, 67; categories of 138;

discrimination of 1, 25, 57, 63, 151, 156, 184, 217, 239, 241; disparities of 13, 100; groups based on 14, 109, 116, 120, 127, 129, 142, 215; hierarchy and dominant 6, 20, 163, 187, 193, 200–04; Hocartian analysis of identity 6, 30, 108, 124–25, 127–28, 150, 172, 241, 243–44; inequalities 140–41; networks of 124; internationalisation of 47, 65; occupations 72, 189, 193; system of 5–6, 12, 20, 72, 201, 204; violence 144; at workplaces 21
caste-based: businesses 124, 128; mobilisation 136, 142, 155; networks 109, 129; occupation 124, 128–29; parties 137, 144; subordination 205
caste-ism 22, 29
Chamar caste 29, 163, 171–72, 188, 239, 246
Chandalas 4
Chandavarkar, Rajnarayan 114
Charmakar caste 29
Charsley, Simon 4–5, 30, 140
Chatterjee, Bankim Chandra 241
Chauhan, Brij R. 198
Chezhian of Allanganallur 144, 148–49, 152
child labour 217, 221–22, 228, 230
children's education 10, 24, 211, 228, 231
Christians 173
Churihaar caste 163
Ciotti, Manuela 10, 239, 246
Cloward, R. 140
Communist Party of India 156, 194
conversion 1, 22; to Buddhism 5

Index व 265

corruption 10, 29, 54, 63, 65, 67, 135–36, 147, 151
Coy, P. 139–40
CPI(M) mobilisation 156
Cycle, Sangam Lal 178

D'Monte, Darryl 112
Dafali caste 163
Dalit Millennium 47
Dalit Panthers 3, 3n2, 111
Dalit Popular Booklets 163–64, 181
Dalits: of affluence 17, 185, 201, (*see also* entrepreneurs); assertion 111, 137, 140, 151; awareness 163, 179; Bahujan politics 179; book centres 174; Bourgeoisie 48; business/industrial class 30, 46, 75, (*see also* entrepreneurs); as capitalists 50; castes 3, 31, 76, 137, 194–95, 197; classification of 5; consciousness 164–65, 168–69, 181; creativity 27; disadvantage 12, 95; economic incorporation of 99–100; empowerment 165; enterprise ownership of 76; feminist groups 29; girls 17, 217, 221, 239; at grassroots 146, 170; households 21, 213, 228; inclusion of 99; liberation 151, 168–69, 171; literacy rates 8; literature 27, 174, 178; middle class 10, 44, 65, 165, 182, 237; occupations 70–71; participation 71, 92, 95, 100; politicians 27, 164; public reading of 168–71; revolution 140; subordination 9, 22, 25, 31, 204; as term 3–4, 30, 111, 246; unity 5, 30

Dalit women: degradation of 24; as domestic labour 217, 221, 224; exploitation of 19–20; health and well-being of 221; as 'house-wives' 220; into manufacturing 215; in labour force 211, 218, 220, 223; in less paid employment 209–10, 213; as mill-workers 114; and NGO funding 229; NREGS and 230; public services and 222; reservations for 229; and self-employment 229; under-representation of 29; wages of 220; withdrawing from paid work 209, 217
Dalitism 28
Dalit-ness 31, 185
Daliton ki Durdasha (Sorry Plight of Dalits) 168
Darzi caste 163
Das, Bhagwan 180
Datt, Gaurav 11
De Neve, Geert 26
Deliège, Robert 201
democracy, and politics of knowledge 171–73
deprivation 7–8, 23; education 169; economic 73, 194; material 7, 9; Oommen on 7; PMK and issue of caste 137
discrimination 10, 46–47, 62–63, 156–57, 246; against Dalits 13, 70, 82, 87, 100, 241; against *thottam* farmers 216; caste 1, 2, 12–14, 25, 57, 63, 141, 151, 156, 184, 215–17, 228, 239, 241; economic 13, 100; in labour market 13, 108, 120, 122; policies of protective 44; positive 87, 133; stage against caste 25

266 द Index

Deshpande, Ashwini 13, 115
development 171–73
Dhanraj, M. 154
Dhanuk caste 172
Dhobis 163, 171–72
Dholi (Dalit musician caste) 191–93, 195–204 (*see also* Sadh); economic security 201; to 'retraditionalise' occupation 195–200
Dickey, Sara 248
Dollar, David 9
domestic work 211, 217, 220, 224, 228, 231–33; valuation of 211, 233
Dr Ambedkar Sahitya Kala Kendra 174
Dravida Kazhagam 135
Dravida Munnetra Kazhagam (DMK) 135–39, 143–44, 147–48, 154, 156
Dravidian parties 137–38, 141–43, 146, 148, 155
Dudley-Jenkins, L. 5
Dumont, Louis 6–7; on caste 5

Education Guarantee Scheme 51
education, attainment of 45, 47–48, 51, 56; and Dalits 10, 45, 47, 54, 58, 67, 168, 182; for girls 239; public reading as 168–71
electoral politics 1, 25, 29, 134, 157
elite, Dalit 10, 184, 204, 254
employment 10, 13, 30, 44, 47, 63–65, 70, 108, 111, 120, 122, 185–86, 197, 209–10, 213, 231–34; MP Dalits seeking 48: opportunities 120, 127–28, 209, 230–31; trends in 120–23
enterprises 54, 57, 62, 74–77, 78–80, 82; culture 15; employment per 80; growth 82

entrepreneurs 15, 19, 45, 50–54, 56–58, 62–64, 67, 74; in Bhopal 54–58; industrial 50; of lower middle class 58–63; partnerships with non-Dalits 64–65; tribal 54, 57–58, 64, 66; upper middle class entrepreneur 63–64
exclusion of Dalits 114–15, 137
ex-mill workers (Mumbai)109, 120, 122; from Nhavi caste 123–24; occupational choices of 109, 128, see also textile industry in Mumbai

fast food business 125, see also street vending, Dalits in
Fitzgerald, Timothy 5
Froystad, Kathinka 12, 99

Galanter, Marc 5
Gamson, W. 155
Gautam, Mohan Lal 178
Geographical Information System (GIS) 78
Girni Kamgar Sangharsh Samiti 122
globalisation 1, 11, 25, 44, 50, 65, 112; benefits of 45; of economy 46, 67, see also liberalisation
Gooptu, Nandini 19
Gorringe, Hugo 25, 29
Gourishankar, V. 150
Gulaamgiri by Jyotiba 175n20
Gundimeda, S. 27, 151

Hans, Buddha Sharan 165, 167; books of 180
Harijans 3–4, 20, 198
Harriss-White, Barbara 8, 13–14, 74, 85, 98

Index द 267

Hasan, Z. 140
Hedeen, T. 139–40
higher education 49, 228, 237, 240, 243, 247, 250; reservations in 45
Holeyas 29
housekeeping work 109, 128

identities 30, 141, 172; 'Dalitisation' of 27; formation of 6; of Dalits 27, 30, 185, 187, 204–05, 237, 243–44, 247, 253;
Ilaiah, Kancha 27
industrialisation 211–12
inequalities 11, 75–76, 135, 140–41, 195; by liberalisation 19; social 73; in Tamil society 135–36
informal sector 80, 108
institutionalisation 142, 144, 147, 151, 155, 157; and Dalit movements 139–41
Integrated Child Development Services (ICDS) 222, 229
intellectuals, Dalit 15, 27, 45, 47, 65, 68,164, 170–72
inter-caste marriage 17, 22
Iswalkar, Datta 122
Iversen, Vegard 100

Jadhav, Narendra 253–54
Jaiswar, Nand Lal 170
Jajmani system 187, 196–97, 200, 202
Jatavs 29, 172
jati 30, 115
Jeffery C. 10, 15, 28, 140, 155
Jeffery, R. 10, 15, 28, 140, 155
Jenkins, R. 139
Jhalkari Bai, Valiant 177
Jodhka 2, 11, 13, 74, 98

Kamalji, Chotey Kitabwale 178
Kannan, K. P. 8
Kapadia, Karin 24, 248
Karanth, G. 140
Karunanidhi 135, 148, 153
Kash Hum Hindu na Hote (If We were Not Hindus) 165
Kashyap, Jaipal Singh 180
Kaushal Vidyarthee 14
Klandermans, B. 139
Klass, Morten 7
knowledge politics 71–73
Kolenda, Pauline M. 196–97
Kolis 115
Kori caste 172
Kraay, Aart 9
Kumar, Sushil 178
Kumbhar caste 185, 187–95, 197–203, 205; elites 205; Jajmani 188–85, 197–98, 202–03; landowners 192, 200; patrons 200–01; political superiority of 203; re-traditionalised occupations of 195–200
Kumhar caste 163

labour 72, 120, 122, 128, 199, 209–13, 218; flexibilisation and informalisation of 12
labour market 13, 47, 72–74, 120, 122, 208; women withdrawing from 209
Lal, Sangam 174
Lal, Bihari 170
liberalisation 1–2, 9, 11–12, 14, 18–19, 25, 31, 47, 71–73, 97–100, 112, 128; dalit occupations and 71–76, (*see also* globalisation); policies of 73

268 द Index

Local Intelligence Unit (LIU) 179
Lohar 163
Long, A. 98

Madan, Guru Prasad 180
Madhya Pradesh 2, 45–46, 51, 53, 58, 65–67, 99, 179; Digivijay Singh government in 46
Madigas 29
Maharashtra Navanirman Sena (MNS) 111
Mahars 29, 113
Malas 29
Mandal Commission 172–73, see also reservations
'mandalisation' of politics 11
Mang/Matang 29, 113
Manohar, R. 155, 157
manufacturing 52, 65–66, 77, 82, 111, 212, 215–16, 222; Dalit participation in 92
Manuwadi Social System 173
Marathas 114–16
Marathi Manus 111; MNS definition of 111n4
marginalisation 1–2, 11, 24, 48, 68, 70–72, 74–75, 99, 156–57, 185, 187–88, 204, (see also economic, marginalisation); political 24–31; social 15–24
market-oriented economy 44, 65
Mauryas 163
Mayawati 24, 28, 164n2, 175, 179, 181
Mayer, Adrien C. 187, 195, 198
Mazhabis and Ad Dharmis 29
Meghvals 185–87, 189–94, 197–99, 201–05; elite 198, 205; landlords 188–95; and marginalisation 203

Mendelsohn, Oliver 3, 63
MGR (M. G. Ramachandran) 135
micro-entrepreneurship, and incorporation of Dalits 75–76, 78, 99–100; margin money under RDS 51, 53, 75
middle-class Dalits 16
Mines, M. 150
mobility 1, 9, 185–88, 204–05, 237–38, 240, 245, 247, 250, 256
mobilisation of Dalits 1, 23, 30, 137, 141–42, 146, 162, 181, 256
Moffatt, Michael 200–01
Mosse, David 7, 24–25, 194, 201, 204
Most Backward Class (MBC) group 136–37
Movements of Dalit 29, 44, 111, 142, 151, 156, 164–65, 244–48, 253–54, (see also Dalit Panther); in South India 27
Mumbai 2, 14, 108–13, 117, 120, 124, 127, 247, (see also textile industry in Mumbai); cotton textile industry and 107–08, 113; names of 107n; occupational choices in post-industrial 117–20; jobbers and textiles mill of 144–15, 123; street vendors in 125
Muslims 12, 14, 108, 115, 120, 125, 156, 163, 173, 198

Nai caste 163, 172, 197, 201
Naimisharay (Dalit writer) 176
Nambath, S. 144
Narayan, Badri 26, 28
Nath, K. 176
National Commission for Safai Karamchari 9

National Rural Employment Guarantee Scheme (NREGS) 9, 212, 230; Tamil Nadu 212
Naudet, Jules 16
Navayuvak Harijan Sangha (Young Harijan Organisation) 180
neoliberal 1–2, 18–19, 31
New Economic Policy 74
Newman, K. S. 13
Nhavi castes 123–24; girls into profession of 124
non-Dalit women 215–18, 220, 223–24, 228–29; in household enterprises 216
non-governmental organisation (NGOs) 98, 248

occupation: by caste 72, 75, 124, 128–29, 189, 193; by Dalits 70–71, 114; distributions for Dalits 218; high-paid professional 44; low-paid 8, 18; of Mumbai's ex-millworkers 109, 120, 122; non-agricultural 215, 223; non-Dalits in cleaning 122; self-employed 109–10, 117, 127–29; traditional 73, 113, 129, 189, 193, 199, 203
Omvedt, Gail 141
oppression 3, 6, 150, 171, 178
organic intellectual 26, 255; Gramscian notion of 247
Other Backward Classes (OBCs) 6, 20, 64, 100, 126–27, 129, 173, 192; of Hindus 120, 123, 125, *see also* Most Backward Classes (MBC)
'own account' enterprises 77, 80

Paatali Makkal Katchi (PMK) 136–38, 143–44, 148

Pai, Sudha 15, 73, 99, 140, 151, 155
Paik, Shailaja 239
Pallars 29, 138
Panchamas 4
panchayati raj institutions (PRIs) 223
Pandian, M. 144
Pannadis 215–16
Panwar Meghvals 188–89
Paraiyars 4, 29, 138
Parsis 173
Parties, Dalit 30, 134, 136–38, 141–43, 151, 155, 157
Pasis 29, 163, 171–72
Patel, B. B. 115, 117, 163; on occupational categorisation 117
Patels 163
patronage 24, 109, 125–26, 128–29; distribution of posts through network of 146; for economic security 201; of Kumbhar Jajmans 202; Mosse on caste 194; political 109, 125–26, 128–29
pauti system 126n15
paying back to society 238, 244–50, 254, 256
Phule, Jyotiba 164, 175
Phule, Savitribai 175n21
Piven, F. 140
political: groups of Dalit 3, 25–26; institutionalisation 134; mobility, 24–30, 204; movements 4, 157; organisations of Dalits 26; participation 133, 140, 142, 145, 155
politics, Dalit and 2, 25, 27–31, 134, 141, 146, 148, 156–57, 164, 178–79, 237; of identity 6; of Uttar Pradesh 164, 181
pollution-line 17–18, 185, 194
pollution, purity and untouchables 7

270 द Index

popular: Dalit booklets 162, 164–66, 171–72, 177; Dalit writers 170, 172
population of Dalits 1, 8, 10, 70, 82–85, 137, 163
poverty 7–8, 12–13, 18–19, 45, 63, 151; characterisation of 19
Prajapat Kumbhars 187
Prakash, Aseem 14, 98
Prasad, Chandrabhan 48, 50
Prashant, Gaya Prasad 180
Premi, Lalji 173–74, 178
Prevention of Atrocities Act 146, 148
private business economy 70–71, 76
private capital 50
private enterprises 74, 79, 82; Dalit ownership of 75. *See also* private capital
private sector 11–12, 45–50, 67, 157, 237, 243–44, 248, 250, 256; affirmative action in 45
protective discrimination (PD) 44–50, 65–66, 68
public distribution system (PDS) 9, 222, 229, 230n27
public service 237, 250
Puthiya Tamizhagam (PT) 138, 156

Quigley, Declan 7

Racine, Josiane 23, 27
Racine, Jean- Luc 23, 27
Raheja, Gloria G. 7
Rahman, Abdul 156
Raidasia/Ramdassia 164
Rajashekar, V. T. 27
Rajasthan 2, 82, 92, 190, 193, 196, 198; reservation system in 192
Rajasthan Tenancy Act 189
Rajasthan, Dalits in 196

Rajputising 196, 201
Ram, Kanshi 27, 164, 175, 179, 181, 245
Ram, Moti 180, 188
Ram, Sant 180
Ramasamy Naicker, E. V. ('Periyar') 135, 152–53, 164
Rani Durgawati Scheme (RDS) 51, 53, 57, 62, 64
Rao Sanjeevan Nath, S. 170
Rashtriya Swayamsewak Sangh (RSS) 179
rationalisation process 115
Ravallion, Martin 11
Ravi (Dalit essay writer) 254; capitalism and 255
Ravidas 164
Ravikumar 133–34, 144, 153–54
reading, writing and Dalit public 168–71
recruitment agency 122–23, 127–28
reservations 10–11, 22, 26, 44–50, 64–66, 99, 116, 151, 157, 165, 172–73, 184, 228–29, 240–41, 244, (*see also* Mandal Commission); in education 95; policies of 45, 48, 66, 244; as recognition of one's inferiority 240
re-traditionalised occupations 195–200
Roberts, N. 137, 141–42; on 'Tamil' 143
Rogers, Martin 19

Sadh (OBC sectarian of temple keepers) 193, 197, 201
safai kam 109, 122, 127–28
Sagar, Sunderlal 165; *Garva se Kaho Hum Hindu Nahi Hai* (Say it with Pride: We are not Hindus)

of 179; *Samman ke liye Dharm Parivartan Karein* of 179
Saglio-Yatzimirsky 26
Samaj Sudhar Prakashan (Social Reform Publication 167
Sanskritisation 196, 198, 201
Sarvajanik Satyadharma 175n20
Satyanaryana 27
Schaffer, B. 98
Scheduled Caste (SC) 4, 6, 13, 113, 116, 156, 173, 192, 242, 244
Scheduled Tribe (ST) 6, 12, 116, 173
schooling 238–40, *see also* education
Scoville, James 72
secondary socialisation: and higher education 240–43; and professional context 243–44
self-employment 109–10, 117, 127–29; trends in 123–28
self-help groups (SHGs) 229
Sen, Amartya 8
service sector 14, 95, 122; economy 108, 110, 122–23, 127–29
Special Economic Zones (SEZs) 151
Shambuk Rishi ki Barahmasi 166
Shiv Sena 110–11, 126; meaning of 110, 110n3
Singh, Digvijay 15, 45, 50–51, 56, 65–67
Singh, Periyar Lalai 179–80; confiscating *Sachhhi Ramayan* of 179
Singh, Sheoraj 176
social: exclusion 72, 76, 140, 184; institutions 14, 98, 108, 120, 129; mobilisation 134; mobility 2, 16, 184, 186, 192, 195, 199–200, 205, 238, 247, 250–51; movements 1, 65, 169

socialisation 238–44
Soshiton ki Samasya aur Samadhan 168
Special Component Plan (SCP) 70
street vending, Dalits in 127
sub-castes of Dalits 11, 24
subordination 3, 7, 23, 31, 201, 204, 208
Subramanian, S. 136–37, 142
Sundaram, K. 9
Supplier Diversity (SD) 15, 45–54, 62–68

Tamil Nadu 2, 14, 27, 29, 67, 133–35, 143, 150, 211–12, 222; caste and politics in 135–39; Dalits against oppressors in 134; politics in 135–36; Scheduled Castes in 138
Tamil Nadu Untouchability Eradication Front (TNUEF) 156
Tamil nationalism 142–43, 150
Tamil Protection Movement 144, 150
Taneja, P. 155
Tarrow, S. 139
Teen Mahaprani 167
Tendulkar, Suresh D. 9
textile industry in Mumbai 122–23, 126; and Dalits 108, 112–17, discrimination against and Muslims in 108; ring-spinning department and Dalits in 114, 116; mill owners of 111–12, 115–16; weaving department and exclusion of Dalits in 114–15; workforce in 108, 115
Tharu, Susie 27
Thass, Iyothee 143
Thiruchendran, Selvy 248

272 द Index

Thirumavalavan 134, 138, 143, 145–46, 148, 152–53, 156; electoral violence in constituency of 142
Thorat, Sukhadeo 13, 47
thottam farmers 216, *see also under* discrimination
Tiruppur garment industry 208n, 214
total millworkers, Dalits as 114
trade 14, 73, 77–78, 92, 95, 126, 212, 215, 222
trading castes 57, 67
traditional caste-based occupations 113, 117, 123–24, 128–29, 189, 193, 197, 199, 203, ex-millworkers and 129
transport 14, 77–78, 92, 95, 217
Trisharan, R. B. 166–67, 178, 180
two-tumbler system 22, 229, *see also* discrimination

UK Equalities Bill 25
unclean occupations 115, 117
Untouchability 3–5, 7–8, 22, 27, 71, 156, 166, 178, 189, 194, 200, 204, 215–16, 228–29, 254; internationalisation of 25
upper castes 8, 12, 16–17, 19, 22, 27, 99, 127, 166–67, 170–71, 177–78, 241–42
upward mobility 2, 16, 27, 228, 237, 246, 248, 251, 255–56
Uttar Pradesh 2, 137, 140, 162, 179; Dalits in 28

Vanniyars 136
Verma, Babu Ram 180
Vicziany, Marika 3

Viduthalai Ciruthaigal Katchi (VCK) 133–34; allegations of 29, 133–35, 137–39, 141–48, 150–57
Vidyarthee, Kaushal 2, 14, 70, 72, 74, 98
Vijayabaskar, M. 150
Vundru, Raja Sekhar 47

wage labour 8, 11, 14, 18, 120
weddings, Dalits at 21
women 19–20, 24, 29, 114, 209–13, 215–18, 220–24, 228–32; as agricultural labour 232; in domestic work 211, 228; and employment opportunities 209; health of 221; labour force and 210; as millworkers 116; participation of 211, 231; and patterns of work 211, 214; position of 208, 210; self-employment opportunities for 229; for staying at home 217, 220, 222, 224, 230; wages of 220, 220n17; withdrawal of 213
Wood, Adrian 9
workforce 48, 108, 112–17, 120, 122–23, 216, 218, 220, 223–24
writers (Dalit) 47, 162, 164–68, 172, 176, 180–82, 204; for freedom of writing 27–28, 165–68
Wyatt, A. 141–42

Yadav 163
Yog, A. K. 179
youth 10

Zamindari and Biswadari Abolition Act 189